Democracy Assistance from the Third Wave

Pitt Series in Russian and East European Studies
JONATHAN HARRIS, Editor

Democracy Assistance from the Third Wave

POLISH
ENGAGEMENT
IN BELARUS AND
UKRAINE

Paulina Pospieszna

UNIVERSITY OF PITTSBURGH PRESS

Published by the University of Pittsburgh Press, Pittsburgh, Pa., 15260
Copyright © 2014, University of Pittsburgh Press
All rights reserved
Manufactured in the United States of America
Printed on acid-free paper
10 9 8 7 6 5 4 3 2 1

ISBN 10: 0-8229-6271-3
ISBN 13: 978-0-8229-6271-7

Cataloging-in-Publication data is available at the Library of Congress.

For my parents and "My Three Men,"
with love and gratitude

Contents

Acknowledgments

I owe a tremendous debt to Barbara Chotiner, because this work could not have been written without her support and encouragement from the beginning. She allowed me the space to shape my own path of professional development without ever imposing a particular perspective. She also offered tremendous assistance when I applied for the University of Alabama Graduate Council Research Fellowship, without which the process of writing this book would have been more arduous. I appreciate her constant feedback and support amid her hectic schedule of teaching as well as advising a large number of undergraduate and graduate students. I have learned from her, both as a scholar and as a teacher, and I hope I will be able to emulate her academic excellence in the future. I would especially like to thank Terry Royed, who, as the director of graduate studies at the University of Alabama, showed me a lot of kindness, support, and understanding from the very beginning.

I also would like to express my gratitude and appreciation to Harvey Kline, who inspired me to explore the topic of democratization. He also showed me that warmth and humanity make academia a friendlier environment. Douglas Gibler exposed me to recent international relations literature on democratization that improved my work and led me to new ideas, and Karl DeRouen introduced me to a new area of study that inspired my postdoctoral research. I would also like to thank Marysia Galbraith, who played an important role in preparing me for my research trip to Poland and advising me with regard to the institutional review board (IRB) process.

I also would like to thank the Capstone International Center, the Department of Political Science, the Graduate School, and the Graduate Student Association at the University of Alabama for generous financial support for my fieldwork in Poland and in the United States.

In my postdoctoral work, I was fortunate to have been embedded in two very stimulating intellectual environments—the University of Konstanz and the University of Mannheim. I thank Gerald Schneider, from the University of Konstanz, who supported me in my endeavors and who helped me establish myself in the discipline in Europe. I also thank Sabine Carey, from the University of Mannheim, who has been an invaluable source of advice. Moreover, I would like to thank all of my colleagues at Alabama, Konstanz, and Mannheim for being great models of support and collegiality and for supplying generous portions of wit and humor amid broader discussions of my research and career goals.

Obviously, this project would not have come to fruition without the input of many civil society activists. I thank each of the many representatives of Polish nongovernmental organizations (NGOs) and the Polish Ministry of Foreign Affairs who agreed to be interviewed for this study. They shared their valuable time and insights, and they generously equipped me with a suitcase full of valuable materials. Thank you also to representatives from the National Endowment for Democracy in Washington, DC, who provided me with data that greatly strengthened my arguments in this study. I must also thank anonymous reviewers for comments that helped me improve the manuscript.

Finally, I could not go far without the love and support of my family and a wide array of friends. Thank you to my parents for teaching me the importance of education and hard work and for demonstrating the value of such in their own lives. Thank you for supporting me in all my endeavors and for encouraging me to climb the academic ladder. I should mention my brothers for their interests in my project and our discussions about life and the future. Many thanks also to my parents-in-law, who always showed great interest in my education and who always had a good word for me. It also is a real blessing to have great friends who have been good listeners and who, sometimes despite geographical distance, offered me a great deal of emotional support. Thank you also for our talks about anything other than my work and for helping me balance an academic career with a personal life. I should express my gratitude to wonderful people from Tuscaloosa for their big hearts, their support from the beginning of my stay there, and for helping me pursue my goals. Thank you to everyone who helped me along the way.

Last, but not least, I must thank my husband, Marcin Smiglak, with whom I have had the great good fortune of sharing this experience. I can honestly say this project would never have been completed without his love, relentless support, and friendship. Thanks also to my children, who keep me sane and make me smile on some difficult days and who always remind me that there are some things that are much more important.

Introduction

■ This book addresses several questions that deal with democracy assistance provided by countries that experienced the "third wave of democracy" and that were recipients of this kind of aid not so long ago.[1] Why does a country that received democracy assistance in the past offer such aid today and when did this shift take place? How does a one-time recipient country go about assisting other countries in their struggles with democracy? How does a young democracy conceptualize democracy and the democratization process and how does its view on democracy assistance differ from approaches used by Western donors? Finally, are democracy assistance efforts effective in terms of their capacity to diffuse democratic norms and practices to other recipient countries?

This book presents a first attempt to investigate the efforts of a young democracy to support democracy in other countries, and it thus contributes to the body of research on democracy assistance. The questions addressed in this work arise largely from ongoing debates in the literature on democracy assistance regarding approaches and strategies used to assist recipient countries with their struggle for democracy. By investigating democracy assistance efforts in an authoritarian versus a democratizing country, this work challenges two major emerging approaches in democracy assistance—political and developmental—and, by presenting cross-border collaborative work between civil societies, it adds to the discussion on how to improve democracy assistance so that it is more in tune with the political reality in recipient countries.

This book also engages many other literatures in political science. It links the concerns of international relations theorists who are interested in the impact of external influences on domestic politics and regional diffusion of democracy with the concerns of scholars of comparative politics in processes of democratization and consolidation, as well as in civil society. Specifically, this study describes nongovernmental networks of actors operating across national borders, and, given the potential of such networks to effect domestic political change, it is important to know more about how they emerge, function, and sustain. This work also points out that, to improve our understanding of democratization processes, it is important to acknowledge the different roles that civil society groups play in authoritarian versus democratizing environments as well as the challenges these groups face.

External Influences on the Diffusion of Democracy

The comparative politics and international relations literatures on democratization and democratic consolidation abound with different explanations about the ways in which a system becomes democratic and solidifies its democratic features, but there is no consensus among political scientists on what affects these phenomena (Tilly 2007, 49). Prior to the 1990s, studies on democratization and democratic consolidation favored explanations that focused on domestic influences (Schmitter 1986).[2] This view began to change, particularly in response to transformations in Central and Eastern Europe (CEE) taking place as part of the "third wave of democratization" (Huntington 1991).[3] The role of external factors in the politics of regime change in postcommunist CEE states made scholars realize that domestic factors do not sufficiently explain how countries democratize. Today, any model exploring the determinants of democratization that does not take external factors into account is lacking in specificity, but the literature devoted to the importance of international forces in democratization is still small.

This study contributes to our understanding of the impact of international influences on democratic change with a special focus on the role of regional diffusion of democracy. Diffusion itself can be defined as a process by which an idea, institution, policy, model, or the like is spread through certain channels to the members of the social system (e.g., within a state or across states) (Bunce and Wolchik 2006; Brinks and Coppedge 2006; della Porta and Tarrow 2005; Rogers 1995, 10; Tarrow 1998, 2005). The fact that democracies expanded in "waves" (Bratton and van de Walle 1997, 29) and that democratization "snowballs" (Huntington 1991) in some regions motivated international relations researchers to investigate the impact of neighboring states and to hypothesize that countries sharing borders with democratizing states or new democracies are far more likely to undergo transition to democracy themselves (Crescenzi and Enterline 1999; Enterline and Greig 2005; Gleditsch and Ward 2006; O'Loughlin et al. 1998; Rasler and Thompson 2004; Starr 1991; Starr and Lindborg 2003). Gleditsch and Ward (2006), for example, find that as the frequency of democracies within a geographic region increases, the more democratic the nondemocratic states in the region become. Thus, the authors argue that "international processes that influence democratization are not particularly to be found at a global level" and that "the global level is an aggregate that masks large regional differences and variation" (Gleditsch and Ward 2006, 913). Therefore, it makes little sense to exclude the regional context.

Scholars find that regional diffusion of democracy has significant effects. However, the question arises as to whether we know what regional mechanism is encouraging actors in authoritarian states to undergo transition to democracy. Despite statistical evidence of regional clustering of democracies, it is difficult to identify the particular causal process behind the correlations between neighborhood influence and democratization. Important questions still remain regarding how regional diffusion of democracy takes place and what drives the regional spread of political change. Without specifying the mechanism behind this regional diffusion, we will have a vague understanding about this process, and diffusion will be just "illusion" (Brinks and Coppedge 2006).

This research may contribute to our understanding of what may be behind the observable diffusion of democracies within a region. This project suggests that, in addition to domestic and other external explanations, an active engagement of democratic neighbors may be one of the mechanisms explaining how authoritarian neighbors imitate and learn and how democratic ideas and behaviors spread geographically. Of course, the mechanisms driving diffusion are usually multiple, but the study suggests that the analysis of diffusion cannot neglect the people on the ground involved in this process. It therefore focuses on cross-border interactions of nonstate actors as a mechanism of diffusion of democracy. Scholars of social movements have become aware of the transnational processes that carry contention beyond borders. Social movement theorists argue that transnational challenges, specifically transnational advocacy networks (TANs), including external and domestic actors and groups, may have impacts on domestic political regimes (Smith et al. 1997; Smith and Wiest 2012; Tarrow 1998). Inspired by Keck and Sikkink (1998), scholars have concentrated on the role of "activists beyond borders" in forging links between social movements and international institutions and organizations (see, e.g., Diani and McAdam 2003). A recent work by Tarrow (2005) that proposes a typology of contemporary forms of cross-border coalitions significantly advances the literature on transnational networks.

Increased scholarly interest in transnational networks can also be observed in the recent literature on postcommunism (Bunce and Wolchik 2006, 2011; Jacoby 2006). Bunce and Wolchik (2006, 288) address the question of why the electoral revolutions in the postcommunist region have taken place since 2000.[4] The authors argue that the process of diffusion occurred through complex transnational collaborations that included not just US democracy promoters but also regional democracy promoters and dedicated local activists. In their recent work, Bunce and Wolchik (2011) analyze the spread of electoral strategies within the postcommunist region as a case of cross-border diffusion. They find that a transnational network, composed of Western democracy promoters, local opposition and civil society groups, and regional democracy activists, was one of the driving factors behind the diffusion of innovative electoral strategies. However, despite such studies, little is known about cross-border collaborative networks. This book fills that gap, identifies these networks, and presents evidence of their origin, evolution, and character and their potential to diffuse democratic ideas and practices to civil society groups across borders. Also, it aims to demonstrate that the inclusion of NGOs from neighboring democratic countries in transnational democracy assistance networks increases the chances for democratic diffusion.

This book addresses the little-researched topic of how democratic ideas and behaviors are transferred via a particular network of actors: civil society activists from beyond national borders. The transnational activities investigated here focused primarily on strengthening democratization processes in Ukraine and facilitating the emergence of democratization in Belarus. Therefore, this study links the concerns of scholars who are interested in foreign influences on domestic politics with the concerns of scholars studying processes of democratization and consolidation.

Democratization and Civil Society in Comparative Politics

Civil society plays a significant role in democratization and democratic consolidation.[5] This work demonstrates that it is instructive to identify the characteristics of different civil society actors, as well as roles and functions that civil society plays, within the context of authoritarian regimes, transitioning regimes, and democracies.

Although scholars and practitioners recognize the importance of civil society, the actual role of civil society in the processes of democratization and democratic consolidation has received little attention in the literature on democratic transition. Scholars have generally agreed that a vibrant civil society is a necessary, although not sufficient, condition for the emergence and sustainability of democracy (Bernhard 1993; Diamond 1994, 1996; Hadenius and Uggla 1998; Linz and Stepan 1996).[6] Deutsch (1961) emphasizes the importance of social mobilization, occurring when a country is moving from traditional to modern ways of life, in facilitating democratization by pressuring the government to respect citizens' growing demands. Putnam et al. (1983) show that the regions of Italy in which democratic institutions function most successfully are those in which civil society was already relatively well developed. In other words, successful democratization processes are possible "*only* if, and only to the extent that, a civil society . . . predates the transition or becomes established in the course of it" (Pérez-Díaz 1993, 40). O'Donnell and Schmitter (1986, 48–56) state that the opening of authoritarian rule usually produces a rapid increase in general popular activation—"the resurrection of civil society"—in which diverse layers of society may come together and form a "popular upsurge" that pushes the transition toward democracy further than it would otherwise have gone. Civil society has played a crucial role in undermining authoritarian regimes and facilitating the establishment of democratic rule in Central and Eastern Europe, sub-Saharan Africa, and South Korea.[7] Linz and Stepan (1996, 9) argue that civil society is crucial in all stages of transition because of the capacity of the third sector to generate political alternatives and to monitor government. A lively and independent civil society can help transitions get started, resist reversals, push transitions to their completion, and consolidate and help deepen democracy.

However, a number of important theoretical questions regarding the role of civil society in supporting democratic institutions remain unanswered. Most authors agree that civil society is the realm between state and family. It is separated from the state (and thus excludes formal "political society" as well as private sector business), is autonomous in relation to the state, and is formed voluntarily by members of society to protect and extend their interests and values.[8] Nevertheless, I argue that scholars focus too much on the role of nongovernmental organizations as a component of civil society in the process of creating and deepening democracy and seem to neglect the role of nongovernmental actors that are not, or cannot be, formally organized (teachers, students, parents) as well as many less formal networks, such as mass media, clubs, associations, and neighboring communities.

Debate regarding the different components of civil society also relates to the discussion concerning the kind of civil society that is desirable and possible in authoritarian states and democratizing countries and to what degree civil society should act as a partner or adversary of the state. I argue that it is important to distinguish between civil society and uncivil society in authoritarian regimes, especially because in authoritarian regimes there may be groups that support the nondemocratic regime and even facilitate the growth of that regime.[9] The truly civil society, however, aims to delegitimize a regime or compel it to be more responsive to its citizens and to guarantee individual and collective liberties. The components of civil society performing these functions are often informal entities, and it is important to support linkages between such groups since a united civil society that forms an active opposition to the regime can mobilize a "popular upsurge" and thus overthrow authoritarianism. In other words, in authoritarian states, civil society plays a more oppositional role, and so it is important to define civil society actors and recognize the role they play or may play in a future transition.

In consolidated democracies, however, although civil society puts curbs on government, the state and civil society are seen more as partners than opponents. For example, Geremek (1996, 250) points out that civil society in a consolidating country "should not be based on emotions" and should not act in opposition to the democratic state but cooperate with it in the building of democratic institutions and involve as many persons as possible in public life, in order to construct a democratic mechanism of stability. During the consolidation of democracy, civil society can be the basis of good and effective government, as well as a partner in resolving problems of successful democratic governance, because civil society serves as a bridge between private citizen and public office, aggregates citizens' interests and articulates their demands, serves as a watchdog for these interests, and widens public debate.[10]

However, scholars argue that certain preconditions must be met in order for civil society to be able to penetrate, fragment, and decentralize government's power. Civil society should be "vibrant" in terms of its pluralism (the number, size, variety, and density of civil society's networks), have a democratic orientation, participate in politics, and, above all, should be autonomous or independent of the state. The argument regarding autonomy and commitment to democratic values is especially important when taking into account Berman's (1997, 424) findings that a robust civil society's alliance with undemocratic elites contributed to the collapse of the Weimar

Republic—Germany's first experience with democracy. I argue that these characteristics should be acknowledged by democracy assistance providers so that civil society can contribute to the consolidation of democracy.

Democracy Assistance Literature

This book focuses on democracy assistance efforts provided by a young democracy, something not previously studied; therefore, the study's major contribution to democracy assistance literature is apparent. The literature abounds with studies on democracy assistance carried out by Western democracies (e.g., Alesina and Dollar 2000; Burnell 2000; Carothers 1999, 2004; Diamond 1992, 1999; Finkel et al. 2006; Kausch et al. 2006; Lancaster 2007; Ottaway 2003; Ottaway and Chung 1999; Pinto-Duschinsky 1997; Schraeder et al. 1998; and Youngs 2008).[11] The literature usually focuses on democracy assistance programs run by quasi-governmental and nongovernmental organizations (NGOs), foundations, and international organizations. The major actors examined in the literature are US government–funded and privately run US-based nonprofit organizations: the Office of Democratic Initiatives attached to the United States Agency for International Development (USAID), the National Endowment for Democracy (NED), the Rockefeller Brothers Fund (RBF), the Soros Foundation, and the Ford Foundation. Other important actors engaged in democracy assistance efforts have been international organizations, such as the World Bank and the Organization for Security and Co-operation in Europe's (OSCE) Office for Democratic Institutions and Human Rights. There is also assistance undertaken by European entities—governmental institutions, civil society organizations, and foundations like Germany's Stiftungen—as well as the European Commission programs, such as the European Initiative for Democracy and Human Rights (EIDHR) (ACAP 1995).

Although the literature on democracy promotion is vast, there is a gap with regard to the way in which third-wave democracies promote democratic values and practices elsewhere. Carothers (2004) just touches on this subject, mentioning that some democracies, such as Chile, Poland, and Taiwan, are also establishing democracy assistance programs in their regions and that these programs are growing and being institutionalized. Hence, this study examines one of these cases in depth. Using Poland as a case, the analysis addresses the question of to what extent, in giving foreign aid, a third-wave democracy is motivated by the desire to spread democracy. Why does the Polish government engage in democracy assistance?

What are the major recipient countries of this assistance? Since there is no comprehensive study on democracy assistance initiatives undertaken by a young democracy beyond its borders, this work fills a gap in the literature.

There are two major debates in the literature on democracy assistance to which this book contributes: one that revolves around approaches to democracy assistance, specifically, which type of assistance and which target sector receives more attention from donors; and one over the best ways to provide civil society assistance.

In general, the democracy promotion literature shows that there are several forms of democracy assistance programs, and they differ based on their particular focus on economic development, political institution building, elections, civil society and the media, and the rule of law. However, support for elections, institution building, and the rule of law has shown that democracy assistance is unsuccessful without taking into the account the role of citizens in democratization.[12] Therefore, most scholars argue that civil society aid is the most important aspect of democracy assistance strategies, because of the merits in mobilizing citizens' demands and strengthening their political participation.[13]

Civil society assistance was not always a major component of democracy aid. The collapse of the Soviet Union and the emergence of opposition from civil society groups in Central and Eastern Europe triggered the expansion of democracy assistance to these groups in the 1980s and 1990s.[14] The growth of civil society in the early 1990s came to show its important democratizing potential when donor agencies realized that their focus on electoral systems and state institutions was inadequate and lacked the ability to strengthen citizens' political participation. Since then, there has been a steady increase in interest among Western democracies' governments, foundations, and organizations in assisting civil society. Donors began to sponsor programs identified as "strengthening civil society" across the developing and postcommunist worlds, with the assumption that civil society is crucial in the transition to and consolidation of democracy (USAID Mission n.d.).[15] However, civil society assistance has received little research attention and needs to be better understood.

The literature emphasizes differences among Western donors with respect to which form of democracy assistance should be given priority. Scholars distinguish two major emerging approaches in democracy assistance: *political* and *developmental* (Carothers 2009; Jarábik 2006, 86; Kopstein 2006). Some policy makers and political observers see US democracy assistance as basically political and the European Union's democracy-building efforts as largely developmental. According to the political approach, democracy aid is directed to political parties, civil society groups, associations, politicians, or politically oriented nongovernmental organizations. Democracy assistance also can be carried out through support to key institutions, such as an independent electoral commission, independent judiciary, or independent media. In Carothers's (2009) opinion, the political approach best corresponds to Dahl's conception of democracy, because this concept highlights the importance of political and civil rights in ensuring that citizens can participate in democratic political processes. The developmental approach, however, perceives democratization as a slow, iterative process of change in a wide range of political and socioeconomic aspects. In Carothers's (2009, 8) opinion, the developmental approach suggests that it is better to achieve a basic level of social and economic development before proceeding with democratization. Thus, particular attention is paid to promoting social and economic development and then building political institutions and good governance rather than strengthening political contestation and openness.

This study helps answer the question of whether democracy assistance provided by a young democracy falls into this typology of approaches to democracy assistance and whether this distinction is still relevant when young democracies provide this support. Moreover, taking into account the importance of civil society assistance and the different roles that civil society plays in generating and sustaining democracy, the question arises as to whether the distinction between political and developmental democracy assistance is equally applicable to both authoritarian regimes and newly democratic recipient countries. For example, if a donor-funded project focuses on strengthening socioeconomic aspects and domestic civil society groups are involved because the project enables them to enhance their role vis-à-vis government, the distinction between political and developmental approaches is not so clear cut. Therefore, this study aims to demonstrate that civil society assistance is a type of democracy assistance that deliberately, directly, and exclusively focuses on societal actors in the recipient country, with the goal of both building their capacity and strengthening their role, regardless of the specific project topic or focus.

Another debate in the democracy assistance literature relates to strategies of providing assistance to civil societies and which methods are most effective in facilitating democratic tendencies in recipient countries. The literature on democracy assistance identifies three strategies, and each has advantages and disadvantages. Carothers's (1999, 257) terminology labels the first strategy the "external project method." This strategy was used by, for example, the USAID for Eastern Europe and parts of the former Soviet

Union at the beginning of the 1990s. This strategy involved providing aid for US NGOs' contractors, such as consulting groups and training specialists (Siegel and Yancey 1992). The proponents of this method may justify it by pointing out that domestic organizations in the recipient countries are poorly institutionalized, lack good reputations and administrative experience, are not developed enough to be able to absorb outside assistance effectively, and thus do not receive direct funds. However, there are also costs associated with this strategy. Much of the funding, instead of being spent in the recipient country, was used by the donor or its domestic contractors. Siegel and Yancey (1992, 52), in their study on assistance to the postcommunist countries, point out that there was "too much of auto-consumption of assistance, because 75 percent of an aid dollar was consumed by the donor." Moreover, such strategies did not find much approval among recipient countries' civil society activists, who were of the opinion that the "Marriott Brigade"—the "fly-in, fly-out" consultants who stayed at Warsaw's five-star hotels—provided training despite having little knowledge about the reality of CEE life (Mendelson and Glenn 2002, 3; Wedel 2001, 1–20). Finally, this strategy is characterized by "lack of local ownership" of assistance projects and a lack of flexibility, when, for example, the real local needs and possibilities turn out to be different from what the donor anticipated (Carothers 1999, 259–65).

The second method of supporting civil society groups in their struggle for democracy is by providing direct grants. US assistance providers have made direct grants to organizations, distributed via a grants competition. In those cases, no American intermediary groups were involved in the implementation of the projects. Direct grants have typically been employed for civil society assistance by the Eurasia Foundation and NED almost from the beginning of their existence (McFaul 2005, 155). The principle in NED work is to provide direct funds for "proposals that originate with indigenous democratic groups."[16] Evaluations of democracy-building work, such as McFaul's writings, seem to favor the NED approach over the USAID model, because the direct grants method has many advantages. Money goes directly into the recipient society, and this method permits greater flexibility in the design and implementation of projects. Although the strategy seems to be more effective in assisting civil society, this approach involves difficulties and limitations as well. In order to avoid any misuse of money, donors might be more likely to finance more Westernized groups that are familiar with grant proposals and are well known by the donor (Carothers 1999, 263, 271–72). It might be difficult to reach local partners, especially in countries with authoritarian governments, and identify whether or not they are worthy recipients. Finally, donors may be more likely to give bigger direct grants for fewer projects to organizations that are well known in the region (Aksartova 2005, 124–25).

The third strategy is represented by the activity of the Soros Foundation, and this strategy may be characterized as "going local." Unlike many other foundations, the Soros Foundation does involve local people in its efforts. The Soros Foundation established local foundations in each target country, and each local organization has a separate identity, along with local boards of directors and local staff. However, this method is costly, because of the expense inherent in providing capital to operate the foundations. Using this approach also entails allocating money to local groups through the individual national foundations, which is problematic because funds may be more likely to be distributed within a tightly knit circle of known associates.

This book addresses questions about how young democracies go about delivering their democracy assistance to recipient countries by examining Polish governmental and nongovernmental aid practices. Is there cooperation between governmental and nongovernmental sectors while they engage in supporting democracy in recipient countries? To what extent are strategies employed in Polish democracy assistance similar to or different from Western democracies' strategies?

The Polish Democracy Assistance Case

In order to examine democracy assistance efforts taken by a young democracy, this study focuses on Polish democracy assistance. The case study method was selected to address the relevant research questions because it allows for fully detailed description, in-depth examination, and explanation of a single example (George and Bennett 2005, 12, 21; King et al. 1994, 4–5). The examination of a single case allows the researcher to look for factors that may not be easily discovered in less detailed studies. With the detailed study of a single democracy assistance case, a researcher may gain a sharpened understanding of why and how such assistance is provided in a particular way and the mechanism by which a young democracy diffuses its newfound approach to governing to other countries. The additional advantage of a case study is that it may reveal elements that demand further research.

There are several reasons why Polish democracy assistance presented itself as an opportune case for answering the research questions posed. First, Poland is known for its active civil society, which was the major force in

bringing down communism and which has influenced other regime altera-
tions in the communist space. The Solidarity movement, which emerged in
1980–81 as an attempt by Gdańsk's shipyard workers to improve labor conditions, was an autonomous civil society organization, a distinct rarity in
the communist region. The movement gave impetus to the Poles' growing
demand for the right to organize and to speak freely. Eventually, Solidarity
became a political movement embracing workers, intellectuals, and dissidents who negotiated and then won the first partially free democratic election, on June 4, 1989. The Solidarity movement not only liberated Polish
people from communism but also sparked the events leading to the fall of
Berlin Wall, the collapse of communism in Central Europe and the Soviet
Union, and the end of the cold war.

A new model of political transition emerged from Solidarity's process
of peaceful resistance to communism. The result is the "roundtable talks"
model of negotiated (pacted) transition.[17] Solidarity is a symbol of citizens
mobilizing to achieve human rights, recognition of the sovereignty of individuals, and freedom of speech and association under dictatorial conditions. This movement provided a model of what is possible if workers,
intellectuals, and civil society activists come together en masse to resist
authoritarianism. The new model Solidarity generated helped shape thinking about democracy assistance and made civil society an important focus
for Western donors.[18]

Another reason why Poland is a good case study is that, among the many
countries that emerged after the collapse of the Soviet Union, it showed
that democratization is achievable and contributes to the prosperity of
the state and its citizens.[19] Poland was a pioneer in political and economic
transformation in the postcommunist region. It is one of the countries of
Central and Eastern Europe in which political and economic reforms were
particularly successful.[20]

A final reason that Poland makes an ideal case study for this research
is that, during the communist era and transformation process, Polish
civil society—including opposition groups, civic groups, and intellectual
and business elites favoring democratization—was the major recipient of
Western aid in the region. Many Polish nongovernmental organizations
were established with major assistance from external funds, and these associations played an important role in Poland's transformation from communism to democracy.[21]

Thus, we can reasonably assume this past experience would impel the
government and nongovernmental organizations toward democracy assistance, particularly civil society assistance. Because of Polish NGOs'

prominent role in the democratic changes in Poland, one may expect that they might also be active in assisting other countries with their democratic transformations. Moreover, Poland's future democracy assistance providers had learned the formula from Western donors who had provided democracy assistance to Poland, and they had even learned lessons from the West's mistakes in delivering assistance. Having gone through political and economic transition themselves and having had experience as recipients of democracy aid, Polish NGOs might have a better understanding of which projects are likely to work better and to produce more substantial results in different stages of movement toward democracy—from the beginnings of change while still under authoritarian rule, through liberalization and increased participation in regime change efforts, and then concerted work toward consolidation.

Utilizing Comparisons

Poland's democracy assistance has focused on Belarus and Ukraine—two post-Soviet states that border Poland—because these two countries figure prominently in Poland's foreign policy priorities, for both security and cultural reasons. The role of Polish diplomacy during the Orange Revolution in Ukraine is well acknowledged in the literature (e.g., Åslund and McFaul 2006; Wilson 2006). Poland proved to be both ready and able to play a key role in Ukraine, and, in doing so, the Polish government raised the EU's own profile in the region and helped place Ukraine high on the EU's agenda.[22] Belarus and Ukraine are important for the security of the whole postcommunist region, and this situation is acknowledged by both scholars and policy makers. Poland's government has many times emphasized its support for Ukraine's future membership in the EU and North Atlantic Treaty Organization (NATO); the Polish government has been actively involved in shaping EU policy toward its eastern neighbors as well. Taking into account these Polish diplomatic efforts, democracy assistance, which is a foreign policy tool, may be used together with other Polish actions. In addition to security reasons, historical and cultural ties with Belarus and Ukraine also are factors influencing the Polish government's decision to grant most of its aid to Belarus and Ukraine.[23]

The diffusion literature suggests that the greater the similarity between transmitters and prospective adopters on one or more sociocultural dimensions, the greater the prospect of diffusion (Bunce and Wolchik 2006; Lahusen 1999; Snow and Benford 1999). This book aims to demonstrate that those similarities facilitate closer ties, which in turn make diffusion of democratic ideas and behavior more likely to happen. A lack of cultural and language barriers, as well as geographical proximity, facilitates the engagement of Polish NGOs to form networks with counterparts in Belarus or Ukraine.[24] Through close partnerships and an almost "personal" aspect in their cross-border work, Polish civil society groups may be better informed about the political situation of the recipient countries and the internal factors that might create obstacles for the provision of assistance. Thus, nearby civil society groups giving assistance may be better equipped to address problems of civil society in the recipient country. Finally, geographical proximity may offer a chance for the development of long-term cooperation and thus may improve the work and status of civil society groups in the recipient country.

Moreover, Belarus and Ukraine present an interesting example of countries that have a shared historical past, including similar circumstances that culminated in the collapse of the Soviet Union in 1991, but ended up with different political systems in the twenty-first century. Belarus has been labeled Europe's last dictatorship (Garnett and Legvold 1999; Marples 2005; Schmidtke and Yekelchyk 2008). Ukraine, however, has only recently begun a difficult road toward democratic consolidation (D'Anieri 2007b; Flikke 2008). Presenting democracy assistance efforts in an authoritarian country versus in a country moving toward democratic consolidation highlights the challenges that these two countries create for democracy-assistance donors and sheds light on the ways in which the political context and relations between the Polish government and each of the recipient governments affect the selection of Polish assistance strategies. Moreover, taking into account the role of civil society in democratization and democratic consolidation, the study highlights the role of the third sector in Belarus and Ukraine and how international support should adapt in order to influence democratic changes in these countries through civil society.

Finally, by studying Poland's efforts to support democracy in Belarus and Ukraine, this book contributes to the debate in the postcommunist literature on democratic transition. It addresses the question of mitigating the so-called "postcommunist divide." Scholars of postcommunist democratization have noted that the communist space in Europe used to be considered "regional," because some countries within this area were politically, economically, and militarily integrated. It is commonly argued that the postcommunist countries witnessed not only a political transformation, from an authoritarian regime to a pluralistic democracy, but also an economic transformation, from a command economy to a free-market economy (Armijo et al. 1994; Offe 2004). However, the transformation paths of these formerly communist countries varied, and today there is a significant variation in political outcomes in the postcommunist space.[25] The differences between postcommunist countries regarding their democratic transition experiences encouraged political scientists to investigate reasons for this "postcommunist divergence" (Crawford and Lijphart 1995; Ekiert and Hanson 2003; King 2000; Kitschelt 2003; Rupnik 1999). This study investigates the possibility that this gap can be narrowed with the help of postcommunist countries like Poland that were more successful in their political transformations.

Time Frame and Methods

This study focuses on the Polish democracy assistance efforts that began in 2003, when the aid program managed by the Polish Ministry of Foreign Affairs was established, as well as on Polish nongovernmental efforts that date back to the 1980s and 1990s. Therefore, this project covers the period when Poland shifted from being a recipient to a donor and evaluates the country's democracy assistance efforts from that time until 2011.

The research findings are based on fieldwork conducted in 2008. The research included interviews with those actors who had the most involvement in democracy assistance activities in Poland. Generating a sample that includes the most important political players who participated in this work—Polish governmental elites and representatives of Polish nongovernmental organizations—avoids selection bias in the research (Tansey 2007, 766–69). Specifically, the book relies on information and opinions expressed in interviews with representatives of the Department of Development Co-operation in the Ministry of Foreign Affairs who manage Polish aid, as well as with staff members of Polish NGOs responsible for establishing policy guidelines and administering projects. The civil society organizations selected for this project work in at least one of the following areas: strengthening the civil society sector, advancing regional cooperation, advocating for democratic reforms, and shaping public policies in socioeconomic and political development pillars. In addition, the interview pool included representatives of the Zagranica Group, which is an association of Polish nongovernmental organizations involved in cross-border work, as well as two representatives from the National Endowment for Democracy, the US democracy assistance organization that financially supports many projects of Polish NGOs in Belarus and Ukraine. (A list of interviews may be found in appendix 1.)

The purpose of these interviews was to gather firsthand information and to go beyond the images, official documents, and statements issued by NGOs and governments. A list of questions was composed in order to find out from interviewees whether democracy assistance in Belarus and Ukraine was part of Poland's foreign policy or the goal of the organization; whether assistance was directed toward specific regions in recipient countries; what the aims of the projects were; and why there were programs targeting civil society in the recipient country. Respondents were asked about their evaluation of Poland's assistance programs for NGO development and civil society in Belarus and Ukraine, as well as about any obstacles that impeded the successful implementation of the project. All interviews were semistructured, allowing for flexibility and for new questions to be brought up during the interview as a result of what the interviewee said. However, for reasons of safety, I do not identify in the text Polish NGOs collaborating with Belarusian civil society groups, and I do not give the names of the Belarusian partners.[26]

In addition to in-depth interviews, the analysis is based upon a variety of materials written by policy makers and documents provided by Polish civil society organizations and European and US democracy assistance organizations. Literature collected during the meetings with interviewees included newsletters, journals, publications, reports, internal memoranda of donors, project documents, and evaluations. This material provides additional background on donors' and their partners' profiles and activities and allows for a better perspective on their projects over time. Based on gathered materials, an in-depth analysis is possible by tracing networks (relationships among donors and recipients) and by demonstrating how these networks function, as well as what strategies Polish NGOs use to disseminate democratic ideas and practices.

Abbreviations

Acronyms for some organizations reflect the spelling of the name in its original language; the names of all organizations are given in English.

ACAP	American Committee for Aid to Poland
ACILS	American Center for International Labor Solidarity
AFL-CIO	American Federation of Labor–Congress of Industrial Organizations
AFPC	American Foreign Policy Council
BEZ	Belarusian Ecological Green Party
BKDP	Belarusian Congress of Democratic Trade Unions
BRSM	Belarusian Republican Youth Union
CASE	Center for Social and Economic Research
CDC	Citizens Democracy Corps
CDiA	Center for Documentation and Analysis
CEE	Central and Eastern Europe
CERF	Central Emergency Response Fund
CIDA	Canadian International Development Agency
CIPE	Center for International Private Enterprise
CIR	Center for International Relations
CIS	Commonwealth of Independent States
CPI	Corruption Perceptions Index
CSSA	Training Center for Local Administration
DAC	Development Assistance Committee
DFID	Department for International Development
DG	Directorates-General in the European Commission
DMK	St. Maximilian Kolbe House for Meetings and Reconciliation
DSE	Democratic Society East Foundation
EBRD	European Bank for Reconstruction and Development
EDIT-Net	Education for Democracy International Network
EEA	European Economic Areas
EEDC	East European Democratic Center
EHU	European Humanities University
EIDHR	European Initiative for Democracy and Human Rights
ENP	European Neighborhood Policy

ENPI	European Neighborhood and Partnership Instrument
EPD	European Partnership for Democracy
ESF	European Social Fund
EU	European Union
EUROSTEP	European Solidarity towards Equal Participation of People
EWI	East West Institute
FED	Education for Democracy Foundation
FH	Freedom House
FSLD	Foundation in Support of Local Democracy
GEF	Global Environment Facility
GONGOs	Government organized NGOs
GSP	Generalized System of Preferences
IBRD	International Bank for Reconstruction and Development
IDA	International Development Association
IDEE	Institute for Democracy in Eastern Europe
IFC	International Finance Corporation
IFES	International Foundation for Electoral Systems
IMF	International Monetary Fund
IPA	Institute of Public Affairs
IRF	International Renaissance Foundation
IRI	International Republican Institute
ISO	International Standardization Organization
KGB	Committee of State Security
KOR	Workers' Defense Committee
KPN	Confederation for an Independent Poland
KPSN	Committee for National Self-Determination
MEDA	Mediterranean Development Assistance
MFA	Ministry of Foreign Affairs
MIGA	Multilateral Investment Guarantee Agency
NATO	North Atlantic Treaty Organization
NED	National Endowment for Democracy
NGOs	Nongovernmental organizations
NZS	Independent Students' Union
ODA	Official Development Assistance
OECD	Organization for Economic Co-operation and Development
OFOP	Polish National Federation of NGOs
OKOR	All-Poland Farmers' Resistance Committee
OSCE	Organization for Security and Co-operation in Europe
OSI	Open Society Institute
PAFF	Polish-American Freedom Foundation
PASOS	Policy Association for an Open Society

PAUCI	Poland-America-Ukraine Cooperation Initiative (later known as the Polish-Ukrainian Cooperation Foundation)
PCA	Partnership for Cooperation Agreement
PCDC	Polish-Canadian Development Co-operation Program
PGCF	Polish-German Cooperation Foundation
PHARE	Poland and Hungary Assistance for Restructuring their Economies
PHO	Polish Humanitarian Organization
PPN	Polish Independence Pact
PSSI	Prague Security Studies Institute
RBF	Rockefeller Brothers Fund
RITA	Region in Transition
ROPCiO	Movement for the Defense of Human and Civil Rights
SDPU	Social Democratic Party of Ukraine
SEED	Support for East European Democracy
SENSE	Strategic Economic Needs and Security Exercise
SIDA	Swedish International Development Cooperation Agency
SKN	Social Committee for Science
SPU	Socialist Party of Ukraine
STP	Study Tours to Poland
TACIS	Technical Assistance for the Commonwealth of Independent States
TANs	Transnational advocacy networks
TKN	Society for Academic Courses
UCIPR	Ukrainian Center for Independent Research
UDF	United Democratic Forces
UN	United Nations
UNDP	United Nations Development Program
US	United States
USAID	United States Agency for International Development
WFD	Westminster Foundation for Democracy
WFP	World Food Program
WIP	Freedom and Peace
WTO	World Trade Organization
YMCA	Young Men's Christian Association
ZPB	Union of Poles in Belarus
ZG	Zagranica Group

1 | Belarus's and Ukraine's Quest for Democracy

■ The political experiences of Belarus and Ukraine since the dissolution of the Soviet Union have broadly diverged, with Belarus backsliding toward authoritarianism and Ukraine struggling with democratization. Paralleling those political experiences are the two countries' situations with regard to civil society, which is the focus of this chapter. The crucial relationship between civil society and democratization and democratic consolidation, as well as aid donors' recent focus on civil society as they assist in the struggle for democracy, makes civil society a critical component of postcommunist transformations. This chapter explores factors behind Belarus's failure to democratize and Ukraine's problems with its transition to democracy and democratic consolidation. The investigation lays the groundwork for the analysis featured in subsequent chapters.

Belarus's Backsliding to Authoritarianism

In this book, the democratization process is defined as a transition that proceeds in a set sequence of stages: from the "authoritarian opening," through liberalization and increased participation, to regime change. Why has Belarus not progressed steadily forward on this gradual scale?

On August 25, 1991, the Republic of Belarus declared independence, and centuries of foreign control by Poland, Russia, and the Soviet Union ended in December 1991.[1] A year earlier, Stanislau Shushkevich, vice-rector of the Byelorussian State University, had been elected first deputy chairman of the Byelorussian Soviet Socialist Republic's legislature. Following the August 1991 putsch against Soviet president Mikhail Gorbachev, Nikolai Dementei, chairman of the Byelorussian Supreme Soviet, was forced to resign, and Shushkevich replaced him. Shushkevich served as head of state from 1991 to 1994. Pluralism became more visible, and new political

1

parties and organizations emerged. However, any positive developments (emerging new political parties and organizations) in Belarus after independence in 1991 were disrupted by the July 1994 election of Alexander Lukashenko as Belarus's first post-Soviet president.[2] This moment marked the beginning of the authoritarian system that has persisted.[3]

In 1994, Lukashenko won Belarus's first presidential elections with promises to halt market reforms, fight corruption, and reestablish Soviet-era social guarantees, which were reasons for his popularity as a candidate. Immediately after taking office, he asserted his main goal of significantly strengthening the power of the presidency in legislative and executive terms through amendment of the constitution in 1996. The amended constitution notably expanded the powers of the president and marked the end of a short period of fragile Belarusian democracy established after the collapse of the Soviet Union in 1991.[4]

The year 1996 was a deciding moment in the history of the state. The new governing structure was a superpresidential republic equipped with all the essential organs of democracy—a parliament, a constitutional court, political parties of various orientations, and trade unions—but controlled exclusively by the president.[5] The constitution, as amended in 1996, vests the president with unlimited prerogatives. The government of the Republic of Belarus is accountable to the sitting president, and he or she has the right to chair the meetings of the government, to determine the structure of the government by appointing and dismissing the deputy prime ministers, ministers, and other members of the government, and to declare any government regulation null and void (Constitution of the Republic of Belarus 1994, art. LXXXIV).

The 1996 referendum also replaced the unicameral Supreme Council with a much weaker bicameral legislature called the National Assembly of the Republic of Belarus. It consists of a 64-seat upper house, known as the Council of the Republic (with 56 seats elected by regional councils and 8 appointed by the president), as well as a 110-seat House of Representatives popularly elected for four years on the basis of single-member districts. Although the parliament officially holds legislative power, the functions of the parliament are also closely connected with the president's administration. The constitution effectively places severe restrictions on the legislative powers of the National Assembly and gives priority to decrees and orders signed by the president. Therefore, the parliament is essentially a rubber stamp mechanically endorsing the decisions of the president. The president may choose to dissolve the parliament and may also take the decision to terminate the powers of both chambers of the parliament (Constitution of the Republic of Belarus 1994, art. XCIII). The constitution gives the president control not only over the government and the legislative process but also over the courts, including the Constitutional Tribunal, and other judicial bodies (Constitution of the Republic of Belarus 1994, art. LXXXIV).

The president is elected for five-year terms, and there are no term limits (Constitution of the Republic of Belarus 1994, art. LXXXI). According to the Organization for Security and Co-operation in Europe (OSCE) and the Council of Europe, electoral regulations in Belarus do not guarantee free and democratic elections. The presidential elections of 2001 and 2006, in which Lukashenko was reelected, were claimed to be undemocratic by the international community. Moreover, presidential elections held in 2006 and in 2010 were accompanied by widespread violence, intimidation, and government repression.[6] After the 2010 presidential elections, seven out of nine Belarusian presidential candidates were imprisoned and one of them, Vladimir Neklyayev, was severely beaten by the security forces. Consolidation of absolute presidential rule in Belarus has eliminated meaningful electoral contestation. All of the declared winners in the parliamentary elections that took place in September 2012 were pro-government and supported the president (BBC News 2012).

The absolute authority of the president encompasses all institutions of power. Since 1994, all levels of local government have been united into a single system of state authority.[7] Lukashenko abolished the autonomy of local governments by having heads of regional administrations appointed by and subordinate to the president (Constitution of the Republic of Belarus 1994, art. CXIX). Local elections in 2007 and 2012 took place without meaningful competition or genuine choice. Opposition candidates faced obstacles in registering their candidacy, and authorities warned some that electoral participation put their jobs in danger.[8]

There is no political space for any real opposition. By strengthening the power of the presidency, the 1996 constitutional referendum eliminated all meaningful political competition and evicted the opposition from the decision-making process. Since then, the opposition has had no opportunities to present its views in parliament or in other state institutions because members of the opposition cannot be elected. Opponents of Lukashenko are also deprived of access to state television and radio. As a result, their contact with society is limited. Opposition leaders make efforts to unite the parties and NGO groups, and for that they are subjected to repression (discussed further below) but are still unable to form a credible alternative to Lukashenko.[9]

Lukashenko has no party affiliation, and political parties play a negligible role in the political process. In fact, they have been deprived of the opportunity to participate in the official political system. As of 2012, six pro-president parties and nine opposition parties had registered in Belarus, but none of the opposition parties secured a seat in the 2012 general elections. The government has also moved to restrict the activities of political parties even further by closing down regional party branches and de-registering several parties. For example, the authorities closed down the small Belarusian Ecological Green Party (BEZ) and a women's party, Nadzeya (Hope), for failure to comply with registration requirements—that is, insufficient membership and lack of the required number of regional branches (Silitski 2008).

Lukashenko's regime also is undemocratic because the president uses the military and police to stabilize the regime. Since the Belarusian judicial system is entirely dependent on the president and his administration, Lukashenko has used the subordinated legal system (just as in the case of actions against civil society) as a tool aimed against both public and private companies, making the private sector very weak.[10] Moreover, the Belarusian authorities seized control over the Belarusian economy: it is highly centralized and controlled by the state, with the private sector generating only about 25 percent of GDP (Gromadzki and Veselỳ 2006).

Belarus's unreformed and extensively bureaucratized economy experienced significant economic growth, as reflected by the GDP, for most of the last decade, but the economy performed strongly owing to a financial upturn in countries traditionally importing Belarusian goods and to generous discounts on energy provided by Russia. Belarus, which does not have its own sources of crude oil and natural gas and is essentially dependent on Russian energy sources, benefited from a rise in oil prices. This benefit was possible because Russia has sold oil to Belarus at lower prices (60 percent below the world price), while Belarus sold petroleum products to the EU at market prices (Gromadzki and Veselỳ 2006, 13). However, the "energy war" between these two countries throughout the winter of 2006–7 shook the prospect of long-term stability for Lukashenko's regime, since socioeconomic benefits are a major source of support for Lukashenko.[11]

Although there is pervasive state control and involvement in the economy, economic stability that the regime of Lukashenko promises may be more important for many Belarusians than opportunities offered by a market economy, according to Marples's (2006) findings. Belarusians are being convinced by the Lukashenko regime to believe that they have been "protected" from the dramatic changes that Russia experienced, such as economic "shock therapy," the presence of oligarchs, mass privatization, and high prices for housing, heating, and food. One Polish NGO activist, Paweł Kazanecki, observed that democracy sometimes has a negative connotation in postcommunist countries because it is associated with poverty, queues, lack of food, and corruption during Gorbachev's perestroika and similar conditions that Poles experienced under the leadership of Wojciech Jaruzelski.[12]

Another focal characteristic of Lukashenko's regime is government control over media in Belarus. Article XXXIII of the Belarusian constitution (1996) declares that "everyone is guaranteed freedom of thought and belief and their free expression" and media law also guarantees these rights, but in practice the Lukashenko regime systematically curtails media freedoms. Media outlets are being silenced by repressive laws and licensing rules, arbitrary closure, discriminatory pricing for print and distribution, and systematic harassment of journalists. The government generously supports the state-owned media. While more than two-thirds of periodicals are private, the state-owned press heavily dominates the information field in terms of copies distributed; the circulation of independent newspapers and magazines is very small in comparison with the government media.[13] As a result, most Belarusians do not have access to independent newspapers, and many are unaware of their existence. The state-controlled media play a key role in shaping public opinion and political views, just as it did during the Soviet era, and poor access to independent or alternative sources of information makes people vulnerable to government propaganda. Belarusian government propaganda also functions as a means of self-preservation for the regime by promoting the national (government's) ideology and strengthening the personal popularity of the president (Marples 2006). Such propaganda creates the impression that there is no difference between the president and the state, which helps rally voters around the president and burnish the image of Lukashenko.[14]

The ideology created by Lukashenko recalls that of Soviet times and is based on the concepts of "friends and foes," political and social myths, and views of the national history. Lukashenko is presented as the father of the nation, as irreplaceable, and as the guarantor of stability. Just as in Russia, there is the commemoration of the Great Patriotic War (1941–45) as the pivotal event in the history of Belarus. Moreover, sports play the same role as in totalitarian countries of the twentieth century. Belarusian authorities use sports as a means of propaganda, because sport inspires patriotism and loyalty to the state. Whereas the authorities underfinance culture and humanities, sports are well funded.

Indoctrination has been intensive at schools, colleges, and universities.

Belarusian students receive twisted facts about history and the current situation of the country. A state ideology course was introduced into schools in 2003. According to official history and ideology textbooks, Belarus has been a buffer for a long period in its history, protecting the eastern Russian-Slavic civilizations from aggression by and attacks from the West. The regime also stepped up its control over the educational system; the culmination came in July 2004, when European Humanities University (EHU) was forced to terminate its activities in Minsk due to government opposition. In an echo of Soviet times, Belarusian authorities deliberately isolate their country from Western influence.[15] There are attempts to consolidate Belarusian society by disseminating the notion that Belarus is threatened by foreign conspiracy. Lukashenko and his staff have alluded to activity by external enemies, namely, just as in Soviet times, the United States and NATO, now including regional allies such as Poland, as well as the European Union and the West as a whole. As expressed in an interview with Lukashenko by representatives of the mass media of the People's Republic of China on November 28, 2005, Belarusian foreign policy priorities are Russia, the People's Republic of China, Venezuela and other countries of Latin America, as well as Arab countries and the Middle East.[16] Russia in particular exercises more influence than other countries over Belarus for not only historical and cultural reasons but also political ones.[17] Since Alexander Lukashenko's election to the presidency in 1994, Belarus has been oriented toward Russia, and the country has expanded existing economic links to Russia through initiatives aimed at bilateral integration within the Union of Belarus and Russia, created in 1997. Russia also uses its leverage to influence internal matters.[18]

Lukashenko's regime has tried to convince Belarusian citizens that a "Color Revolution" would not improve their lives. During an annual address to the country's National Assembly on April 19, 2005, President Lukashenko said categorically that he was opposed to democratic changes that the West favors. Referring to the Rose Revolution in Georgia in 2003, the Orange Revolution in Ukraine in 2004, and the Tulip Revolution in Kyrgyzstan in 2005, Lukashenko said that no such option would be feasible in Belarus: all those regime changes were in fact not revolutions but "they are banditry under the guise of democracy" and the limit of such revolutions was fully exhausted by the Belarusian people in the past century (East View Information Services 2005, 14).

In order to ensure political loyalty to the regime, the government has established a propaganda and ideology system that pervades Belarusian society. All people who apply to work in the state administration must pass ideology tests before being appointed to a position. The ideology offices and departments are headed by so-called "ideology workers" (Usau 2007b, 43). Those workers, however, regularly participate in seminars and workshops organized by the Management Academy of the President—the major training center—so that they stay informed about changes in the official position of the government.

Lukashenko holds the Soviet-style view that the Belarusian identity, especially language, is something secondary, temporary, and transitional. When Belarus gained independence, Shushkevich put in place some measures to build a distinct Belarusian identity: Soviet symbols were replaced in favor of a white-red-white flag and a coat of arms depicting a knight on horseback, and Belarusian was declared to be the state language. However, after the election of Lukashenko as president in July 1994, nation-building went into reverse.[19] One of Lukashenko's first acts upon coming to power was to replace Belarusian national symbols, which included the coat of arms of the Grand Duchy of Lithuania, with Soviet Belarusian ones, except without the communist hammer and sickle.[20] He also declared Russian to be the official language.

Whereas the Belarusian language is not employed in politics, it did dominate in speeches, songs, and signs during the protests in the wake of the 2006 election. The Belarusian language is also frequently used by oppositionists and young people, and thus the fates of both Belarusian language and culture seem to be inseparable from the fate of democracy. Such an argument corresponds with scholars' analyses of Belarusian national identity. Eke and Kuzio (2000), in their analysis of failures of democratization in Belarus, point to lack of national identity as a factor that prevents Belarus from having democracy.[21] Jocelyn (1998, 73–93) argues that, in Belarus, the notion of national consciousness is highly problematic and fragmented. Throughout the history of Belarus, there have been many efforts to destroy Belarusian society, its sense of statehood, and cultures; as a result, no single Belarusian identity has ever had a chance to develop (Ioffe 2003). During the Soviet period, while there was a strong Ukrainian identity, the Byelorussian Soviet Socialist Republic had a much weaker identity and thus was less prepared for independence than was Ukraine.

The Belarusian regime thus features heavy-handed treatment of the opposition, disregard for democratic institutions and procedures, control over the economy, growing reliance on the police and special forces, efforts to destroy nascent civil society, and violations of the civil liberties and human rights of the Belarusian people, who classify Belarus as an authoritarian country. This movement away from democracy to authoritarianism caused the European Union and the United States to label Belarus as "Europe's last dictatorship" or an "outpost of tyranny."[22]

Belarus is considered an authoritarian regime not only by scholars but also by international nongovernmental organizations that conduct research and advocacy on democracy, such as Freedom House (FH).[23] FH ratings take into account political rights and civil liberties, which scholars consider basic to democracy. Dahl (1989, 233) argues that political rights enable people to participate freely in the political process, including through the right to vote, compete for public office, and elect representatives who have a decisive impact on public policies and are accountable to the electorate. In turn, civil liberties allow for the freedom of expression and belief, associational and organizational rights, rule of law, and personal autonomy without interference from the state. According to Freedom House, Belarus has been considered "not free" since 1996.[24] In 2012, its political rights rating was 7 and its civil liberties rating a 6; these ratings mean that the Belarusian regime is considered extremely oppressive and that the Belarusian people have severely restricted rights of expression and association.

Lukashenko's War against Civil Society

Belarus is one of the countries of the postcommunist world in which observers clearly see the preservation of a Soviet model of cooperation between state and society. Like socialist state regimes, the Belarusian government imposes its repressive capacity and institutional and ideological control on its citizens' everyday lives. From the beginning of Lukashenko's regime, the government aimed to destroy civil society, and primary targets of the Belarusian regime have been nongovernmental organizations.[25]

The Belarusian government sends the signal that it is not interested in the development of organizations independent of the state and their activities in the third sector. Government officials in Belarus have the right to control and monitor the work of local NGOs. Whereas, between 1994 and 1996, the number of socially and democratically oriented NGOs grew dramatically, circumstances have changed since Lukashenko was elected president (Wilde 2002). Some of the organizations that have been persecuted include the Youth Movement for a Democratic and European Belarus, Zubr (Bison), and Malady Front (Young Front). Also persecuted were human rights NGOs and other organizations, such as the well-known Vyasna (Spring); Grodno-based Ratusha (Town Hall), headed for a long time by opposition candidate Aleksandr Milinkevich; Civil Initiatives of Homel; Vezha, operating out of Brest; the Association of Belarusian Students; the

Belarusian Helsinki Committee, founded in 1995; and many more. Many of those civic organizations have been closed down or condemned to financial ruin using a variety of different methods, including politically motivated fines for holding unauthorized seminars or distributing nonregistered information materials.

The regime implemented a number of regulations targeting nongovernmental organizations. The Belarusian government has full rights to harass existing NGOs by denying or delaying the registration that is required by law. A civic organization is required to register with the government, which involves providing the personal information of all members. Between February 1 and July 1, 1999, the government required the entire third sector to re-register, and many NGOs and political parties were forced to cease their official activities. During this process, 211 organizations were refused registration (Zhuchkov 2004).

Due to government fears about the role played by the independent civic sector in the democratic, so-called "Color Revolutions" in Georgia and Ukraine, the Belarusian government launched another major campaign to liquidate NGOs in 2003–4. The regime forced almost one hundred NGOs to close down, and another one hundred, under pressure from the Lukashenko regime, decided to liquidate themselves in 2003 and 2004. The most widespread reason for liquidations was failure to obtain a legal address or a lease and to meet stringent and effectively impossible requirements demanded by laws regarding rents.

While denying registration to independent groups, the government has continued to create its own special interest organizations that the regime fully and directly controls. According to the Ministry of Justice of Belarus, as of January 2009, as many as 15 political parties; 36 trade unions, 2,221 NGOs (224 international, 702 republican, and 1,295 local); 22 NGO unions (associations), and 75 foundations (8 international, 3 republican, 64 local) were on the register in the Republic of Belarus.[26] Most of these organizations represented nonpolitical NGOs loyal to the regime. The spectrum of the Belarusian NGOs' activities is very broad. Most of them focus on education, issues involving youth, children, and veterans, and problems of women and the disabled. Some organizations focus on culture and art. The majority of NGOs operate in Minsk and the surrounding region.

The Belarusian government-organized NGOs (GONGOs) enjoy generous support from the government, including office space and preferential presidential attention. These entities are excluded from many repressive regulations applied to independent organizations. Two well-known organizations with this preferential status are the Belarusian Republican Youth

Union (BRSM) and the Belarusian Union of Women. BRSM is a replica of the Soviet-era Komsomol, imitates its predecessor in structure and ideology, and serves as a tool to instill loyalty among the younger generation. BRSM tries to attract members with privileged university admission and various discounts (Charter 97 2007).

These government-controlled entities also serve two purposes. First, by means of GONGOs, authorities co-opt civil society, just as they did under communism. The creation of GONGOs demonstrates that Lukashenko wants to create an uncivil society, one in which the behavior and opinions of the members are regulated and controlled by the regime. Second, through the network of government-controlled entities, authorities seek to gain control over authentic NGOs, as well as the activities of citizens.

The Belarusian authorities still tolerate civil society organizations as long as they do not have a significant impact on public opinion. However, the authorities closely monitor the situation to make sure that the influence of NGOs does not increase. Such a hostile environment in Belarus affects the public image of independent NGOs and threatens their existence. The few such organizations that still function today have lost many of their members and volunteers. The NGO Sustainability Index for Central and Eastern Europe and Eurasia reports on the strength and viability of NGO sectors in each country in the region and demonstrates that the overall conditions of the NGO sector in Belarus are worse than in other countries of the region (USAID 2007). Because of the hostile environment in which Belarusian organizations operate, they have problems with defining their missions, strategic planning, management structure, financing staff, modernizing office equipment, and so forth, as the NGO Sustainability Index reports. Organizations also suffer from a poor administrative and communication skill base.

Financial viability also remains the weakest aspect of "sustainability." Domestic funding sources are almost nonexistent. A weak private business community in Belarus supports the NGOs, but funds are scarce mainly due to government disapproval and sanctions against business activity. Belarusian NGOs receive financial and technical support from foreign donors, from membership fees, and through partnership with foreign NGOs for specific projects. Żejmis (2003, 279) reports that Belarusian civil society depends substantially on foreign funding—80 percent of the financing for organizations in Belarus has been raised from foreign foundations, associations, and private companies.

However, external donors face many problems in Belarus. First, it is difficult for donors to determine, for example, which organizations are truly independent women's NGOs. Second, the Belarusian government restricted access to international assistance as an attempt to limit the independence of Belarusian organizations. In fact, since 1997, when Lukashenko issued a decree regulating foreign aid for NGOs, from year to year it has been more difficult to support civil society in Belarus. Lukashenko also uses direct methods of punishing pro-democratic social activists for their cooperation with external donors by influencing family members and the activists' personal lives, such as threatening dismissal from workplaces, schools, and the like.[27]

In 2001, Lukashenko issued Presidential Decree No. 8, which limited conditions under which organizations could receive aid and restricted the circumstances under which foreign aid could be used for special purposes. Many Belarusian organizations were forced to end their cooperation with foreign partners and donors, putting them in a very difficult financial situation. Moreover, Lukashenko authorized almost every governmental body to exercise control over the ways foreign aid was used. In addition to the State Control Committee, the Ministry of Internal Affairs, the Ministry of Taxes and Charges, the State Technical Committee, and the Administrative Department of the President, the Committee of State Security (KGB) has also possessed the right to control since December 12, 2003 (United Way/ Belarusian National Non-Governmental Organization 2003). Later, another decree prohibited organizations and individuals from receiving and using assistance for preparing and conducting elections, referenda gatherings, rallies, street marches, demonstrations, picketing, and strikes, as well as for producing and distributing campaign materials and other forms of mass politicking among the population (International Center for Not-for-Profit Law 2006).[28]

The NGOs' record of influencing public policy is almost nil, and Belarusian NGOs have no means of communicating their messages through the media to the broader public. Also, because of this difficult access to media, the ability to reach people and to expand organizational membership is a problem for Belarusian independent organizations. Moreover, as the result of negative reporting in the government-controlled media, a positive public image of NGOs, including a broad understanding of and appreciation for the role that NGOs play in society, is also hampered (USAID 2007). The public image of the NGO sector in Belarus is relatively negative, since many perceive these entities to be interconnected with the opposition— which is dangerous. Any affiliation with independent organizations brings risk, especially since the Criminal Code of the Republic of Belarus (art. 193.1) calls for criminal penalties for anyone conducting activities under the auspices of nonregistered organizations or associations (Human Rights House Network 2009).

The question arises as to why Lukashenko does not like NGOs. Undoubtedly, the repressions against independent organizations have been meant to consolidate Lukashenko's power, but they also show that Belarusian authorities acknowledge the potential of civil society groups to bring down the regime as the Color Revolutions did in the postcommunist region. Therefore, the Belarusian government has tried to discourage NGOs from involvement in politics, so that "there will be no rose, orange, or even banana revolution" in Belarus (Gershman and Allen 2006, 38).

The Belarusian government's battle with civil society goes beyond harassment of nongovernmental organizations. The authorities target groups that have been involved in election campaigns and election observation and those linked to political parties, human rights activists, and journalists. The Law on Mass Events in the Republic of Belarus seriously restricts the freedom of assembly and freedom of expression. Lukashenko's regime classifies any activities not controlled by authorities as antistate. This means that not only political leaders and their activists, NGOs, and journalists but also ordinary people are seen by authorities as opposition forces and have been subject to criminal prosecution and administrative persecution for participation in demonstrations. For example, many teachers were fired in 2006 because of their political activity.

The regime has become increasingly repressive toward independent journalists. The Belarusian government closed down many independent newspapers, and these measures were accompanied by large-scale harassment of journalists.[29] The Committee to Protect Journalists lists Belarus as one of the most dangerous places for journalists and as one of the most censored countries in the world.[30] Independent journalists have faced arbitrary lawsuits under Criminal Code article 367 (slander against the president), article 368 (insulting the president), and article 369 (insulting government officials) (Council of Europe 2008). These articles stipulate large fines and prison sentences for those found guilty. For example, during the week of protests following Lukashenko's reelection for a third consecutive presidential term, in March 2006, authorities arrested more than forty journalists in an unprecedented crackdown. They were sentenced to jail for up to fifteen days. Radio station workers operate in conditions almost as difficult as newspaper journalists do. In contrast, state media journalists are well paid and socially secure as long as they do not write something that may put their careers and personal lives, as well as privileges, at risk.

Also vulnerable to repression from the Lukashenko regime are trade unions. Traditionally, trade unions seek better conditions and living standards for their members, but in Belarus the independent trade unions also focus on defending human rights. Independent unions have made efforts to expand their influence and have formed the Belarusian Congress of Democratic Trade Unions (BKDP) as an alternative to the state trade union center.

In response, Lukashenko has sought to restrict the rights of trade unions affiliated with the BKDP by using police and military forces to disperse workers' demonstrations, intervening in trade union conferences, and making an attempt to bring these groups under the government's control. Although Lukashenko's large-scale campaign against independent trade unions weakened them (e.g., membership fell drastically), he failed to eliminate them completely. The BKDP continues to function and relies on international support.

The situation of independent women's organizations is similar to that of other nongovernmental organizations. Such organizations as the Belarusian Organization of Working Women, the Women's Independent Democratic Movement, the Belarusian Women's League, and the Belarusian Association of Young Christian Women are struggling for survival and find it very difficult to work together. Nevertheless, despite all impediment and repression, they continue to exist and work, because they have one thing in common—each is too small to have a real impact on the women's political, economic, and social situation in the country.

Repression has also reached Polish minorities living in Belarus. In Brest, located at the border with Poland, there are many organizations representing the Polish and Ukrainian minorities. For example, nationally, there is the organization of Polish minorities called the Union of Poles in Belarus (ZPB), established in 1990. Through its activity, diversity, and innovative action, the union could add a positive element to the third sector in Belarus; thus, Belarusian authorities took action against ZPB. In 2005, the Belarusian government cracked down on the union and its activities, accusing Poland and the EU of trying to create an uprising similar to the Orange Revolution in Ukraine. Belarusian authorities do not officially recognize the organization and its leader, Anzhelika Borys, who openly criticizes Lukashenko's regime.[31]

Since 2005, all activities, including meetings and congresses, of ZPB have been regarded as illegal (Radio Free Europe/Radio Liberty News 2009). Some Belarusians are too frightened to participate in projects organized with Polish money, because, according to Belarusian propaganda, the Poles are agents of NATO and the United States and Poland are major enemies of Belarus (Zagranica Group 2003).

The Belarusian government's attitude toward the Roman Catholic Church is also determined by the "Polish syndrome" (Uładamirski 2007). The Roman Catholic Church, which represents the largest "minority," or non-Orthodox, religion in Belarus, has a shortage of Belarus-born priests because the number of men being trained in the country's only two seminaries (in Grodno and Pinsk) is insufficient to satisfy all the needs of the Catholic church, and those priests who come to Belarus from other countries are often denied visa extensions by the Belarusian government. At the end of 2006, seven Polish Catholic priests and five nuns were forced out of Belarus. The authorities have also harassed other religious minority groups, such as various Protestant groups, suspecting them of being instruments of Western influence in Belarus.

To conclude, one may argue that the Belarusian government's actions against civil society, which, encompasses nongovernmental organizations, trade unions, women's groups, dissident groups, academics, students, independent media, minority groups, and so forth, demonstrate that Lukashenko's regime is afraid of organized groups and independent initiatives and instead prefers to deal with an atomized society.

Signs of Hope for Democratization in Belarus

Given the oppressive nature of the Belarusian regime, one may ask whether civil society exists and can exist in the context of such an authoritarian state. Despite all of these negative tendencies in Belarus, it is apparent that civil society actively works in opposition to Lukashenko's regime. Some of those illegal (unregistered) organizations that the authorities closed, such as Ratusha, led by presidential candidate Aleksandr Milinkevich, did not cease their operations. Organizations that operate without official approval define themselves in opposition to the government and work underground. Even in such difficult conditions, in Milinkevich's opinion, they pursue the process of de-communization, de-sovietization, Europeanization, and democratization, and thus these NGOs are the future democratic elite of Belarus.[32]

The illegal (unregistered) NGOs are sometimes personally linked with the political opposition, because many politicians seem to use nongovernmental activism when other political channels are closed. For this reason, some organizations are directly involved with politics. Most of the participants in the Opposition Congress that was held in Minsk on October 1 and 2, 2005, were drawn from NGOs. Just after this congress of democratic forces, the Ministry of Justice started collecting data on members of NGOs who took part.[33] It is strongly suspected that such information was used by the security forces to complete lists of people to be arrested on the eve of the March 19, 2006, presidential election (Sannikov and Kuley 2006).

Undoubtedly, illegal NGOs engaging in oppositionist activities can be a useful and even indispensable force in the political process working toward the democratization of Belarus, since these organizations play a key role in the fight against the regime of Lukashenko. Developments accompanying the 2006 and 2010 presidential elections can be appreciated as an encouraging step toward change in Belarus. During the preparation for the presidential election of 2006 and afterward, coordination and cooperation between different groups increased substantially. In the fall of 2005, the Congress of Democratic Forces nominated Aleksandr Milinkevich to run in the Belarusian presidential election on March 19, 2006. As the election approached, state authorities exerted massive pressure on the democratic opposition and civil society by arresting key leaders and activists (especially those taking part in the "For Freedom" campaign), depriving organizational structures of financial resources, and creating obstacles to keep activists from influencing Belarusian society at large (Forbrig et al. 2006).[34] The election results granted an overwhelming victory (83 percent) to Lukashenko, compared with 6 percent for United Democratic Forces (UDF) leader Aleksandr Milinkevich, 4 percent for pro-presidential leader Siarhej Hajdukevich, and 2 percent for Belarusian Social Democratic Party leader Alexander Kazulin (Central Election and National Referendum Commission of Belarus 2006). Lukashenko won a third term, but the OSCE declared that the elections were neither free nor fair and that the voting did not meet democratic standards. Alexander Kazulin's criticism of Lukashenko in the media led to his imprisonment for organizing mass disorder, but, together with other Belarusian political prisoners, he was released by the Belarusian government in August 2008.[35]

The elections provoked the largest public protests since Lukashenko took power in 1994, bringing ten thousand to fifteen thousand activists onto Minsk's October Square on election day (BBC News 2006; Freedom House 2008a). The wave of popular protests against the rigged elections lasted for a week. Peaceful demonstrators withstood both threats of violence by the regime and icy temperatures. Milinkevich (2006, 9) himself said that "the tens of thousands of ordinary Belarusians that came out into the freezing streets of Minsk sent a message not only to the regime but to the whole country and the wider world. The content of that message is clear and unambiguous: We refuse to be lied to! We demand to be free! We are no longer afraid!" The repression has been gradually beginning to affect a growing number of Belarusian citizens, rather than just isolated and small groups of activists. During the crackdown, hundreds were insulted, abused, imprisoned, fired from jobs (women are especially vulnerable because they tend to work in professions controlled by the state, such as schools and hospitals), and expelled from universities (Vidanava 2007, 35). The majority of young people who took part in the 2006 mass protests emigrated.[36]

Similarly, during the 2010 presidential elections, between ten thousand and twenty thousand people took part in an anti-Lukashenko rally in Minsk in December. Thousands of protesters gathered to decry unfair elections and Lukashenko taking a fourth term in office. Hundreds of civil activists faced arrests, interrogations, and prison sentences or heavy fines. One of the candidates was beaten unconscious (Radio Free Europe/Radio Liberty 2010).

In sum, the events surrounding the presidential elections demonstrated that Belarusian society has been gradually expanding and becoming capable of organizing nationwide campaigns. The demonstrations showed that civil society is visibly engaged in the struggle for democracy in Belarus, thus creating prospects for democratization. However, despite those positive signs, scholars and practitioners acknowledge the weakness of opposition forces, resulting mainly from the extremely difficult environment in which they operate. Gromadzki and Veselỳ (2006, 17–19) find significant differences between the situation of the Ukrainian opposition before the Orange Revolution and the Belarusian counterpart. First, the Belarusian opposition was deprived of participation in the official political system in 1996, and it has no representation in parliament. The Ukrainian opposition, however, belonged to the Ukrainian political system; its politicians were members of the parliament. The leaders of the Orange Coalition had held high office, and they led parties. Second, opposition forces in Belarus do not have the typical channels of communication with the public, given the movement's total absence on television and radio and lack of support from business circles. Although the opposition in Ukraine also had no access to state media before the Orange Revolution, there were private channels; most of them more or less openly supported Viktor Yushchenko. Part of the private business community in Ukraine supported Yushchenko's "Our Ukraine" movement. Moreover, Yushchenko also was known before 2004 because of his public service and opposition to the incumbent, Leonid Kuchma. Thus, the Ukrainian opposition leader was a popular politician and well recognized in society. However, Belarusian opposition leaders are less well known.

In addition to the overall context in which the opposition has to oper-

ate, there are also internal problems and contradictions that make the opposition forces weak, as was visible during the political campaign of 2006. It
could be observed that not all representatives of the pro-democracy forces
accepted the choice of Milinkevich as the coalition's presidential candidate,
and some partners became more self-centered and sought to advance their
specific interests. Moreover, the oppositional coalition failed to create an
attractive picture of Belarus without Lukashenko and was reluctant to ad-
mit new members and partner organizations (Karniajenka 2007).[37]

Despite those weaknesses among opposition forces, the 2006 and 2010
elections demonstrated that civil society is the best hope for change in the
country.[38] The opposition did not win, but civil society showed a strong will
to resist injustice and election fraud and to mobilize, the For Freedom campaign being one example. This positive trend could be further encouraged.

Ukraine's Transition to Democracy

Consolidation remains a contested if not controversial concept in the
comparative politics literature. Scholars point to the difficulty of specifying
precisely when a consolidation begins or when a democracy is consolidated
(Diamond and Plattner 2001; Gunther et al. 1995; Linz and Stepan 1996). In
light of the scholarly literature on democratic consolidation, we might ask
what problems Ukraine has experienced with democratic consolidation.

From Hybrid Regime to Democratic Breakthrough

Like other post-Soviet countries, Ukraine faced the historic challenge
of creating a state with the rule of law, democracy, a civil society, and an
economic market. Scientists studying postcommunist transition argue that
Ukraine's paths of development after the collapse of communism, under
Leonid Kravchuk, as well as under his successor, Leonid Kuchma, could
be explained in terms of an aftereffect of the "Leninist legacy."[39] Political,
economic, and social arrangements stemming from communist times, specifically, the absence of a successor elite, the persistence of old institutions,
and the legacy of the command economy, could be observed in Ukraine.
Soon after Ukraine gained independence, new national institutions were
built very much within the existing institutional framework. Moreover, a
culture of corruption and nepotism from the former Communist Party of
Ukraine had strong influence on policy making. In other words, former
Soviet institutions together with post-Soviet elites created the greatest impediment for reforms.

The absence of clear institutional rules, as well the fact that some people were trying to keep the president in check, resulted in constant tensions between the president and the Verkhovna Rada (the Supreme Council, or parliament), which in turn delayed the adoption of a new constitution and agreement on the fundamental "rules of the game." Until the mid-1990s, the constitution of the Ukrainian Soviet Socialist Republic remained in force, yielding supremacy to the legislature. Perceiving the parliament as an obstacle to his consolidation of power, Kuchma, who won the 1994 presidential elections, issued a decree to strengthen the position of the president and place the government under his control. Moreover, contradicting his electoral promises of decentralization, he issued another decree aimed at subordinating local councils to the president, under the rationale that economic reforms could not be implemented without political reforms. Although Kuchma was in favor of expanding the economic powers of the regions, he was against granting them political autonomy and was thus trying to curb the powers of local authorities.[40] Because only the president had the power to issue decrees, he used that power extensively to regulate and strengthen the position of the president relative to the parliament. A new constitution, adopted on June 28, 1996, further strengthened the position of the president by giving him the right to issue decrees that reduced the role of the legislature.[41] Kuchma was thus able to regulate many fields of executive power.

Another feature of Kuchma's regime was that individuals, not institutions, dominated politics. The network of Kuchma's followers linked the state administration and the parliament, various political parties, the media, and economic actors.[42] Kuchma also used linkage with oligarchs to boost his status and political power—partly in exchange for access to state resources—and oligarchs helped to mobilize political support for Kuchma.[43] The expansion of opaque networks into the political sphere also included the parliament. Oligarchs and businessmen made full use of parliament to gain power over some political parties. Under Kuchma's regime, political parties received low state funding for their electoral campaigns, and insufficient legal rules and a lack of law enforcement encouraged some oligarchs to establish their own parties or "buy" candidates. Thus, political parties as a potentially balancing force in politics remained weak in Ukraine. Because of Kuchma's strategies to strengthen his position and his use of many informal practices, Ukraine under Kuchma came to be regarded as a "competitive authoritarian" regime with uncertain prospects for further transition to democracy.[44] Ukraine had many features of a hybrid regime.[45]

Suspicion focused upon Kuchma's government because of a scandal over

the murder of a journalist, Heorhiy Gongadze, a longtime critic of the regime and a crusader against corruption (D'Anieri 2007b, 92; Wilson 2006).
After Gongadze's murder and the release of transcripts of tapes that a security guard named Mykola Melnychenko had secretly made in the president's office, Kuchma's popularity began to diminish.[46] However, the most
significant change in the political arena in Ukraine occurred with the parliamentary election in 2002, when Viktor Yushchenko's Our Ukraine bloc won
the party-list vote, marking the first electoral success for the democratic
opposition since independence. This election helped polarize Ukraine's
political landscape. Other anti-Kuchma forces included the Socialist Party
of Ukraine (Sotsialisticheskaya Partiya Ukrainy, or SPU), led by Oleksandr
Moroz, and the Bloc of Yulia Tymoshenko (Blok Yulii Tymoshenko). The
election also was accompanied by popular protests called "Arise, Ukraine!"
and "Back to Europe!" It also might be argued that without the elite conflict
that began in 2000 and without the establishment of the Our Ukraine bloc in
the 2002 parliamentary elections, Yushchenko's victory in the presidential
elections of 2004 might not have occurred.[47]

The presidential election in 2004 represented a watershed in Ukraine's
political system. Kuchma could not run but instead put forth as a candidate Prime Minister Viktor Yanukovych, former governor of the Donetsk
oblast in eastern Ukraine. Yanukovych had a reputation as "a hard-liner
with little respect for the democratic rules of the game" (Fritz 2007, 180).
Yanukovych's main opponent was Viktor Yushchenko, who represented a
new image of a politician—energetic, professional, and Western-oriented
(Tudoroiu 2007, 328).[48] After the 2004 presidential election, there was a
run-off and Yanukovych was declared the victor. Protesters immediately
gathered in Kiev's Independence Square (the Maidan), marking the beginning of a democratic breakthrough dubbed the "Orange Revolution."[49]
Conciliation meetings were arranged between Kuchma, Yanukovych, and
Yushchenko, to which Lithuanian president Valdas Adamkus and Polish
president Aleksander Kwaśniewski, High Representative Javier Solana of
the EU, and Boris Gryzlov, speaker of the Russian state duma, were invited.
The Constitutional Court issued a critical decision when the tribunal overturned the Ukrainian Central Election Commission decision and declared
the second round of the presidential elections null and void. The rerun of
the second round was carried out in a new political and social atmosphere.
As a result, Yushchenko won easily with 52 percent of the vote over Yanukovych's 44 percent (Central Election Commission of Ukraine 2004b),
marking a new period in Ukraine's struggle for democracy.[50]

Civil Society Upheaval during the Orange Revolution

The fall of Kuchma's regime and the peaceful election of Yushchenko in 2004 were clearly due to an exceptional role of civil society and mass mobilization. Ukraine has one of the most vibrant civil societies of any post-Soviet state, and it existed even before the Orange Revolution. Already in the mid-1980s, as soon as it became possible to register NGOs under the new policies of glasnost and perestroika, a large number of civic organizations and initiatives emerged.[51]

Conditions in Ukraine were more favorable for the emergence of civil society than in Belarus, especially because the third sector was more autonomous, well organized, and better financed. This development was allowed because local authorities, especially in western Ukraine, were more permissive. An important feature of civil society was the tendency to form coalitions, such as Pora (literally, "It's time"). Pora was founded as a national council of nongovernmental organizations to mobilize civil society, with a special focus on young people. The association demanded free and fair elections in 2004 and succeeded in getting several hundred thousand people into the streets of Kiev during the Orange Revolution, contributing to its triumph.[52] Moreover, although major media outlets were owned by pro-president oligarchs, some critical media managed to survive, thanks to the support of dissident business owners like Petro Poroshenko. His TV Channel 5 proved to be very important during the Orange Revolution.

Despite these developments, some scholars were skeptical about the future expansion of civil society and its ability to influence political changes in the country (e.g., Kupryashkina 2000; Nanivska 2001; Sułek 2003). Civil society in Ukraine was described as weak, passive, fragmented, and demobilized (Kuts et al. 2001; Narozhna 2004, 256). Also, some scholars remain skeptical about the NGOs' role in the Orange Revolution. Yet, the question arises as to whether such massive social mobilization visible on the Maidan would have been possible if NGOs were not powerful enough to motivate citizens. Moreover, one should stress that civil society in Ukraine did not comprise only nongovernmental organizations. The success of the Orange Revolution was, foremost, a popular movement, one that would not have been possible without millions massed peacefully in Kiev and other cities to protest fraud in the second-round vote. As one observer noted, "Though the role of some Ukrainian NGOs, such as Pora, For a Clean Ukraine, Know How, and others, in mobilizing and triggering activism during the Orange Revolution should be acknowledged, this was above all the revolution of the people, not of the agencies" (Stepanenko 2006, 579). The active part of

Ukrainian society that contributed to the success of the Orange Revolution included local officials, some state university deans, and city administration officials who helped to organize transportation for those trying to get to Kiev. The support of the business and political elite for the opposition was a decisive factor. Journalists constituted another important and powerful civil society group (Prytula 2006).

A significant development in Ukrainian civil society during the Orange Revolution concerned the actions taken by the mass media, especially television stations. A few days after the second round of elections, they provided objective information and apologized on the air for having misinformed people over the previous few years. In the opinion of one Polish NGO representative, Jan Fedirko, the media's openness encouraged people, especially those in small towns without access to the opposition's Channel 5, to protest rigged elections.[53]

In addition to civil society, the second important factor in the Orange Revolution was an external one—international support.[54] Many international NGOs and civil society groups provided key assistance to their Ukrainian counterparts before and during the Orange Revolution. The youth-oriented group Pora, which played a crucial role in the protests, had received funding from external actors. International assistance also included political declarations, foreign observation missions, and mediation during the November political crisis. International election observers, as well as domestic observers trained by foreign NGOs, made a critical contribution by exposing and reporting election fraud and voting irregularities. Also, some prominent Americans, including Madeleine Albright, Zbigniew Brzeziński, George H. W. Bush, and George Soros, chose to exert direct individual influence on Ukrainian authorities by visiting the country in 2004. The United States also used the threat of sanctions. Authorities from new EU member countries in Central and Eastern Europe very actively and strongly committed themselves to helping Ukraine follow a democratic path. Presidents of new EU member states Poland and Lithuania, Aleksander Kwaśniewski and Valdas Adamkus, provided the impetus that led to the EU intervention in Ukraine in December 2004, and they asked EU High Representative for Common Foreign and Security Policy Javier Solana to travel to Ukraine to resolve the ongoing dispute over the presidential vote (RFE/RL Newsline 2004).

New EU member states not only provided assistance through mediation but also mobilized support in their countries. The Polish Sejm sent an appeal to its Ukrainian counterpart, the Verkhovna Rada, calling for a free and transparent election in Ukraine (*Gazeta Wyborcza* 2004; RFE/RL

Newsline 2004). Similarly, the Slovak government declared that the elections should be conducted in a free and fair manner and then sent election observers (Sushko and Prystayko 2006, 131). Poland also expressed support for Ukraine's future role in the EU and in NATO.

The Difficult Road toward Democratic Consolidation

The Orange Revolution marked a new period of Ukrainian political development and identified the end of the previous political era of the hybrid Soviet-type system. A civil society uprising against fraud-tainted elections, international mediation, and the elite pact that followed together opened up the possibility of a resolution of conflict by means of changes to the political system. Based on Linz and Stepan's (1996), Diamond and Plattner's (2001), Przeworski's (1991), and Dahl's (1997) criteria for the consolidation of democracy, Ukraine's recent political status indicates that it has yet to achieve democratic consolidation, despite the dramatic changes brought about by the Orange Revolution.

Problems with Commitment to Democratic Rules

Diamond and Plattner (2001, xiii) argue on the basis of Linz and Stepan's definition of democratic consolidation that there might be problems with governance in Ukraine. Under conditions of democratic consolidation, no significant political or social actors attempt to achieve their objectives by illegal, unconstitutional, or antidemocratic means. Unfortunately, Ukraine does not meet these criteria for democratic consolidation. Between 2005 and 2007, Ukraine entered a period of protracted conflicts among elites in government, and the frequent shifts of officials into and out of power not only paralyzed decision making in Ukraine but also, more importantly, resulted in unconstitutional actions (Flikke 2008, 376; Kuzio 2007b, 30).[55]

However, the beginning of 2010 brought new changes to the political scene and raised the question about the future of democracy in Ukraine. The presidential election winner was Viktor Yanukovych, the villain who sparked Ukraine's Orange Revolution.[56] He promised to rewrite the country's constitution to strengthen the powers of the president.[57] As a result, in October 2010, the Constitutional Court of Ukraine overturned the 2004 amendments, labeling them unconstitutional, and reinstated the semi-presidential system of government called for in 1996 by Ukraine's original constitution. Also, the change in the electoral law was the first step that Yanukovych's party, the Party of Regions, undertook to keep him in power, and this move demonstrates lack of adherence to democratic rules. Moreover, the continuing practice of the political instrumentalization of state in-stitutions, which was demonstrated by the imprisonment of former prime minister Yulia Tymoshenko and the harassment of other politicians, shows that Ukraine's democratic consolidation is uncertain.

Moreover, although the 2010 presidential election was the cleanest election the post-Soviet space has ever seen, the 2012 parliamentary vote received a strongly negative assessment by international observers. Un-like the two previous elections, this election used a mixed voting system (50 percent under party lists and 50 percent under simple-majority con-stituencies) and the ruling Party of Regions emerged as the clear winner. Walburga Habsburg Douglas, the head of the monitoring mission for the OSCE, blamed ruling politicians for using administrative resources to in-fluence the outcome of the vote (Radio Free Europe/Radio Liberty 2012a). She also expressed her opinion that the campaign was marked by biased media coverage and a lack of financial transparency. The results were criti-cized by the United Opposition coalition led by Batkivshchyna (meaning "Fatherland"), the party of jailed former prime minister Yulia Tymoshenko, which accused the government of rigging the vote and illegally taking away mandates won by opposition candidates (Shurkhalo 2012). Tymoshenko went on a hunger strike to protest the manner in which the 2012 election was conducted.

The abuse of power and the excessive role of money in parliamentary elections demonstrate that competitive and fair elections have not become the rule, and democratic progress in this sphere appears to have reversed in Ukraine. The erosion of meaningful competition in the post–Orange Revo-lution period, through different methods used against competitors, as well as weak institutions, may further undermine democratic consolidation in Ukraine.[58]

Moreover, institutional confusion and constant constitutional changes may paralyze Ukraine's politics. Unfinished political reforms at the local level create unclear lines of accountability, which further undermine dem-ocratic consolidation. Schmitter (2005) and Rose-Ackerman (2007) argue that accountability is an important dimension of democratic consolidation. Political accountability must be institutionalized if it is to work effectively, and it should be embedded in a mutually understood and established set of rules. The current division of rights and obligations creates confusion as to who is responsible for actions taken at the local level. Although the territo-rial division is clear, precise divisions of power among bodies at different levels, including administrative bodies such as urban communities, village councils, and township councils, are less clear.[59] Decentralization, that is, the process of expanding the functions and authority of the local government bodies, is very uncertain. The duality of authority at the local level, which dates back at least to Kuchma, lies in the conflict between the locally elected self-governance authorities and local administrations appointed by the central government. At the *raion* and the oblast levels, self-governing bodies and central state governing bodies collide. Oblast heads, called governors, are nominated by the prime minister. At the raion level, the head is nominated by the central government and confirmed by the oblast administration. There is a direct dependency of the raion on the oblast. Such "vertical dependency" is also reinforced by the way the oblast and local budgets are set. In other words, local and regional actors are dependent both with regard to budget resources and with regard to career opportunities and political survival.

Problems with Adherence to Democratic Practices

A real challenge for Ukraine's democratic consolidation is reversing the legacy of the Soviet Union and features of the old regime, because "informal" practices still dominate Ukraine's politics. Ukraine has modernized at a relatively rapid pace, and the business climate is improving, albeit confusingly. Some reforms, such as the privatization of land, have been done in a chaotic and larcenous way. Members of the government fought over land privatization issues, with many officials implicated in a variety of scandals (Emerson 2007). The number of firms involved in the privatization scheme, as well as the criteria for choosing them and the mechanics of privatization, is unclear (*Economist* 2005).[60]

Corruption, one of the country's biggest problems before the Orange Revolution, is little better. According to the Transparency International Corruption Perceptions Index (CPI), Ukraine was ranked 144 out of 176 countries surveyed, with the score of 26 in 2012. Corruption also reaches local governments; it is widespread at all levels of public administration, including the health and education systems. It pervades political parties, the legislature, the police, public officials, and the judiciary. In May 2012, the Ukrainian government created the National Anti-Corruption Committee, but it has yet to produce any results. Moreover, Ukrainian society can be characterized as a one with a high tolerance for corrupt practices.[61]

The tactics used by Leonid Kuchma are still prevalent and are adapted to new political circumstances. One of them is nepotism or, *kumivstvo,* which could be observed during the 2012 parliamentary vote. A significant number of incoming and returning Verkhovna Rada deputies were close relatives of high-level political candidates in Ukraine. They could profit from the endorsements (both personal and financial) of these relatives, which helped them to win elections.[62]

Opaque groups continued to play an important role in the new post–Orange Revolution era. As in post-Soviet Russia, there is group of oligarchs who acquired tremendous wealth and significant political influence in Ukraine. Yet, since the end of Kuchma's regime, the oligarchs' assets and political influence have been cut back only to a limited extent. Debates about privatization, as well as accusations of corruption in the first government after the Orange Revolution, were closely linked to the relative power and influence of the oligarchs in Ukraine. The Party of Regions continued to collaborate closely with oligarchic groups, especially with Rinat Akhmetov, Ukraine's wealthiest businessman; he and managers of his company were entered on the Party of Regions' election list.[63]

Linz and Stepan (1996, 3) argue that consolidation of democracy has been accomplished when the executive, legislative, and judicial powers are not constrained by other actors. The dominance of oligarchs, as well as Russia's influence on Ukraine's politics, suggests that Ukraine does not meet this criterion for democratic consolidation. Jan Piekło, a Polish NGO activist from the Poland-America-Ukraine Cooperation Initiative (PAU-CI), argues that "the fruits of the Orange Revolution are wasted in this moment mainly due to Ukraine's large neighbor—Russia, who in all possible ways wants to prevent these efforts . . . and the term 'season state' used by Putin toward Ukraine demonstrates Russia's attitude toward changes in Ukraine."[64]

Ukraine is heavily dependent on Russia's energy resources.[65] But this dependency stretches to the political sphere and poses a threat to the stability of Ukraine's democratic system.[66] Russia has a strong influence on the eastern regions of Ukraine—especially its heavy industries. In the Ukrainian oblasts of Luhansk, Dnipropetrovsk, and Donetsk, the Russian influences can be detected in daily life, because they are long term and deeply rooted.[67] Yanukovych, former governor of the eastern Ukrainian Donetsk oblast, was endorsed by Russia's President Vladimir Putin, who went to Kiev the week before the first round of the 2004 election and supported Yanukovych's candidacy (Lozowy 2004). Thus, Russia's presence contributes to political cleavages in Ukraine. Less economic dependence on Russia would mean less political leverage for Russia.[68] Jan Fedirko and Paweł Kazanecki, Polish NGO activists, observe that some oligarchs seem to be aware of this leverage and have become more interested in modernizing the country through their business contacts with the West, which will help Ukraine to be less economically dependent on Russia.[69]

Although oligarchs largely seem to have a negative impact on democracy consolidation, some oligarchs did support the Orange Revolution.[70] They also want the West to have a good impression of Ukraine. Prior to President George W. Bush's visit to Kiev on April 1, 2008, there were protests on the city's streets. Akhmetov, the wealthy businessman, immediately persuaded demonstrators that it would not be good for Ukraine's image if protests were taking place while the US president was visiting Ukraine.[71] Moreover, one of the two biggest Ukrainian companies owned by oligarchs, the Sistema Company, funded a conference organized by a Polish NGO in Ukraine.[72]

Despite the recent setback in democratic rules and practices, some observers and analysts across the region remain optimistic, believing that Yanukovych's rule will not end the progress toward democratization.[73] One of the reasons for optimism is that the transition to democracy started twenty years ago, and it may be very difficult to reverse this process. A second reason for optimism is that the civil society empowerment of the Orange Revolution, once experienced, is less likely to be taken back. However, the first signs of a rollback of civil liberties in the post–Orange Revolution period undermine this optimism.

The Weakness of Civil Society and Problems with Political Culture

The Ukrainian Orange Revolution demonstrated how important civil society can be in democratic transformation and that the involvement of civil society can stimulate mobilization against authoritarian regimes and lead to the creation of a democratic political system. Clearly, the Orange Revolution has improved the chances for liberal democracy in Ukraine, but it did not automatically generate the desired outcome. The eventual outcome of transition also depends on the civil society, the role of which does not stop when a transition point is reached.

After the huge street protests in December 2004, many Ukrainians said that they were much freer, and the new government's critics were not afraid to give their names to journalists, as they had been during the previous regime (*Economist* 2005). Ukrainian media reported the biggest improvement in its situation since the pre-revolutionary period: the media sector grew (with many new independent newspapers) owing to the appearance of new domestic and foreign investments and the development of the advertising market (Freedom House 2008b).

However, despite the growth of the media, freedom of speech and the press is doubtful because political and economic groups continue to have a strong influence in the media sphere. The National Union of Journalists of Ukraine publicized a list of officials and judges silencing the press in Ukraine, which indicates that censorship and government pressure are still present in Ukrainian media (ZIK 2009). The Independent Media Trade Union in Kiev also raised the issue of the many unsolved murders of journalists in Ukraine since the country gained independence (Radio Free Europe/Radio Liberty 2009a). Moreover, investigation of the infamous murder of investigative journalist Gongadze in 2000 has been hampered by the inconvenient deaths of key witnesses (*Economist* 2005). Lack of information regarding this and other murders creates a blurred picture of how dangerous it is to work as a journalist, and it implies that those who ordered the killing could be in high offices (Radio Free Europe/Radio Liberty 2009b). Such developments run counter to the notion that Ukraine is now a recognizable democracy with free media and a strong opposition led by civil society.

After the Orange Revolution, civil society grew, especially in terms of the number of organizations that emerged. Ukrainian NGOs provide services in many areas—consumer rights, women's rights, Chernobyl, HIV/AIDS, human rights, and environmental protection. For the most part, authorities do not interfere with the activity of NGOs, and organizations rarely face harassment. NGOs register only through the Ministry of Justice, and it takes usually ten days to three months to register, depending on the type of NGO at issue. However, it is still easier to register a business (US-AID 2011).

Undoubtedly, Ukrainian organizations grew in terms of number, size, and variety, but the third sector also presents some internal weaknesses. It should be recognized that the majority of these organizations are based in the capital (Kiev)—the center of political and economic activity—and in a few urban and industrial areas, such as L'viv, Dnipropetrovsk, and Donetsk or the Crimean Autonomous Republic (Sushko and Prystayko 2008). Agricultural regions, which make up the majority of Ukraine, have few NGO networks. There is still a low public image of NGOs and weak links with their constituencies overall. Moreover, although improved over the few years, financial viability is impaired. Financial viability improved because of increased diversification of domestic funding (especially from the business sector), but contributions are still scarce relative to international assistance.

The presence of NGO experts in both electronic and print media is generally visible, but a large number of NGOs still lack training in media outreach (Sushko and Prystayko 2008). Moreover, the collaboration between NGOs and media in Ukraine has become a bit problematic. The question also arises as to whether nongovernmental organizations' strength and involvement in political matters relates directly to the quality of democracy in Ukraine.[74] Diamond (1994, 8–9) argues that civil society's strength can generally be measured by how much it can influence all levels of government. After the Orange Revolution, the NGOs' advocacy efforts were delayed, mainly due to political stalemates. In 2011, the NGO Sustainability Index for Central and Eastern Europe and Eurasia (USAID 2011) reported that civil society organizations lobbied for the Law on Public Access to Information and amendments to the tax code, and they also developed the Draft Law on Freedom of Peaceful Assemblies to replace the existing law. However, it is too early to say whether this positive trend will last. Whereas local government authorities have become more open to working with civil society organizations, there is still not much improvement in the organizations' interactions with national authorities.

When US Secretary of State Hillary Clinton expressed her opinion that governments in the former Soviet space were "becoming much more aggressive" in trying to stifle dissent and prevent the free expression and exchange of views, it sparked heated public debate over the situation of civil society in Ukraine (Radio Free Europe/Radio Liberty 2012b). Scholars who examine the overall role of Ukrainian civil society in the post–Orange Revolution context also remain skeptical about the strength of the activist opposition. They have concluded that although civic activists made an important contribution to the mass mobilization underlying the revolution and leading to political change, civil society did not play a dominant role afterward. Tudoroiu (2007, 316) argues that the struggle for power within the ruling elite under Yushchenko negatively affected civil society's chances to participate in the political transformation and participate in debate over reforms. Many scholars are of the opinion that this weakness of Ukrainian civil society in the postrevolutionary political environment stems from divisions in Ukrainian society at large with respect to the democratic transition and that these divisions were also apparent during the Orange Revolution.[75]

Geopolitical, historical, and economic factors play a role in this polarization of Ukrainian society. Ukraine is a country of three culturally different units, but the western and eastern parts are particularly distinct. The west is dominated by Ukrainian-speaking people with pro-Western views. The east is occupied by Russian-speaking people living in the Donetsk basin (Donbas) and Crimea and identifying predominantly with Russian or even Soviet-style political culture (van Zon 2005b, 394). Many residents of russophone eastern Ukraine feel closer to Moscow than Kiev and consume

Russian popular culture, including television programs, books, and newspapers (Osipian and Osipian 2006, 500). According to one Polish NGO activist, Paweł Bobołowicz, in some eastern regions of Ukraine, Russian TV, radio, and press predominate; it is difficult to find even Russian-language Ukrainian mass media. As Bobołowicz reports, "'Who is interested in what is happening in Kiev?' said a waitress when asked about the newspapers covering Ukrainian politics. People know names of Russian politicians better than Ukrainian ones."[76] In central Ukraine (in terms of geography and culture) people speak both languages.[77]

The issue of regionalism in Ukraine and its impact on politics has been extensively discussed by scholars.[78] The fact that those linguistic and regional divisions drive Ukraine's political development was especially visible during the 2004 presidential election. Viktor Yanukovych is representative of the eastern, Russian-speaking Donbas region, where economic oligarchs tightly control the local media and political life, while Yushchenko seemed to represent a Western-oriented politician. Thus, eastern and southern Ukraine largely but not exclusively voted for Yanukovych; the western part of the country supported Yushchenko. The vote not only reflects a political preference but also a political culture. The Orange Revolution, which was mainly based in western and central Ukraine, created the impression that the revolution was conducted by western and central Ukrainians and was therefore not a collective action on behalf of the whole nation. Ukrainians with a more pro-European national identity have been easier to mobilize than those with an eastern, more Slavic identity.

The question remains how polarization of society with respect to democratic transition affects the strength of civil society and eventually democratic consolidation. Scholars point out that a democratic system requires a political culture—consisting of citizens' behaviors, practices, and norms concerning political life—that is consistent with that political order (Almond and Verba 1963, 369; Inglehart 1988; Putnam et al. 1983). Particularly appealing here is the work of Inglehart (1988), who finds that such elements of political culture as interpersonal trust, satisfaction, and support for the existing social order are important factors affecting democratic stability. Thus, essential differences and distrust among various sectors of society may have negative political consequences. If all citizens share a common political culture, better governance and democratic consolidation may result. Putnam et al. (1983, 65) explain that when society is interested in social and political issues and shows "more commitment to modern, secular and democratic values," then society is less willing to approve of political systems other than democracy.

O'Donnell (1988, 283) suggests that, "if political democracy is to be consolidated, democratic practice needs to spread throughout society, creating a rich fabric of democratic institutions and authorities." In this vein, Linz and Stepan (1996, 16) point out that a democratic regime is consolidated when a strong majority of the public, even in the midst of major economic problems and deep dissatisfaction with incumbents, believes that democratic procedures and institutions are the most appropriate way to govern collective life, as well as when support for antidemocratic alternatives is quite small. Finally, Dahl (1997) argues that the consolidation of democracy implies and requires the emergence of a democratic political culture: political trust, tolerance and willingness to compromise, and belief in democratic legitimacy. Unfortunately, this is not the case in Ukraine yet. It is thus fair to say that divisions in Ukrainian society with respect to democratic transition translate into the weakness of civil society that undermines democratic consolidation.

Undoubtedly, one also cannot ignore in this analysis Lijphart's consociational mechanism, which argues that reinforcing cleavages can be managed beneficially (Lijphart 2004, 96). However, it should be stressed that this mechanism is not in place in Ukraine since political elites, instead of mitigating disparities among groups, regularly pursue polarizing strategies. Ukraine's regional divisions were apparent not only during the Orange Revolution but also during demonstrations in 2007, when Ukrainian leaders were using the polarization of society with respect to democratic transition as a tool in their struggle for political power.[79] Moreover, the presidential vote of 2010 also demonstrated the territorially aggregated basis of support and polarized views between western and eastern Ukrainians.[80] Thus, it seems that overcoming co-optation and the problem of alienation of civil society may be crucial for reducing the potential for system volatility observed in Ukraine and the establishment of liberal democracy in Ukraine.

Belarus and Ukraine, having similar initial conditions for democratization following the collapse of the Soviet Union in 1991, ended up with different political situations; one has consolidated authoritarianism and the other is aiming toward an uncertain democratic consolidation. Taking into account the differences between these two countries and the challenges they face, the states provide interesting cases for democracy assistance studies.

Analysis shows that political power in Belarus is concentrated in the hands of the president, who, with prerogatives given to him by the constitutional referendum of 1996, controls the government, the legislative process, and the judicial branch. Electoral fraud and manipulation are rampant, too. President Lukashenko disregards democratic institutions, does not allow any opposition, and relies on the police and special forces to ensure loyalty to the regime. Human rights abuses, indoctrination through the media and the educational system, and reluctance to build Belarusians' cultural identity are some of regime's features.

Most apparent, however, is the Belarusian regime's attitude toward civil society groups, such as nongovernmental organizations, journalists, trade unions, the Polish minority, and the Roman Catholic Church. Belarusian civil society faces increasing repression—constant surveillance, closure of independent organizations, and harassment—by the government. Whereas government-organized NGOs, supported by the Belarusian authorities, are in good shape, the situation of many independent civil society groups is poor; they are merely tolerated by the regime, unless their influence increases. A series of laws has restricted public gatherings and significantly limited civil society activities.

Despite all of these negative tendencies in Belarus, civil society persists, and it continues to work against Lukashenko's regime. Those organizations considered "illegal" by the Belarusian authorities are working underground and in alliance with opponents who were visible during the Opposition Congress in 2005. Moreover, the protests before and after the presidential election of 2006 demonstrated that civil society is capable of organizing itself against the regime amid the risk of being imprisoned or expelled from the universities. Also, Belarusian oppositionists find means of communicating with each other, especially via the Internet, and they have unifying symbols, such as the Belarusian language.

Ukraine shifted from a regime in transition in the early 1990s to a hybrid regime with growing concentration of power in the hands of President Kuchma in the late 1990s, and it then shifted toward a democratic regime in late 2004, although it remained unconsolidated. Kuchma's ten years of presidency and its impact on institution-building and the conduct of politics in newly independent Ukraine cannot be ignored. The Constitution of 1996 created the semipresidential system, with strong presidential powers reaching down to lower administrative units. Although the amendments to the constitution introduced in 2006 reduced some presidential powers, the "vertical dependency" that goes from the lowest local level up to the central government still exists. Moreover, Kuchma's informal practices—clientelism, control of the media, and opaque elites—echo in current Ukrainian politics.

Thirteen years after its independence from the Soviet Union, Ukraine finally found itself on a democratic vector started by the Orange Revolution in 2004. Ukraine shows many features of political and civil liberty, but it is at the beginning of a difficult road toward democratic consolidation that will not be successful if Ukrainian elites do not show commitment to democratic rules and adherence to democratic practices. Moreover, whereas civil society in Ukraine is strong in comparison to that of other post-Soviet societies, as demonstrated during the Orange Revolution, in the postrevolutionary environment Ukrainian civil society remains weak vis-à-vis the government and is culturally and ideologically divided.

In light of this analysis, a key question is whether democracy assistance providers recognize these challenges and to what extent the Polish government and its partners take them into consideration.

2 | Polish Governmental Aid Programs

■ The Polish government provides aid for democracy assistance in various areas, through multiple channels of aid distribution, and with various partners. Drawing on data from the Polish Ministry of Foreign Affairs (MFA) that has not previously been addressed by scholars, the analysis in this chapter shows how Poland, as a young democracy, conceptualizes democracy assistance. It also discusses whether the choice between different approaches to supporting democracy, emphasized in democracy assistance literature, is relevant in the case of new donors. Some policy makers and scholars observe that there are two distinct approaches to democracy assistance—political and developmental. US democracy assistance is seen as basically political, while the European Union's democracy-building efforts are viewed as largely developmental. A political approach highlights the importance of citizens' participation in democratic political processes and focuses on assisting civil society groups and politically oriented NGOs. A developmental approach, however, gives more emphasis to assisting socio-economic development in the first place, rather than supporting political openness.

The analysis here shows that projects financed by the Polish government in Belarus and Ukraine do not fall neatly into these categories. Rather, this study demonstrates that the Polish government seems to understand the difference between actions leading to democratic breakthrough versus actions leading to democratic consolidation and that these actions require the employment of different types of assistance. In other words, the Belarusian reversion to authoritarianism and Ukraine's difficult path toward democratic consolidation, discussed in chapter 1, are reflected in Polish democracy assistance to these countries. This chapter also highlights the role of civil society, both as a source and a recipient of democracy assistance,

in Polish efforts to aid Belarus and Ukraine and in efforts to influence the
EU approach.

Poland among Other Donors

Democracy assistance is no longer the exclusive domain of Western advanced democracies; many young democracies, once recipients of aid, now
act as donors themselves. In the context of this analysis of the Polish approach to providing democracy assistance to its neighbors, it is instructive
to show how Poland, as a new donor, has entered the international arena
and what motives and means the Polish government has for engaging in
aid provision.

According to the Organization for Economic Co-operation and Development's (OECD) data on Polish Official Development Assistance (ODA)
going back to 1998, Poland, in comparison to Western countries, provided
more aid in 2010 than New Zealand and was only slightly behind Portugal,
Luxembourg, and Greece.[1] As compared to other young democracies, Poland, as a non–Development Assistance Committee (DAC) OECD country,
provides fewer financial resources for international assistance than Korea
but clearly stands out as the major donor from the postcommunist region,
outpacing Hungary, the Czech Republic, and the Slovak Republic.[2]

Total ODA provided by Poland in 2010 was $376 million, the equivalent
of 0.08 percent of Poland's GDP.[3] Year by year, the Polish government has
increased funds allocated to foreign assistance. These funds support multilateral assistance (assistance provided through international organizations)
and bilateral assistance (provided directly through Polish institutions, organizations, and other bodies).

One might ask why the Polish government is providing assistance to
other countries. As emphasized in public documents and in an interview,
both international commitments and domestic interests have influenced
the Polish government to grant aid.[4] Poland has an obligation to provide
aid that stems from its membership in international organizations. By obtaining membership in the OECD in 1996, Poland demonstrated its aspirations to join a "club" of the developed countries (the world's wealthiest),
which are actively involved in aid provision. Because of this membership in
the OECD, it is Poland's obligation to provide aid to developing countries.
Moreover, the Polish government endorsed the United Nations Millennium
Declaration in 2000, the Political Declaration and Plan of Implementation
adopted during the World Summit on Sustainable Development in 2002, as
well as the Paris Declaration, emphasizing the effectiveness of aid imple-

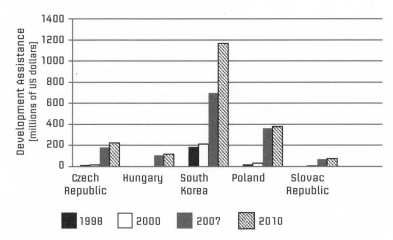

FIG. 2.1. The amount of official development assistance provided by some young democracies. Development Co-operation Reports are available at OECD iLibrary, and the data represented here are from October 4, 2012. Note that the official development assistance net disbursement is the sum of grants, capital subscriptions, and net loans (loans extended minus repayments of loan principal and offsetting entries for debt relief). There are no data reported for Hungary from 1998 and 2000 or for the Slovak Republic from 1998.

mentation.[5] By supporting these international initiatives, Poland pledged to share responsibility and become involved in actions aimed at solving global economic, social, and humanitarian problems.

However, above all, membership in the European Union has had an impact on Poland's aid provision. With its accession to the European Union on May 1, 2004, Poland demonstrated that the state is politically and economically ready to join a club of major European aid donors and to undertake initiatives, including aid provision, not only at the European but also at the global level. The EU is considered one of the world's largest donors, and it requires countries that join this organization to commit to provide help to developing countries. Like other member states of the EU, Poland is obligated to have an institutionalized system of providing aid and to co-finance EU assistance programs. Therefore, since Poland's accession to the EU, much of Polish aid has been channeled through institutions and programs managed by the European Commission. According to the annual report of the MFA in 2009, the Polish share in the EU total assistance budget in 2009 was 3 percent and was the largest of all the new member states. The Polish contribution exceeded that of some of older members of the EU, such as Sweden, Denmark, and Austria.

The EU not only requires Poland to contribute to the European Community's multilateral aid provision and to actively participate in common initiatives undertaken by the EU but also shapes Polish bilateral aid. The development policy of the European Union, termed the European Consensus and adopted in December 2005, laid out common objectives, rules, and values guiding assistance efforts undertaken by all EU members. The European Consensus, for the first time since the existence of the EU, defines the framework of common principles within which the EU and its member states will implement their development policies.[6] According to this major policy, the volume of assistance and the expected increase in the volume of Poland's assistance is subject to close coordination within the entire EU. As a result of its membership in the EU, Poland committed itself to reach the ODA/GDP ratio of 0.17 percent by 2010 and 0.33 percent by 2015.[7]

Despite the fact that assistance provision is a new area of Poland's international activities, Poland was able to expand channels of aid distribution in a short time. Figure 2.2 demonstrates the current model of Polish aid provision. The Ministry of Foreign Affairs is the predominant governmental body dealing with Polish aid, because it sets the direction and priorities of Polish aid policy and manages the implementation of bilateral and multilateral project assistance. Specifically, within the MFA there is the Development Co-operation Department, which is responsible for managing aid and cooperation with international organizations, such as the EU, UN, and OECD. The department has been operating within the MFA since September 2005. Prior to that date, all assistance-related activities were carried out by the UN System and Global Problems Department at the MFA. The Development Co-operation Department comprises the Development Policy and Programming Unit, the Unit for Implementation of Development Cooperation Programs, and the Democracy Support Unit.

Whereas the volume of Polish foreign assistance and Poland's overall engagement in assistance activities are a function of its membership in the EU, the choice of recipient countries is within the EU members' domains. The European Union does not interfere in the geographical distribution of financial resources; it allows its members to define the direction of their assistance. According to the European Consensus on Development, the member states enjoy some freedom to choose not only the geographic but also the sector priorities for their assistance activities. Therefore, like other EU members, Poland chooses its priority countries and areas of assistance based on their compatibility with Polish foreign policy goals and the so-called Polish "comparative advantage," that is, its specialization in certain types of assistance.[8]

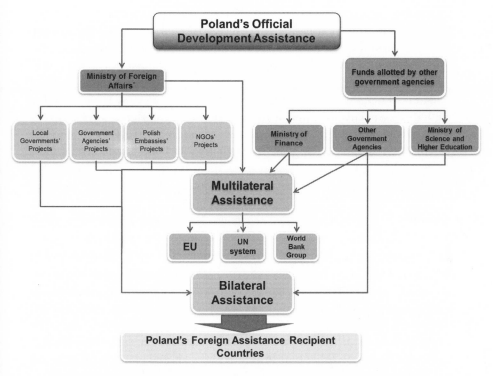

FIG. 2.2. Poland's foreign assistance channels. Source: Polish Ministry of Foreign Affairs 2006.

Since Poland has less expertise, as well as fewer organizational and logistic capacities for providing aid to distant countries, than older democracies, the government is more likely to provide aid through multilateral channels. The bulk of financial resources allocated for multilateral assistance are payments made into the budget of the European Union. The remainder constitutes financial resources allocated for multilateral assistance in the form of projects managed by the United Nations System, World Bank Group, the International Monetary Fund (IMF), the European Bank for Reconstruction and Development (EBRD), and the European Investment Bank. However, Poland has recently reduced the number of multilateral assistance institutions to which the state contributes, limiting the recipients to those that have the greatest capacity for delivering effective aid. This move is motivated by the fact that the MFA wants to raise Poland's profile in these institutions and thus its ability to exert more influence on their activities.[9]

The bilateral aid, however, focuses on countries located in Poland's neighborhood, where Poland's experience and organizational capacities may be of particular use. The Ministry of Foreign Affairs is the predominant governmental body dealing with bilateral assistance.[10] In 2010, the percentage of the funds allocated for multilateral assistance provided by the MFA was only 3.5 percent, as compared to 89.5 percent allocated for bilateral aid. The remaining 7 percent of the MFA assistance was for other activities associated with aid provision, such as promotion of the Polish Aid Program or evaluation and monitoring (Polish Ministry of Foreign Affairs 2010). In 2011, due to the growing participation of Poland in development cooperation and democracy assistance, the minister of foreign affairs took the initiative to revitalize the Solidarity Fund PL, established in 2001. According to the Act on Development Cooperation of August 16, 2011, the minister of foreign affairs may delegate tasks relating to development cooperation to the Solidarity Fund PL.[11]

Documents emphasize that Poland embeds the country's national foreign policy interests in bilateral aid. Through aid provision, the Polish government supports its diplomatic initiative, and undoubtedly the Ministry of Foreign Affairs' involvement in dealing with Polish aid demonstrates that that aid is an important tool of the Polish government's foreign policy. This statement leads to the question of what countries receive Polish governmental bilateral aid, what type of aid they receive, and to what extent it goes for democracy assistance purposes.

Engagement in Democracy Assistance

The Ministry of Foreign Affairs, as the main governmental body that makes decisions about Polish aid, each year decides on priority recipients of Polish assistance and announces them together with the amount of assistance to be spent on each country.[12] Usually, the bulk of bilateral aid has been targeted to Belarus, Ukraine, Georgia, Moldova, Afghanistan, the Balkan countries, and the remaining countries of the Commonwealth of Independent States (CIS). These countries are labeled as priority recipients of Polish aid. Two recipient countries that receive a significant share of Polish bilateral aid assistance administered by the MFA are Belarus and Ukraine. In 2010, almost half of bilateral foreign assistance administered by the MFA was devoted to Ukraine and Belarus (Polish Ministry of Foreign Affairs 2010).

Why are Ukraine and Belarus the main recipients of Polish governmental bilateral aid? MFA documents underscore the fact that these countries are targeted recipients of aid because of Polish foreign policy priorities, geopolitical location, and their impact on stability and peace in the whole postcommunist region. As expressed by the MFA's representative, Mirosław Sycz, the situation in the postcommunist region, especially in Poland's close neighbors—Belarus, where basic human rights and democratic values are violated, and Ukraine, in which ongoing transformation faces many obstacles—creates precedence for the allocation of Polish bilateral aid to these countries. In addition to this ideological reason, there are also practical reasons (probability that the aid will be used effectively) and national interest reasons (such aid raises the profile of Poland as a donor, both internationally and domestically).[13]

Polish government documents provide information not only about the geographic focus of Polish aid but also about goals that the Polish government wants to achieve with its assistance. The Ministry of Foreign Affairs assistance activities carried out until 2006 were based on a policy document called "The Strategy for Poland's Development Cooperation," adopted by the Council of Ministers in 2003. The main goals for MFA assistance presented in this document were support for sustainable development, poverty reduction, and the promotion of democracy, rule of law, and human rights. However, since 2006, Polish foreign assistance within the MFA has been classified into two main areas: development assistance and support for the process of building democracy and civil society. This new classification means that the assistance programs implemented by the MFA not only include actions that can be qualified as official development assistance but also encompass support for democracy.

Analysis of the contents of the new strategy for Polish government assistance that will replace the old one, as well as other documents issued in Poland after 2006, makes it clear that the Polish government's goals of aid provision are to promote democratic standards, the rule of law, good governance, and respect for human rights, and to enhance the independence of civil society in recipient countries. The new strategy considers the need to make Poland more involved in the democratization processes of Eastern Europe, the southern Caucasus, and Central Asia. Of pivotal importance also is promotion of European integration and Euro-Atlantic cooperation. Once approved, the new strategy will replace the existing strategy of 2003. In addition to the new aid strategy, there are plans to prepare what are called country strategy papers, each of which will be a concise document describing the assistance strategy for a particular Polish aid recipient. These documents, which will be prepared in close cooperation with recipient countries and Polish NGOs actively involved in aid provision, will lay the groundwork for aid provision to each state in years to come. There are expectations that, by focusing on a limited group of countries, Poland will get a chance to use its comparative advantage and thus to achieve a greater impact (Polish Ministry of Foreign Affairs 2006).

Government officials also indicate that the broadening scope of Polish activities for promoting democracy reflects a growing donors' consensus and belief that sustainable economic development of aid recipient countries depends on progress in the functioning of state institutions, as well as respect for democratic standards and human rights.[14] However, there are also domestic reasons for engaging in democracy assistance. The MFA official documents stress that the Polish focus on democracy assistance, in addition to the activities aimed at improvement of the social and economic situations of recipient countries, also stems from Poland's "comparative advantage" in this area of support since Poland was a recipient of Western democracy assistance and was a leader in bringing about democratic changes in the postcommunist region. Poland's role in the historic changes in the region, Europe, and the world stemmed from Solidarity, the movement that sparked systemic and economic transformation in Poland and served as inspiration for other countries in the communist bloc: "In the name of Solidarity we [the Polish people] will grant all-round assistance to countries in need, particularly our close neighbors: Belarus, Ukraine, Moldova, and Georgia" (Polish Ministry of Foreign Affairs 2007b).

The actions of Polish political elites have emphasized the role of Poland in sharing its experience with other countries and in bridging the gap between postcommunist countries. For example, former president Aleksander Kwaśniewski became a mediator in the political conflict in Ukraine during the Orange Revolution in late 2004 and actively supported democratic tendencies in the country. Moreover, the Polish government undertook an initiative to expand forms of cooperation with the East within the International Visegrad Fund and to launch the Visegrad 4 Eastern Partnership Program 2011.[15] Also, the Polish role has occasionally been emphasized in public statements, such as former Polish president Lech Kaczynski's address to the UN General Assembly on September 19, 2006, when he underlined Polish efforts in supporting eastern neighbors in their reforms: "Poland, which in Central and Eastern Europe paved the way toward a market economy and toward the building of civil society, has extensive experience in these matters. We are prepared to share this experience even further with countries that are transforming their economies and state institutions or intend to embark upon the reform track."[16] Moreover, Poland provides aid because the country was a major recipient of foreign aid during its own transformation process. The fact that West-

ern aid significantly contributed to the success of the systemic transformations, as well as to social and economic reforms initiated in 1989, is well
acknowledged not only among scholars but also among Polish intellectuals
and politicians (Balcerowicz et al. 1997; Pridham 1999; Pridham et al. 1997;
Sachs and Lipton 1990, 49; Regulska 1998, 40; Schimmelfennig 2007). Since
Poland's socioeconomic success to some extent can be attributed to the
foreign assistance that it received for many years from Western countries
and international organizations supporting the Polish struggle for freedom,
the Polish government indicated that it was a "privilege and obligation" for
Poland to provide aid to others (Polish Ministry of Foreign Affairs 2007b,
3).[17] Also, the Polish finance minister, Jacek Rostowski, in an interview for
the BBC said, "We have received a significant contribution from the international community in the past and our view is that it's important we give
something back, now that relatively we're not too badly off" (Hanrahan
2009).[18] Finally, it became clear while analyzing the official documents that
Polish elites are proponents of democratic peace; the link between democratization and stability and peace in the whole postcommunist region is
often emphasized. Poland exists in a dangerous neighborhood, and history
has taught that Polish democracy would not be secured if the state were
not protected by democracies surrounding it. Such a belief was spelled
out by Jerzy Giedroyc, political activist, writer, and editor of the very influential Polish political journal *Kultura*, published from 1947 to 2000 in
Rome and later in Paris. Giedroyc believed that Poland cannot be truly free
and be safe without freedom in Lithuania, Belarus, and, above all, Ukraine.
However, relations with these countries should be based on tolerance and
friendship and not on Polish imperialism and dominance over its neighbors. Poland's "Eastern policy" should be amended, in his opinion, so that
Poland has a chance to play an important role in Europe. Giedroyc was the
first to declare that the Poles should recognize the right of Ukraine to the
city of L'viv, and of Lithuania, to Vilnius.[19] Such bold statements, made by
Giedroyc in 1952, were very unique. His vision for the Polish Eastern policy
became a reference point for the generation of intellectuals and politicians
in independent Poland, including Bronisław Geremek, the minister of foreign affairs.[20]

   Poland's engagement in aid provision for democracy assistance in
Ukraine and Belarus underscored the influence Giedroyc's views had on Polish foreign policy. But how does Poland conceptualize democracy assistance
to these countries? The answers may be found in an examination of the types
of activities financed and the organizational structure of the assistance—that
is, how the MFA bilateral aid is channeled to recipient countries.

Political versus Developmental Approaches

In order to examine Poland's approach to democracy assistance for young democracies, it is instructive to analyze the European Union's developmental approach and the United States' political approach. This analysis will help to answer the question whether Polish democracy assistance fits neatly into one of these two categories. Another possibility is that the Polish government views democracy assistance in a different, third way.

The EU for a long time focused on developmental aid, and democracy assistance was not a top priority (Carothers 2009, 13; Jarábik 2006). The first recipients of EU assistance were the ACP (African, Caribbean, and Pacific Group) countries—most of them colonies of Great Britain, France, and Belgium.[21] Colonial heritage, common historical ties, religion, and/or ethnic ties play important roles in aid allocations and might have little to do with rewarding democratic trends in recipient countries. Scholars find that the older EU members, especially Britain and France, have been more likely to exert influence on the EU to provide aid to nondemocratic former colonies than to other countries (Alesina and Dollar 2000; Lancaster 2007; Schraeder et al. 1998).

Such an image of European assistance is still present among some democracy assistance practitioners. Joanna Rohozińska of the National Endowment for Democracy (NED) argues that the majority of Western European NGOs are not interested in democracy work but in development assistance.[22] She also claims that most European countries are not interested in working in Eastern Europe—the priority is Africa. Scandinavians are the only Western Europeans really interested in working in the same places as NED, but with a less political approach. The United States is still the major donor in this region, in Rohozińska's opinion.

The EU as a regional actor assisting democracy on the European continent and beyond was given credit for facilitating democracy after the EU eastern enlargement that included former communist countries in Central and Eastern Europe. The political conditionality regarding democratization and marketization that the EU for the first time attached to eligibility for pre-accession funds, such as PHARE (Poland and Hungary Assistance for Reconstructing their Economies) and future membership, was a dominant force behind the consolidation of democracy in CEE states that joined the EU in 2004 and 2007 (Burnell 2008; Crawford and Lijphart 1995; Henderson 1999; Schimmelfennig 2007; Schimmelfennig and Sedelmeir 2005).[23] Because of the success of the EU enlargement policy, the European Community extended political conditionality in aid provision to the Western

Balkans and also to countries lying in the EU's immediate neighborhood—countries that do not have a chance for EU membership or whose membership lies in the distant future.

The EU hopes, in the case of the European Neighborhood Policy (ENP), to influence democratic progress through political conditionality.[24] The ENP was developed in 2004, and its main objectives have been an avoidance of new dividing lines between the enlarged EU and its neighbors and, instead, the strengthening of prosperity, stability, and security in the neighborhood (Mingarelli 2006). The ENP financial instrument is the European Neighborhood and Partnership Instrument (ENPI), which replaced the TACIS (Technical Assistance for the Commonwealth of Independent States) and MEDA (Mediterranean Development Assistance) programs. The ENPI is simply a new single cooperation instrument for the EU's eastern and southern neighbors plus Russia. These states became the EU's direct neighbors after the 2004 and 2007 enlargements. ENPI continues the objectives of TACIS and MEDA and refers to specific cross-border cooperation between the EU neighbors and border regions in the EU member states (European Commission: External Cooperation Programs 2009).

If the recipient countries meet political conditionality specified in the ENP, they can be granted better access to the EU market, more privileged status in bilateral trade relations, and so forth. Most ENP instruments are based on the presumption of partners' goodwill and their interest in integration into the EU. However, scholars point out that political and aid conditionality exerted by the EU seems to be effective only when the reward at stake is accession to the Union (Burnell 2008; Ethier 2003; Schimmelfennig and Sedelmeir 2005). Even if future membership is a realistic goal, as in the case of Ukraine, this incentive is too distant for this country at this moment to compel its government to comply with the EU requirements (Lynch 2006; Zhurzhenko 2005).

The impact of the EU on the democratization of countries ineligible to join the EU reveals many shortcomings, and there seems to be no other incentive instrument to push reform forward that would be as successful as EU membership (Crawford 2000; Cremona 2004; Emerson 2005; Emerson and Noutcheva 2004; Ethier 2003; Gillespie and Youngs 2002; Haukkala and Moshes 2004; Kelley 2006; Milcher et al. 2007; O'Brennan and Cox 2006; Olsen 2000; Pinder 1991). The EU intends to provide assistance to not only Ukraine but also Belarus through the new European Neighborhood and Partnership Instrument, and "conditionality" is a key tool in relations with Belarus within this policy. In the ENP's main document, published in May 2004, it is concluded that with radical change and economic policies, Belarus will be able to fully take advantage of the ENP.[25] Yet, the political system in Belarus is now authoritarian, so offering Belarus the full advantages of the ENP is not yet possible. Thus, in accordance with current policy, the EU should wait for positive change in Belarus and then engage more intensively.[26]

It seems that the major problem is that the ENP does not provide instruments adequate to deal with nondemocratic neighbors, because the policy envisions cooperation only with the governments, rather than directing inducements at society.[27] EU programs in third world countries are implemented in cooperation with the government of the country, and financial support is dispersed through government structures. Where the government of a recipient country has no interest in cooperating with the EU in the field of democracy, assistance cannot take place. The ENP does not contain a specific analysis of the role of civil society and a way to support it.

Given the critical role civil society has played in democratization activity in Central and Eastern Europe, the importance of the third sector is not sufficiently taken into account by EU democracy assistance to Ukraine and Belarus. Whereas in the case of the CEE countries, their third sectors were embraced by way of PHARE assistance, in the case of Belarus and Ukraine, the EU still looks for channels to target civil society there. According to OECD data, the EU has been the largest Western multilateral donor to Belarus ($13.7 million) and Ukraine ($228.1 million), with only a maximum of 40 percent and 21 percent, respectively, of that assistance going to the civil society sector in those countries (OECD Aid Statistics 2009). The low level of assistance to civil society is particularly problematic in the case of Belarus, because, in an authoritarian regime, democracy assistance has to be directed to nonstate actors, whereas, in Ukraine, the EU has been able to support democratic reforms carried out by the government (Raik 2006, 170).

In recent years, the EU has begun to recognize deficiencies in its democracy assistance and the lack of effective instruments for promoting democratic change in countries that have no prospect for membership in the near future. The EU has increased its pressure on Lukashenko's government, while at the same time seeking to identify approaches to engage with Belarusian citizens, civil society, and independent media, acknowledging the important role that civil society can play in the democratization process (Tapiola 2006). As it has become impossible to allocate EU funds to civil society in Belarus for both political and institutional reasons, most of the money is used for activities outside the country, such as the work of the

European Humanities University (EHU) in Vilnius (Raik 2006, 175). The European Humanities University is a nonstate establishment, which was located in Belarus from 1992 to 2004, until the institution was forced to terminate its activities there. However, thanks to political, administrative, and financial support from the government of Lithuania, the government of the European Union, NGOs, as well as US and EU foundations, the EHU managed to resume its operations in Lithuania and open bachelor's and master's degree programs for Belarusian students in autumn 2005. The MacArthur, Heritage, and Open Society Foundations in the United States were among the donors to the EHU as well, but the EU initiated the idea.

Moreover, the EU has started to finance television and radio programs for Belarus, with organizational assistance provided by Deutsche Welle Bonn and Media Consulta Berlin (Lindner 2007, 72). Another project was supporting scholarships for Belarusian students wanting to study abroad. Finally, in 2008, the EU established an independent European organization, the European Partnership for Democracy (EPD), to remedy the problem that occurred when the European Commission gave funds directly to NGOs and civil society groups; the system of financial controls was so complex that the programs became rigid.[28] The EPD was created according to the model of the National Endowment for Democracy in the United States. The idea behind this initiative is to enable the EU to boost its activities in promoting democracy and civil and political rights vis-à-vis its neighbors.

Explanations for the changes in the EU's recent approach to Belarus and Ukraine should address the role of new member states, which will be discussed in the final section of this chapter.

While for a long time the EU did not pay serious attention to the question of democracy in former Soviet states, the United States had already begun supporting civil society in Ukraine and Belarus and other postcommunist countries in 1992–93 (Conkievich 2002, 421; Forbrig et al. 2006; Narozhna 2004; Stent 2007; Sushko and Prystayko 2006, 132). Americans have been leaders in providing such democracy assistance, through the United States Agency for International Development (USAID), the National Endowment for Democracy, and through major private donors such as the Open Society Institute (OSI) and a small group of other private charitable foundations. The other principal funders of US democracy aid include the International Foundation for Electoral Systems (IFES) and Freedom House. According to the OECD, in 2007 alone the US government gave 86 percent of its total aid to Belarus and 46 percent of all aid to Ukraine to the civil society sectors in these countries, two times more than the EU gave.

US relations with Ukraine and Belarus changed when the two postcommunist countries were moving away from democracy toward authoritarianism. Despite the situations in these countries, the United States has continued to be involved in assistance to civil society. The United States had long seen Ukraine at the forefront of democracy in the post-Soviet space. After the election of Kuchma in July 1994, Ukraine became the third largest recipient of US assistance in the postcommunist region, and some of this support went to the NGO sector (Kuzio 2007b, 26; Sushko and Prystayko 2006). American NGOs have been active in Ukraine and played an important role during the Orange Revolution through their training of Ukrainian electoral monitoring groups (Stent 2007, 18). Civic groups working on pro-democracy issues in Ukraine received international funding for their operations and preparation for the popular movement that became the Orange Revolution (Diuk 2006, 82; Kelly 2004; Mulvey 2004).

Lukashenko's resistance to democratic reform led the United States to announce its decision to pursue a "selective engagement" policy with the Belarusian government (Wilde 2002, 435). Since neither the Belarusian government nor the business sector in Belarus held significant intent for achieving democratic change, the US government decided that it would expand contacts with Belarusian civil society—nongovernmental organizations, political parties, independent trade unions, and other associations not directly linked to the Belarusian government—to promote democratization (Wilde 2002, 429–30). Emphasis was on the development of a civil society with the capability and willingness to interact with the government and business sectors (USAID Assistance Strategy for Belarus, 1999–2002).

Subsequently, in response to the worsening political record of Belarus, the United States defined its disapproval of the ruling regime in the Belarus Democracy Act, passed by the Congress and then signed by the president in October 2004 (US Congress 2004).[29] The legislation has become the main US policy regarding the Belarusian regime. This legislation condemns political developments under Lukashenko's leadership and refers to the referendum in November 1996 as "illegal and unconstitutional." It calls upon Lukashenko's government to "cease its persecution of political opponents or independent journalists and to release those individuals who have been imprisoned for opposing his regime or for exercising their right to freedom of speech" (US Congress 2004). The act envisions imposing sanctions against Belarus, if the Belarusian authorities fail to stop repression of the opposition and independent media and investigate cases of politically motivated disappearances. Moreover, the law states that strategic exports to Belarus and investments will not be permitted and that the United States opposes international institutions' providing any financial assistance to Belarus. Finally, the act provides for support to Belarusian democratic forces, such as the independent press and nongovernmental organizations.

On December 8, 2006, the US House of Representatives renewed an amended version of the Belarus Democracy Act of 2004 (US Congress 2006). The Belarus Democracy Reauthorization Act of 2006 extends and specifies approval for appropriations for democracy and civil society activities and for radio and television broadcasting to Belarus. This law establishes specific economic and US governmental sanctions against the Belarusian government until it makes progress in meeting certain conditions, such as the release of political prisoners and accounting for the disappearances of opposition leaders and journalists, cessation of political harassment, prosecution of senior government leaders for embezzlement of state assets and administration of fraudulent elections, and holding free presidential and parliamentary elections under independent supervision (US Congress 2006).

The US government's assistance to Belarus continues to be subject to the policy of "selective engagement" under which little bilateral assistance is channeled through the government of Belarus, except for humanitarian assistance and exchange programs involving state-run educational institutions (US Department of State Bureau of European and Eurasian Affairs 2009a, 2009b). The US strategy for assistance used to focus predominantly on restructuring government and state enterprises and, in general, developing the private sector, as well as addressing security issues. However, due to concerns over human rights violations committed by the government of Belarus, the United States provides no direct assistance for economic growth and peace and security issues (US Department of State Bureau of European and Eurasian Affairs 2009a). Today, most US assistance goes to support the transformation of Belarus into a democracy that respects human rights and the rule of law by building and strengthening civil society (US Department of State Bureau of European and Eurasian Affairs 2009a, 2009b; US Congress 2004).

The United States is the biggest donor in terms of assistance to civil society; it is therefore argued that US democracy assistance follows the political approach (Carothers 2009; Jarábik 2006). However, there are significant differences among the US donors. For a long time, USAID followed the developmental approach, but today it sometimes uses a more political approach as well (Carothers 2009, 14).[30] The USAID missions to Ukraine, Moldova, and Belarus focus mainly on increasing citizens' awareness of their rights, as well as providing training and technology to small rural communities and offering small grants to provide special support for independent media activities. In order to achieve these goals, the USAID works through its regional offices.

In addition to the USAID, there are many US-based foundations, such as NED or the Open Society Institute, which have their own ways of assisting democracy, demonstrating that the USAID approach does not dominate American democracy assistance. These other organizations support elections-related work, bolster civil society, provide aid to independent media outlets, and so forth.

A significant player in democracy assistance to the post-Soviet states is George Soros's Open Society Institute. Unlike many other foundations, the OSI involves local people in the recipient countries and has been financially independent of the US government. The Soros Foundation has established local foundations in each postcommunist country, and each of the local foundations has a separate identity, with local boards of directors and local staff, and they are informally coordinated by Open Society Institute offices in New York and Budapest. The Soros Foundation was the first Western donor to open such an office in Belarus. The Belarusian Soros Foundation (BSF) provided grants, training, and equipment to educational, political, and local social projects (Wilde 2002). Despite its local approach to civil society support, as well as some achievements in assisting civil society in Belarus, this entity encountered significant barriers to building democracy there. As it became more and more complicated to support Belarusian NGOs from outside, the Soros Foundation, as well as representatives of other donors, finally gave up their long battle with the Lukashenko administration and closed their offices in Belarus (Hill 2005; Zagranica Group 2003).

The creation of the National Endowment for Democracy in 1983 marked a new trend in providing direct assistance for human rights activists and democratic organizations abroad (McFaul 2005, 155). NED receives money from the federal government, but the endowment remains independent in its operation and style. Unlike USAID, which has focused on developmental aid, NED was created to do democracy work exclusively. In an interview, Rodger Potocki, director for the Europe and Eurasia region in NED, said that NED had never used a USAID "cookie-cutter" model in which it is assumed that democracy develops similarly in all spheres or that one can apply the same approach anywhere.[31] The USAID approach reflects the old development model from the 1960s onward, and it has also been widely used by German *Stiftungen* and other Western European donors. Moreover, USAID has been known for bringing consultants to recipient countries; NED, however, has always provided direct funds to the recipient countries' civil society groups. This approach distinguishes NED's tactic from USAID's external project method, widely criticized by practitioners and scholars: "The NED is very different, very unique. . . . NED was based on the principle that local partners know best what should be done in the country. . . . They ask us 'is that a good idea?' But it is not us telling them what needs to be done in their country. We do not believe in a donor-driven mentality; we really think that idea[s] should come from those places."[32]

The evaluations of democracy-building work, like McFaul's writings, seem to be more favorable to the NED approach than to the USAID model, because the direct-grants method has many advantages. In direct grants, money goes directly into the recipient society, and this method permits greater flexibility in the design and implementation of projects.[33] However, NED's mode of operation entails difficulties and limitations as well. An obstacle to reaching smaller local organizations in a recipient country is the absence of a representative office. In order to compensate for this lack, NED sends its employees on short trips to the regions. However, NED's employees cannot get visas to Belarus, so the organization has difficulty reaching local communities. Moreover, in order to avoid any misuse of money, donors have been more likely to finance Western groups whose members speak English and are familiar with grant proposals and so forth (Carothers 1999, 263, 271–72). These practices, in turn, contributed to the emergence in Ukraine of new types of grant-oriented NGOs, known as *grantoid*s (literally, "grant-eaters"), which were the first to receive financial support (Narozhna 2004, 243).[34]

The Polish Government Approach to Democracy Assistance

The Polish government is most likely to channel its democracy aid, as figure 2.2. shows, through partners, mainly central and local administrative units, Polish embassies, and civil society organizations.[35] However, the question arises as to why the Polish government creates a network of assistance involving governmental and civil society agencies and whether such a web of bureaucracy is necessary for democracy aid provision.

The MFA cooperates with these entities, because their expertise allows for the realization of different MFA democracy assistance goals. For example, the importance of offering assistance at the lowest administration levels in recipient countries and reaching specific groups of recipients induces the MFA to cooperate with local government entities. All official organs of Polish lower-level administrative units are qualified to apply for MFA funds to finance projects.[36] These administrative agencies usually cooperate with their counterparts in the recipient countries and predominantly focus upon strengthening local administration, supporting civil servants of the local governmental bodies, and helping to sustain regional economic development through cross-border cooperation. Polish local government bodies try to achieve their program goals through study visits, publishing multimedia presentations, local administration meetings, job training, exchange of experiences through disseminating information on local administration reforms in Poland, and the like. The number of MFA-financed projects with local government increases each year.

Projects implemented by Polish central government agencies are directed toward institutions of the same kind in the recipient countries and thus allow the Polish government to reach public officials and politicians.[37] Projects between Polish central institutions and those in Ukraine, for example, have involved such efforts as strengthening the agricultural sector and the justice sector, developing the institutional capacity of central administration, improving safety on the border, and supporting economic transformation and European integration through the organization of training, study visits, and conferences. Taking into account the potential of Polish central government institutions to strengthen links between central government agencies in donor and recipient countries, these entities are very important partners in providing assistance; each year the number of projects financed by the MFA has increased.

To some extent, the MFA also involves Polish embassies in carrying out democracy assistance projects. In the embassies are Polish diplomats who have developed significant knowledge about the local situation in the recipient country. Polish embassy staff might have a better understanding about needs and obstacles; therefore, their projects have more chance to be successfully implemented than projects designed in Poland.[38] A significant portion of MFA funds distributed through the Polish embassies is spent on activities initiated and managed at the local level in recipient countries and thus more likely to be well implemented.

However, the main domestic partners for the Polish government's provision of bilateral aid to the priority countries are Polish nongovernmental organizations. Polish NGOs are especially active in Belarus and Ukraine.[39] The interest of the Polish government in offering civil society assistance causes it to share this responsibility with Polish nongovernmental organizations, which are the most reliable partners due to their experience in this field. Polish NGOs do not deal with the politics of the recipient countries in the strict sense, as the associations prefer to leave this sphere in the hands of the relevant authorities. Rather, the NGOs aim to assist recipients at the social and local levels, to support civil society with specific solutions and projects. Since most NGOs focus their activities on supporting democracy, without these partners, the Polish government's efforts in providing democracy assistance would be less apparent.

It should be mentioned that, thanks to Polish nongovernmental organizations, in fact, Poland has been actively involved in assistance activities in neighboring states since the early 1990s. The Polish government involvement in aid provision extended the scope of activities, number of recipient countries, and the volume of assistance.[40] According to the Polish Ministry of Foreign Affairs (2006, 26), "The potential of Polish civil society organizations, co-operating with partners from developing countries, has been considerably strengthened. Their activities are not only limited to projects co-financed from the official development budget, but, in a great measure, they are a result of these organizations' own efforts. In addition to the added value represented by their knowledge of specific developing countries' realities and abilities to undertake effective and flexible actions, NGOs have intensified the humanitarian aspect of Polish assistance activities." As one of the representatives of Polish NGOs said, the reason why the MFA made a decision to disburse its funds for aid through NGOs is that the MFA realized that Polish NGOs have an important role to play in Polish aid.[41] Polish NGOs have been active in the postcommunist region since the 1990s, and Belarus and Ukraine were the first countries from the region to receive assistance from Polish organizations. But for the MFA, cooperation with Polish NGOs is important for more practical reasons as well. According to Polish law, the MFA is not authorized to send money to the foreign account of any organization; therefore, cooperation with Polish NGOs is essential.[42] Paweł Kazanecki, a well-known Polish civil society activist, pointed out that Polish activities in the postcommunist region could focus on development aid, humanitarian initiatives, and assisting democracy. The first two types of aid require cooperation with the authorities of the recipient country, but the situation looks very different in the case of democracy aid. Democratizing activities can be implemented by consent and together with authorities, as in Ukraine, but the situation becomes complicated when the regime of the recipient country is authoritarian, as in Belarus. Therefore, in case of hostility from the authorities, Polish NGOs can perform an important role in democracy assistance by targeting civil societies and reaching local communities.

Given the methods the Polish government uses to channel aid, one can then turn to the question about priority areas in democracy assistance. In the case of authoritarian Belarus, the Ministry of Foreign Affairs argues that support aimed at promoting free media and strengthening civil society and Belarusian identity is a crucial element in the promotion of democratic change. For example, one of the biggest aid projects is the creation of the satellite television channel Belsat TV, which broadcasts throughout Belarus. Of the total bilateral MFA assistance to Belarus in 2008, 87 percent was spent on direct subsidies for this television channel. The station is an undertaking on an unprecedented scale—in terms of its complexity, the number of people involved in its implementation, and in terms of its potential impact on Belarusian society. According to the MFA, this initiative is meant to address the needs expressed by, among others, Belarusian democratic circles, as well as Belarusian and Polish journalists (Polish Ministry of Foreign Affairs 2008b). Belsat TV began broadcasting in December 2007 and is the first foreign satellite channel of Polish television. Programming is developed by a team of Belarusian and Polish journalists and broadcast in the Belarusian language. This initiative is the largest project of this type in Europe. Belsat TV is meant to provide information and opinion programs, documentaries, serials, and feature films. The satellite channel has a chance to become one of the biggest and most famous individual foreign projects promoting democratic change in Belarus.

Additionally, there are media projects that are dedicated to promoting Belarusian culture. It has been stressed during interviews and in projects directed toward Belarus that Belarusian cultural identity should be strengthened and that it may play an important role in Belarus's struggle for democracy by providing a sense of social solidarity.[43] One such initiative is the Belarusian Internet Library—Kamunikat.org—which provides information about Belarusian culture, history, literature, and the social and political situation in Belarus (all publications are provided in the Belarusian language). It has been operating since 2000 and has been able to attract a wide group of users.[44] Another Internet service is Belarus-Live, implemented by the Center for International Relations Foundation. The initiative also is dedicated to promoting Belarusian culture; therefore, in addition to daily news, there is a weekly summary of the most important cultural events. The information is put into an electronic format and sent to interested parties (fifteen hundred different addresses), including European Parliament deputies, officials from ministries of foreign affairs of the EU member states, international organizations, and others who have some influence on policies toward Belarus (Polish Ministry of Foreign Affairs 2006).

The Polish government also seems to recognize the democratizing potential of young people, because the biggest directly funded governmental project, the Konstanty Kalinowski Scholarship Program, is directed toward them.[45] This program offers help to Belarusian students expelled from their universities because of participation in activities in favor of democratic values, and it provides the opportunity to continue studies in Poland. The program was launched in March 2006 after the conclusion of a letter of intent between the Polish government, represented by former prime minister Kazimierz Marcinkiewicz; Aleksandr Milinkevich, presidential candidate in the 2006 elections and a representative of the Democratic Bloc in Belarus; and representatives of the Conference of Rectors of Academic Schools in Poland and the Conference of Rectors of Polish Universities. The Kalinowski program is directed toward three hundred expelled students who, in addition to receiving scholarships, are also offered tuition waivers, housing expenses, and Polish and English language courses. Students are also invited to participate in a cultural program. The Center for East European Studies of Warsaw University, together with the Ministry of Science and Higher Education, has been implementing the program.[46]

However, in addition to direct grants, the Polish government finds it important to cooperate with Polish NGOs to support civil society groups and the free media (radio, television, and Internet) that are subjects of Belarusian government harassment. In 2008, close to 60 percent of MFA aid to Belarus distributed through the MFA partners was channeled via Polish NGOs (Polish Ministry of Foreign Affairs 2008a; see also appendix 3). As figure 2.2 has shown, in addition to Polish NGOs, the MFA cooperates with other central administration entities and with local government agencies.

In the case of Ukraine, the Polish government emphasizes the importance of supporting the state's capacity to enforce its decisions associated with political and socioeconomic reforms, as well as European integration. There are more MFA funds allocated to projects of Polish central administration to be spent in Ukraine than in Belarus. In 2008, almost as many of the MFA funds for Ukrainian projects were allocated to Polish central and local government projects together (47 percent) as to Polish NGOs (50 percent).

The Polish government-funded programs in Ukraine focus on Ukraine's integration into the European Union. Some projects aim to share with representatives of Ukrainian media the Polish experience in information campaigns on the EU and the integration process. For example, within the "Europe in the Ukrainian Media" project, implemented in 2008, Ukrainian local television and press journalists could get internships at *Gazeta Wyborcza*—one of the biggest newspapers in Poland and one with important democratic credentials.[47] These internships would allow Ukrainian journalists to learn how the newspaper has presented the European integration process and reported the referendum on Polish accession to the EU, as well as events after Poland's entry into the EU.[48]

Whereas political and economic reforms are not the primary interest of Polish NGOs, the focus on those areas in the postcommunist region, particularly in Ukraine, is encouraged by the Polish governmental program led by the MFA, which finds these areas important in the overall aid to Ukraine. The MFA, for example, financed projects submitted by the Center for Social and Economic Research (CASE) that focused on economic reforms in Ukraine. These projects instructed authorities on how to deal with economic problems that are typical for countries in transition, such as macroeconomic turmoil involving currency, financial, and balance-of-payment crises. For example, in order to prevent macroeconomic problems that might affect the well-being of a population and trigger public unrest, CASE offered a project entitled "Development of the Early Warning Indicators of Economic Crises for Ukraine."[49]

Another CASE project that aimed at economic reforms in Ukraine was entitled "Preparation of the Strategy for Social Benefits Monetization Reform in Ukraine." It consists of the following steps: (1) an analysis of available reform strategies; (2) the construction of a comprehensive picture of the functioning of the social benefit system in Ukraine; (3) an analysis of the direct social benefits schemes applicable to the current institutional background; and (4) recommendations about a strategy for Ukraine's social benefits system reform.[50]

Since 2006, the most expensive Polish central government project has been SENSE (Strategic Economic Needs and Security Exercise), which instructs civil servants, representatives of the legislature, and members of business associations and NGOs in Ukraine about the country's economic development. The project is organized by the Ministry of National Defense (in cooperation with the MFA) and the Center for East European Studies at Warsaw University. The training consists of a computer simulation that presents the functioning of an imaginary country with a market economy. Participants are also introduced to problems of social, political, and economic transformation.

The Polish government has focused its aid efforts on economic and political reforms in the postcommunist region while paying scant attention to social issues. Polish NGOs, however, recognized the impact of social problems in postcommunist countries (Polish Ministry of Foreign Affairs 2007a). Thus, some Polish NGOs have undertaken social reforms with special focus on changes in educational systems, reforms of pension and health services, and combating HIV/AIDS and drug abuse. The Institute of Public Affairs in Warsaw organizes fellowships for young policy researchers from Ukraine, Russia, Moldova, Georgia, or Azerbaijan who come to Poland to work in Polish think tanks. During their stays, fellows gather materials, do interviews, and then write their observations on certain social policy solutions adopted in Poland and make policy recommendations for their own countries.[51]

Many Polish projects are directed toward Ukrainian authorities, in order to instruct them about reform in particular sectors of the economy. For example, supporting the creation and development of an agricultural advisory service is one of the most important elements of Polish outreach provided to Ukraine. The initiative responds to the Ukrainian partners' need to broaden their knowledge of the possibilities of agricultural development and local communities' activation in rural areas. Similarly, a few projects implemented by Polish central administration units refer to Ukrainian authorities' need for solutions regarding internal security, cross-border cooperation, and combating organized crime.

Many Polish government-financed NGO programs focus on transparency and governmental accountability, especially at the local level. The Polish government believes that strengthening the role of local governments will greatly contribute to improving state capacity, which is critical for the survival of democracy in Ukraine. Recognizing that the quality of administrative management is of crucial importance in countries undergoing transformation and that endemic corruption is an obstacle to achieving this goal in Ukraine, the MFA has supported anticorruption programs such as "Transparent Ukraine: Building Effective and Ethical Self-Government in Ukraine," managed by the Foundation in Support of Local Democracy. In this project, Polish local governments shared their experiences using modern management systems in public administration with their Ukrainian counterparts (Polish Ministry of Foreign Affairs 2006). Within this program, mayors of Ukrainian cities and public administration professionals, who later conducted similar workshops in their country, made study visits to Poland, where they received training about efficient methods of preventing corruption as well as about the introduction of new procedures and norms in administrative entities.

Moreover, the list of NGO projects financed by the MFA shows that the Polish government places decentralization of the political system high on the list of priority activities in Ukraine. Polish NGOs place particular importance on local governance, also recognizing it as one of the major conditions for democratic consolidation. The rationale behind these projects is that contemporary decisions must be taken as close as possible to the problem they resolve and as close as possible to citizens affected by these problems. Therefore, along with the expanded third sector, local governance creates conditions for strengthening democratic tendencies or reversing the so-called "democratic deficit."[52] Representatives of Polish NGOs believe that the state wishing to be fully democratic should delegate power to the territorial levels (state, region, district, and commune) because, in terms of democratic theory, such dispersion of power stresses checks and balances, or accountability of the central government.[53]

Such emphasis on state capacity in Ukraine recalls Tilly's (2007, 15) argument that state capacity is an important feature of democratic regimes and that "no democracy can work if the state lacks the capacity to supervise democratic decision making and put its results into practice."[54] An emphasis on economic reforms, however, is grounded in the discussion on the relationship between democratization or democratic consolidation and economic development. Modernization theory postulates that economic development is a domestic factor that may lead to political democratization (Bunce 2000).[55] Przeworski and Limongi (1997, 156) and Przeworski et al. (2000) argue that the emergence of democracy is not a by-product of economic development. Instead, they find evidence to support the view of Lipset (1959, 75) that "the more well-to-do a nation, the greater the chances it will sustain democracy."[56]

An examination of the Polish government's approach to democracy assistance in Belarus and Ukraine does not mitigate the difficulty in tagging Polish aid as belonging to either of two types of democracy assistance approaches—political or developmental. Instead, it presents elements of each approach, with the addition of specific features evident in programs that carefully fit the political landscape in Belarus and Ukraine. Authoritarian Belarus is mostly aided by assistance that emphasizes support for civil society. In this aspect, Polish democracy assistance matches Carothers's (2009) definition of a political approach to democracy assistance and resembles the US approach. However, in the case of Ukraine, in its efforts toward democratic consolidation the Polish government's democracy assistance presents a mix of political and developmental approaches. There are different types of assistance bundled together because of the complexity of democratic consolidation. Linz and Stepan (1996, 7–13), for example, recognize five interconnected and mutually reinforcing conditions that must exist for a democracy to be consolidated. Democracy is more than a regime; it is an interacting system in which no single arena can function properly without some support from one or often all others. First, the conditions must exist for the development of a free and lively civil society. Second, there must be a relatively autonomous and valued political society. Third, there must be rule of law that ensures legal guarantees for citizens' freedoms. Fourth, there must be a stable bureaucracy that is usable by the new democratic government. Fifth, there must be an institutionalized economic society. Some conditions mentioned by Linz and Stepan (1996) would be aided by developmental help and others by political assistance, and therefore the Polish government's democracy assistance to Ukraine presents a mixed approach. This assistance is based on the recognition that the civil society that emerged after the Orange Revolution needs a functioning state, including effective policing. Therefore, the best avenue for developing domestic civil society in democratic consolidation is to strengthen the state by establishing stable and efficient social and political institutions.

Taking into account the emphasis of the Polish government on civil society both as a sender and recipient of assistance, the question is whether and how Poland, a member of the EU, is changing the European Community's approach to democracy assistance, which has always been developmental in orientation.

Efforts to Shape the EU Approach

Before the EU enlargement of 2004, the member states saw Belarus and Ukraine as distant countries (Kubicek 2005; Pavliuk 2001). The situation changed once Belarus and Ukraine became direct neighbors of the EU after the eastern enlargement. The role of the new EU members was especially visible during the Orange Revolution in Ukraine, when the presidents of Poland and Lithuania stimulated EU interest in the Ukrainian conflict. Vilnius and Warsaw strongly support the democratization of Belarus and Ukraine. Both Lithuania and Poland have had close contacts with the democratic oppositions and civil societies in these countries. There are, however, significant differences in the treatment of the Lukashenko government by Lithuania and Poland. Lithuania supports informal meetings with the highest Belarusian officials. In contrast, Poland is less likely to maintain such contacts and prefers to support meetings with lower officials in the Belarusian regime (Gromadzki and Veselý 2006, 23–24).

Polish interest in supporting its direct neighbors has been stronger than that of other countries because of history, culture, and its geographical location between east and west, as well as because there are large Polish minorities in these countries and large Belarusian minorities living in Poland and Ukraine (Sushko and Prystayko 2006). Polish elites are urging the EU countries to assist its eastern neighbors financially. For example, Poland's participation in the EU's decision-making mechanism enables the state to have an influence on the distribution of the Union's assistance funds through its financial instruments. For the period 2007–13, the EU has earmarked more than 11 billion euros to promote cooperation with the neighboring countries—both in Eastern Europe and in the Mediterranean region (Cieszkowski 2007). According to the Polish government, resources for Eastern Europe are not sufficient, but with the involvement of Poles, among others, in persuading the EU partners, allocations have been increased to these countries for the 2007–13 period. Ukraine received 75 percent more as compared with the previous budget period, while Moldova and the Caucasus countries each received more than 200 percent above the previous level of funding. Planned expenditure on aid to Belarus also grew, by 85 percent (Cieszkowski 2007).

However, Poland actively participates in European Union assistance not only financially but also with its expertise. Every year representatives from the MFA participate in the Belarus Donors Forum. This meeting brings together all countries actively involved in providing assistance to Belarus, including EU nonmember states such as the United States and international organizations. Polish elites representing the government and the nongovernmental sector call on the EU to make better use of the instruments at its disposal. They criticize the EU's conditionality approach toward its eastern neighbors, arguing that this approach does not correspond to either the new situation in the EU after enlargement in 2004 or the deteriorating situation in Belarus.

Polish elites agree that important and appropriate methods for the EU to use in influencing the situation in Belarus include applying pressure on Lukashenko's government, while at the same time supporting civil society groups (not limited to officially recognized organizations) and facilitating contacts between societies through meetings, visits, and educational programs, as well as business and social contacts. In their opinion, such an approach is speeding up democratic processes in these countries and stimulating transition (Cieszkowski 2007). In this vein, Poland also acknowledges a need for significant help in the movement of people between the EU and the countries of Eastern Europe. Since there is some freedom that new member states have in issuing visas, for example, Polish NGOs lobby the Polish government for an agreement on visa facilitation and the softening of visa regulations (Rettman 2011).[57] Moreover, recognizing the economic sphere as one of the most important areas of cooperation between the EU and countries of Eastern Europe within the ENP, Polish elites have suggested a new generation of agreements that do not focus exclusively on a liberalization of trade in goods and services but would also ensure the removal of nontariff barriers (Cieszkowski 2007).

Although civil society has played a critical role in democratization activity in Central and Eastern Europe, the importance of the third sector was not sufficiently taken into account in the European Union's democracy assistance to Ukraine and Belarus, according to Polish elites. The European Union does not have any equivalent to the Belarus Democracy Act of the United States, which supports Belarusian democratic forces, opposition parties, NGOs, and youth organizations. According to Gromadzki and Veselý (2006), the EU policy toward Belarus should combine both forceful measures against Lukashenko's regime as well as positive actions to promote civil society and democracy. Aleksandr Milinkevich made the following remarks about EU assistance:

> I have just been to Brussels, where the European Commission debated on how to deal with Belarus. When Belarusian NGOs were being assessed, we heard that the only successful ones are those capable of cooperating with the authorities in the current situation. We do understand that such cooperation is important, and sometimes we do so at the local level, but it won't succeed on a bigger scale because the authorities do not want an active society; they are interested in its passivity. Belarusian organizations shouldn't be assessed for their ability to cooperate with the authorities. Let us take human rights organizations, for example; for obvious reasons they, will never initiate contact with the authorities. . . . At the abovementioned meeting in Brussels, there was also talk of isolating Minsk. We argued that it wouldn't mean isolation, but only supporting self-isolation of Belarus, which makes all the difference. If Minsk is unwilling to cooperate with Europe, it should not be aided in its policy. Help should be offered to those willing to cooperate, namely the democratic third-sector forces. (Komorowska and Kuzawińska 2004, 60–62)

The most tangible result of Polish efforts to change the EU's approach to democracy assistance is the creation of the European Partnership for Democracy (EPD) and the Eastern Partnership policy. With these two initiatives, the new EU member states advocated for a stronger presence of democracy assistance on the EU's agenda and greater focus on the EU's eastern neighbors.[58]

The Eastern Partnership policy was presented by the Polish government with assistance from Sweden at the EU's General Affairs and External Relations Council in Brussels on May 26, 2008, and launched by the EU in May 2009 (BBC News 2009; De Quetteville 2008). This program maintains the principle of the ENP, and the development of relations with each country continues to depend on the progress made by the partners in their reform and modernization efforts. However, with the Eastern Partnership, the EU offers its eastern partners more specific support for democratic and market-oriented reforms (European Commission: External Cooperation Programs 2009). The initiative is directed toward EU neighbors such as Armenia, Azerbaijan, Belarus, Georgia, Moldova, and Ukraine. The new points in this policy worth highlighting are the inclusion of new association agreements encompassing comprehensive free trade agreements, border management programs, increased people-to-people contacts, and greater involvement of civil society. The initiative stresses that the development and involvement of civil society are key factors for the success of democratic and market-oriented reforms in countries embraced by the Eastern Partnership. Thus, the European Commission proposes to support civil society actors and to engage them in the initiative through the establishment of an Eastern Partnership Civil Society Forum, which will promote contacts between civil society actors as well as facilitate their dialogue with public authorities.[59]

An important opportunity for Poland to have an influence on the EU approach toward the eastern partners was Poland's presidency of the Council of the European Union, which Poland held between July and December 2011. The Polish government contributed to the extension of the Erasmus student exchange program with the Eastern Partnership countries, the adoption of a European directive on victims of violence, and finalization of negotiations on the Association Agreement as well as on free trade with Ukraine. Above all, the most important achievement of this presidency was the organization of the Warsaw Eastern Partnership Summit in 2011. The Warsaw meeting with European leaders confirmed its support for the development of the Eastern Partnership—a project initiated by Poland and Sweden that aims to strengthen the European Union's cooperation with the six eastern neighbors.[60]

Polish NGOs also try to attract the EU's attention to challenges and obstacles for democratization in Belarus and democratic consolidation in Ukraine. Publishing is one means of gaining the EU's attention, and some Polish NGOs disseminate periodicals dedicated to a broad range of subjects on postcommunist matters—politics, the economy, society, and culture in the former Soviet republics—with articles by authors from both East and West, such as Liliia Shevtsova and Timothy Snyder.[61] Other NGOs work to raise awareness among longtime EU members about the Belarusian situation by issuing annual analytical bulletins on Belarus's civil society sector or organizing international exhibitions that showcase the achievements of Belarusian civil society.[62] Other NGOs organize conferences on various topics related to the situation in Belarus or Ukraine and that match the plenary session of the Parliamentary Assembly of the Council of Europe.[63]

Moreover, Polish NGOs often actively cooperate with their counterparts from the EU in order to exchange opinions and views on the situation in the EU-adjacent countries. For example, the Stefan Batory Foundation participates in informal meetings organized by its German counterparts, such as Stiftungen Wissenschaftlich Politik in Berlin. During such meetings of the Polish-German group, which consists of twenty to forty people, the topic of discussion is always policy toward the eastern neighbors. Different perspectives (German, American, and Polish) are analyzed, and recommendations for EU policy are developed. Another example is cooperation with the Prague Security Studies Institute (PSSI) on shaping EU policy toward the eastern neighbors. The joint activities involve organizing conferences, preparing analyses, and publishing the papers. The results of their efforts are presented to the Western members of the EU in Paris, as well as in Brussels.[64]

Those interviewed for this study have pointed out that it is difficult to specify precisely to what extent such Polish activities can be transformed into ideas and solutions that lead to certain decisions in the EU. However, what can be observed are the ways in which the European donors start to think about democracy assistance in Belarus—for example, that it is important to invest not in the registered organizations in Belarus but in people.[65] Under pressure from Poland, the Union decided to support, among other measures, independent radio programming for Belarus transmitted from abroad and the establishment of an EU Representative Office in Minsk.

Poland, as a new aid donor, has well-institutionalized ways of providing aid. Whereas Polish multilateral assistance usually goes to distant countries and to specific areas of assistance defined by international organizations, the bilateral aid goes to countries that are important from the point of view of Polish foreign policy and to areas of assistance in which Poland has an expertise.

The Polish governmental aid program emphasizes democracy assistance to the country's two eastern neighbors, Belarus and Ukraine, for moral as well as political and strategic reasons. Political and strategic considerations stem from the belief that democratic neighbors will be safer for Poland, the region, and Europe. Moral considerations stem from a feeling of obligation to pay assistance forward, because Poland received considerable assistance during its own struggle for democracy and after the commencement of its transformation in 1989. This assistance contributed to the success of the political, economic, and social transition.

Taking into account both Polish experience as a recipient of aid and the fact that Poland was a leader in democratic transformation in the postcommunist region, democracy assistance is one of Poland's areas of assistance in which the state has a "comparative advantage." However, the way Poland perceives democracy assistance to Belarus and Ukraine is in fact unique and does not fall neatly into the dichotomy suggested by scholars, since the Polish approach is neither strictly political nor solely developmental. Instead, it responds to the particular situation in the recipient country. Given the fact that longtime EU members have dominated the Union's approach, the question is whether CEE countries that entered the Union have shifted EU democracy assistance away from a focus on the developmental approach. A short examination of Polish efforts shows that new member states have likely had an impact on the EU approach to democracy assistance to Belarus and Ukraine. As this study shows, Poland's strong focus on civil society empowerment aims to influence the EU's approach toward Belarus and Ukraine, pressuring not only for more attention to the EU's neighbor states but also for solutions that engage citizens instead of governments.

There are major differences in the Polish government's democracy assistance efforts in Ukraine versus Belarus, both in terms of types of assistance and choice of project partners. In the case of Belarus, there are great efforts by Polish NGOs to support not only civil society but also culture and language, recognizing as they do that cultural identity is pivotal for Belarusian nation-building and identity. In Ukraine, the Polish government-funded programs focus on the state's capacity to enforce decisions associated with complex political (especially local governance), economic, and social reforms, as well as on Ukraine's integration into the European Union; in order to achieve this goal, the Polish government cooperates with not only Polish NGOs but also local and central entities. It seems that Polish elites recognize that a healthy civil society is the sign of a well-functioning state and that the best avenue by which to foster the emergence and development of domestic civil society is to strengthen the state by establishing stable and efficient political and economic institutions. However, it should also be mentioned that the focus on state capacity is not given priority over civil society assistance; these two areas are being bundled together, and it is therefore difficult to classify this assistance as developmental. Given that, the usual debate that argues that we must choose between two approaches to democracy assistance then sets up a false dichotomy.

The Polish government recognizes that, whether a country is authoritarian or going through the democratic transition, it is important to reach civil society groups in recipient countries. The Polish government works toward this goal through its cooperation with Polish NGOs. Through contacts with nongovernmental entities in recipient countries, Polish NGOs have the opportunity to achieve foreign policy goals that might be difficult for the Polish government to attain, and they do so by targeting the authorities of recipient countries. Such cooperation between the Polish government and NGOs allows Poland to become an important player in democracy assistance.

Given that Polish NGOs have been active in Belarus and Ukraine since the 1990s, their role in Polish democracy assistance requires a closer investigation.

3 | The Solidarity Movement's Lasting Legacy

Polish NGOs' Engagement in Democracy Assistance

■ Although nongovernmental organizations are major partners in implementing the Polish government's democracy assistance, they began their own such activities in the postcommunist region in the 1990s, before the government's program was established. Polish NGOs' involvement in democracy assistance can be considered a legacy of the Solidarity movement, and the historical overview offered here details Polish civil society's role in democratic transformation, not only in Poland but in the whole region, and its links with Western donors. These international donors, as well as the Polish government, have recognized the important role of Polish NGOs in democracy assistance.

The Solidarity Movement, Foreign Assistance, and Civil Society Development in Poland

Polish civil society was very active long before the democratic revolution of 1989. In order to have a complete picture of the Polish nongovernmental sector today, it is important to take into account its history prior to 1989.

The communist People's Republic of Poland actively attempted to eliminate the institutions of civil society and control the work of special interest organizations. The official organizations that existed, such as the women's, sports, environmental, or youth associations, were usually controlled by the Communist Party and could not qualify as civil society organizations. These officially sanctioned groups were quasi-state structures, receiving funds from the state budget and the party elite. However, at the same time, Polish communist authorities did not completely isolate Polish society from external influences. For example, the Polish United Nations Associations were the strongest in Central and Eastern Europe. From the 1950s to the end of the 1980s, they had succeeded in building up a grassroots network with active local branches.[1] The Polish institution most independent from the communist government, however, was the Catholic Church, especially the Catholic Intelligentsia Clubs, established in 1956, and, later, other Catholic communities popular among young people (Weigel 1992; Sadowska 1996). The Catholic Church had relatively significant autonomy, around which different intellectual circles could unite (Michnik 1993). The church's position became even stronger after the Krakow archbishop, Cardinal Karol Wojtyła, was chosen to become pope in 1978 and when, as Pope John Paul II, he visited Poland in 1983 and 1987 (Weigel 1992, 16). Moreover, as Juros et al. (2004, 562–63) observe, for many civil society activists the Catholic Church was a "legacy of the Old Polish Era" and postwar history: "It is thanks to the Catholic Church that Poland's culture of social activity could preserve itself in a more or less latent form across the decades following World War II in order to rise again in 1980 in the form of the Solidarity movement."

The origins of contemporary civil society in Poland lie in the dissident movement, which emerged in the 1970s and 1980s. The first organization established under communism was the Workers' Defense Committee (KOR), created in 1976 by a modest number of workers and intellectuals. KOR later grew into Solidarność (Solidarity)—the world's best-known mass civic movement, which undermined the Polish communist government (Kenney 2002). Other groups that played an important role in shaping civil society were the Polish Independence Pact (PPN), the Movement for the Defense of Human and Civil Rights (ROPCiO), and Freedom and Peace (WIP), as well as student and youth groups and organizations concerned with education, such as the Independent Students' Union (NZS) and the Society for Academic Courses (TKN) (Kantorosinski 1991; Kenney 2002).[2]

When the Polish pope made his first visit to Poland, his support for the Solidarity opposition movement, led by Lech Wałęsa, provided a strong impetus for change in Poland. The emergence of Solidarity in 1980 "signaled a new stage of civil society development across the region and was a harbinger of the processes that eventually led to the overthrow of the communist regimes and the reunification of Europe" (Leś et al. 1999, 325). Solidarity was registered as a trade union in November 1980, but it was a union not only of workers but also 10 million persons, including members of other organizations, such as the Movement of Young Poland, Znak (literally, "The Sign"), and people opposed to the communist regime (Leś et al. 1999, 325).[3] The initial brief emergence of Solidarity in 1980–81 paved the way toward the rebirth of organizations that had been dissolved under the communist regime, such as the St. Brother Albert Aid Society and the Committee for Protection of Children's Rights. The Solidarity movement was also involved in the creation of an independent sector of some autonomous groups, such as publishing houses, newspapers, and study circles that evolved in the 1980s into civil society (Siegel and Yancey 1992).

Solidarity's growing popularity represented too great a threat to the communist regime, and it was of particular concern to Soviet leaders. As the result, on December 13, 1981, General Wojciech Jaruzelski introduced martial law. The imposition of martial law, which was viewed as a sign of possible military intervention by the Soviet Union in a manner similar to earlier interventions in the satellite countries, suppressed the development of this burgeoning civil society in Poland.[4] Overnight, Solidarity became an illegal organization. A thousand people were arrested, Poland's borders were sealed, and political and civil rights were severely curtailed. Most of the self-governing organizations were made illegal, but many of them, including the Solidarity trade union and the Independent Students' Union (NZS), continued their operations underground.[5] Recognition of the significance of the movement not only for Poland but also communist opposition throughout Eastern Europe came when Lech Wałęsa, one of Solidarity's founding members, received the Nobel Peace Prize in 1983. The Catholic Church was also an important element of the activation of Polish civil society during martial law, as it tried to prevent isolation or exclusion of interned persons or victims of repression (Ćwiek-Karpowicz and Kaczyński 2006).

From 1982 to 1989, civic activity was possible only for those mass organizations remaining under the control of the regime. However, the Polish regime took slow steps to lift some repressive actions, often in response to international pressure. According to a report by the Commission on Security and Cooperation in Europe in 1994, the rights to freedom of movement, freedom of speech (independent publishing), and freedom of assembly (nonviolent demonstrations) qualitatively improved from 1983 to 1988 (CSCE 1994, 2).[6] All known political prisoners were freed during this period, a civil rights commissioner was appointed, and Voice of America, Radio Free Europe, and the British Broadcasting Corporation's World Service ceased to be blocked.[7]

By 1989, the political situation in Poland had improved (in contrast to other communist countries), and Solidarity, which functioned mainly as an illegal political opposition movement, finally managed to reach a compromise with the communist authorities. This ability to cooperate facilitated the peaceful regime change. Solidarity pushed for the Roundtable Talks, and the historic meetings between the communists and the democratic opposition took place in 1989.[8] The main resolutions of the Roundtable Talks included legalization of the Solidarity trade union (through amendment of the Law on Association, which made the registration of Solidarity possible); creation of a senate (an upper chamber of the parliament); establishment of the office of president of the Republic of Poland, chosen by both chambers of the parliament for terms of six years; legalization of some opposition media outlets; and an agreement to give the Catholic Church full legal status (Osiatynski 1996, 44–47). Most significantly, however, terms for the first quasi-free parliamentary elections in the postcommunist space were negotiated.[9] The election of June 4, 1989, brought a victory to Solidarity. This event marked the end of communist rule in Poland and was an indication of the processes that eventually led to the fall of the Berlin Wall and the overthrow of communist regimes across Central and Eastern Europe (Leś et al. 2004).[10] A year later, Lech Wałęsa was elected president of Poland.

After the 1989 Roundtable Agreements, there was a rapid increase in the number of civil society groups (Mansfeldová et al. 2004; Sadowska 1996). Also, some organizations that had existed in Poland before World War II were revived. New political circumstances allowed for changes in the functioning of associations; based on compulsory membership during the communist times these groups now had voluntary memberships and fostered a true civil society. The loose, informal structure that characterized civil society in 1982 gave way to formal, professional NGOs in Poland. Registration of new organizations was especially rapid in the first three or four years after 1989. According to the Klon/Jawor Association's database, at the beginning of the 1990s there were approximately twenty thousand nongovernmental organizations involving two million people.[11] In 1993 and 1994, the distinction between political parties and NGOs became more clear-cut, and the main actors and forms of activities began to change. Freedom of association was recognized in the new Constitution of the Republic of Poland, adopted in 1997.

The remarkable renaissance of civil society in Poland during the 1980s and of nonprofit organizations after 1989 would not have been possible without the actions of Solidarity activists and all who contributed to the movement's success, both the religious and the secular formal and informal networks (Leś et al. 2004). Another factor that has influenced the development of the third sector in Poland was foreign assistance. It is unlikely that Solidarity and democratic change in Poland could have arisen without considerable Western assistance (Ćwiek-Karpowicz and Kaczyński 2006). That assistance came in many different ways. Western donors played an important role in strengthening the opposition in Poland through numerous contacts with Solidarity and frequent visits by representatives of Western NGOs and trade unions to meet with the Polish opposition leaders. Also, the flow of information and know-how (especially organizational know-how) facilitated formation of the democratic opposition. Finally, financial support, mainly from Western trade unions, assisted Solidarity during martial law. The largest share came from the American Federation of Labor–Congress of Industrial Organizations (AFL-CIO).[12] Another important source of assistance in the mid-1980s was the National Endowment for Democracy, established by the US Congress on the initiative of President Ronald Reagan. It was mainly monies from NED (about half a million US dollars) that the AFL-CIO was channeling to the underground Solidarity movement in 1985–86 (Friszke 2006, 110).

Western assistance continued after the breakdown of the communist government, and it played an important role in the emergence and sustainability of many Polish NGOs. Although civil society grew substantially in Poland at the beginning of the 1990s, the third sector in Poland and other CEE countries was facing challenges, such as the need to create legal and fiscal structures to regulate and support the third sector.[13] Other challenges included organizational development, management, and networking. Also, there was need for greater information sharing among organizations in Poland, as well as with the third sector in CEE and Western nations. Groups were often unaware of like-minded organizations and unable to identify needs. In many cases, efforts overlapped when groups could not collaborate. Finally, lack of money, blurred lines between nonprofit and for-profit work, and lack of modern technology were other challenges with which the Polish third sector had to cope (Siegel and Yancey 1992, 43–46).

Facing these many challenges, the third sector relied heavily on the aid and experience of their Western partners. Polish NGOs received substantial funding from multilateral agencies, governments, and private foundations based in Western Europe and the United States.[14] The major multilateral assistance project to support the emerging third sectors in CEE countries (especially Poland and Czechoslovakia) was provided by the PHARE (Poland and Hungary Assistance for Restructuring their Economies) initiative of the European Union. PHARE was one of the three pre-accession instruments to assist the Central and Eastern European countries in their preparations for joining the European Union. The objective of the program was to facilitate economic restructuring and political change in these countries, and the third sector was automatically embraced in order to safeguard and develop the democratic process.[15]

The majority of Western European assistance efforts were disbursed by national government offices, such as the Department for International Development (DFID) in the UK, which between 1993 and 1999 launched the British Know-How Fund of bilateral technical assistance provided to the countries of Central and Eastern Europe and Central Asia. This British program aimed to support the process of transition to pluralist democracy and a market economy by promoting civil society development.[16] Also, private organizations such as the Fondation de France—established to help organizations to carry out philanthropic, cultural, environmental, or scientific projects and social activities—gave significant grants to social service NGOs in the region. The German political foundations (*Stiftungen*) have also played an important role in extending public debate in Poland by opening offices in Warsaw, publishing books, sponsoring seminars on policy matters, and the like.

The most substantial help came from the US government and US private foundations that addressed such areas as human rights protection, freedom of the press, and citizens' participation. Poland was one of the largest CEE recipients of American assistance (Siegel and Yancey 1992). The US government granted support to NGOs in CEE through several different entities, such as USAID, which supported the initiatives of such nonprofit organizations as the Young Men's Christian Association (YMCA) and Project Hope. Congress tasked USAID to disburse funding under the Support for East European Democracy (SEED) legislation of 1989.[17] The SEED Act of 1989 also provided funding to the Citizens Democracy Corps (CDC) and the National Endowment for Democracy. CDC focused on supporting economic development and aiding private enterprises. NED, however, specialized in providing grants to political parties, trade unions, and media organizations, as well as to NGOs in CEE countries (Siegel and Yancey 1992, 76).

Notable US private financial sources for Polish organizations included the Ford Foundation, the Andrew W. Mellon Foundation, the Charles Stewart Mott Foundation, the Pew Charitable Trusts, the Rockefeller Brothers Fund, the German Marshall Fund, and the Open Society Fund–Soros Foundation (ACAP 1995; Siegel and Yancey 1992, 76–77). These US foreign organizations and institutions contributed materially to building up the infrastructure of civil society. In the mid-1990s, foreign donors began to scale back their support to the civil society sector in Poland, arguing that Poland was a fully fledged democracy that no longer needed support from abroad (Juros et al. 2004, 566). US financial assistance ceased to flow in the mid-1990s, and European Union sources became more visible when the EU shifted from focusing only on development assistance to assistance in the form of pre-accession programs such as PHARE.

From Democratic Transformation to Consolidation

This supportive regulatory framework for the operation of civil society, as well as Western assistance, contributed to a rapid increase in the number of business associations, foundations, and church organizations. By 1997, the estimated start date of the withdrawal of US funds from Polish civil society, there were more than twenty thousand registered NGOs (Quigley 1997, 44).

Once US aid ceased to flow into the country, there was a qualitative shift in the character of participation in organizations and in funding for civil society; participation was not on such a popular, mass scale and funding was less broad based, being directed instead toward specific (selected) organizations for specific purposes (Juros et al. 2004, 568). Many NGO activists were ready to engage themselves in the public interest sphere, and they did this for a variety of reasons: hobby, passion, or sense of social duty (Chimiak 2004). The Polish third sector entered a phase in which it strengthened its position vis-à-vis the government and society. This attempt, however, was undermined by periods of stagnation in government policies toward the third sector (Gliński 2006; Leś et al. 2004; Rymsza 2007). The complexion of the various governments and political instability in the first years of Poland's transformation made the focus on civil society even more difficult.

The impact of EU financial assistance and pre-accession conditionality started to play a steadily increasing role in the development of the Polish nongovernmental sector in the mid-1990s. The EU's standards regarding the treatment of the nongovernmental sector facilitated institutional changes in Poland (Koźlicka 2002). The process of strengthening the role of Polish NGOs was also supported by the third-sector activists themselves, who in 2001 established the Delegation of Polish NGOs in Brussels.[18] This institution strongly lobbied, both in Brussels and in Warsaw, on behalf of NGOs as a group (for example, inclusion of Polish NGOs when earmarking European funds) and also initiated several campaigns directed at both the NGO sector and society overall.

The process of lobbying the government resulted in significant institutional changes. The reform of local self-government in 1999 was actively supported by Polish NGOs, such as the Foundation in Support of Local Democracy (FSLD) and its founding chairman, Jerzy Regulski.[19] In 1989, the first noncommunist government, under Tadeusz Mazowiecki, set up a representative office to administer the reforms that were a provision of the Roundtable Talks, but at that time there was no discussion about territorial self-governance, since the Polish system was very much centralized (and self-governance was associated first with citizens building their own neighborhoods). Regulski was nominated for the representative office, and then the FSLD was created in 1989 to support the development of local democracy and governance in Poland and abroad.[20] The organization prepared a reform plan years before any administrative changes in Poland took place; therefore, the text of the reform could be written and submitted to the parliament very quickly, accelerating the whole process and making the reform implementation successful.[21] The foundation's involvement in the development of local democracy in Poland also had substantial implications for strengthening the role of civil society. This advocacy gave a signal to the government that Polish NGOs could not only serve as a forum for discussion about political, social, and economic issues but also propose practical solutions. Moreover, FSLD engagement encouraged other NGOs to pressure political elites to force legislative and institutional changes.

Polish NGOs began to lobby the government intensively. As a result of such efforts, a program to monitor election promises was implemented during one of the nongovernmental forums. Moreover, permanent positions for NGOs in a number of the lower chamber's committees were created.[22] One such position is the Parliamentary Group for Cooperation with NGOs within the Parliamentary Committee on Social Policy (Skrzypiec 2008).

Furthermore, Polish NGOs not only engaged in activities helping Poland to consolidate its democracy but also responded with flexibility to the demands of the community they represented. The nongovernmental sector undertook a number of very important initiatives that filled a gap in state politics. For example, Polish NGOs helped to organize aid deliveries to Poles affected by a severe flood in 1997. The fact that NGOs were the first to engage such important social issues demonstrated the professionalism of civil society organizations, and their high level of involvement could no longer be overlooked by authorities.

Polish NGOs also lobbied for some changes favorable to the third sector. One result was the Public Benefit and Volunteer Work Act of 2004. In 2004, the government also established the Civic Initiatives Fund, the first long-term governmental program to support the third sector. Finally, Polish NGOs played an important role in building a model of intersectoral cooperation in the finalization of Poland's accession to the EU, which improved NGOs' access to European funds and programs, especially the European Social Fund (Koźlicka 2002).

Polish organizations were aware of the importance of building bridges not only to the state and public sector but also among themselves. Whereas in the mid-1990s, as Sadowska (1996) points out, Polish NGOs were not actively cooperating with one another, this situation changed at the beginning of 2000, once again on the initiative of third-sector activists. Polish organizations learned that in order to change their situation for the better, they had to combine their efforts. Information and communication institutions were highly developed by the creation in 2000 of a nongovernmental Internet portal, www.ngo.pl, administered by the Klon/Jawor Association. Also, the Polish National Federation of NGOs (OFOP) was established to integrate and consolidate their relationships. This association promotes legislative changes to improve conditions for the functioning of the sector and works on improving civil society advocacy through partnership and cooperation of federation members.[23]

The NGOs also became an important factor in the shaping of Polish foreign policy. At one time, foreign policy comprised merely efforts in diplomacy, and no actors outside the government played any substantive role in formulating policy. Today, there is "social diplomacy," in the opinion of Renata Koźlicka-Glińska of the Polish-American Freedom Foundation (PAFF).[24] Events such as the Orange Revolution teach us that NGOs can play an important role in shaping Polish policy toward the East (Stanowski 2005b). Think tanks are particularly active in the debate on Polish foreign policy, preparing analyses in policy papers and participating in roundtables with ambassadors and other representatives of the MFA.[25] Likewise, the Ministry of Foreign Affairs participates in conferences organized by NGOs on such topics as Polish foreign policy toward Eastern countries.[26] For example, the Center for International Relations (CIR) founded the Foreign Policy Club—an influential forum for foreign policy analysis and debate involving hundreds of leading politicians, diplomats, civil servants, local government officials, academics, students, journalists, and representatives of other NGOs. The College of Eastern Europe, however, in cooperation with governmental institutions, organizes the international Warsaw East European Conference (WEEC) for scientists and the annual Poland East Policy Conference, which brings together politicians, diplomats, academics, and representatives of nongovernmental organizations. Participants, to mention a few, include Bogumiła Berdychowska, Zdzisław Najder, Agnieszka Magdziak-Miszewska, Henryk Wujec, and Paweł Kazanecki, as well as others who deal with Polish foreign policy on Eastern countries and have played a prominent role in shaping these relations.[27] It also happens that people who work in Polish think tanks later sometimes work for the government and vice versa.

To sum up, Polish NGOs have broad experience in promoting democratization and democratic consolidation, having played an important role in the democratic transformation of the country. Polish civil society also served as a center for the technological transfer of resistance in the 1980s, which led to democratic changes across Central and Eastern Europe. Polish civil society, after demonstrating its democratizing power, later became formally subdivided into NGOs that have promoted democratic consolidation mainly by complementing the official process, building and strengthening relations with people and engaging in dialogue (socialization and education), engaging in advocacy and public communication, and using its deep familiarity with local conditions—a crucial component for democratic consolidation. In the twenty-first century, Polish NGOs, which are often led by former Solidarity activists, have gone east to engage in democracy assistance activities in Ukraine and Belarus.

How Former Recipients Became Democracy Promoters

While engaging in democratic transformation and consolidation activities and strengthening their position in Poland in the mid-1990s, many Polish NGOs were developing the desire and the skills to share their experience beyond Poland's borders (Juros et al. 2004). A growing number of organizations that previously worked mainly in Poland became active in the East, including the Foundation for the Development of Local Democracy, the Foundation for the Development of Civil Society, the Institute of Public Affairs, and the Foundation for Socioeconomic Initiatives.[28] Polish NGOs' first target countries were Ukraine and Belarus, and later the organizations also became more involved in Russia, Mongolia, and various countries in the Balkans, the Caucasus region, and Central Asia.[29]

One might ask why NGOs decided to direct their democracy assistance activities to the postcommunist region. When asked that question, representatives of Polish NGOs gave answers that can be grouped in six categories. First were idealistic reasons; interviewees indicated they have an obligation to help, because Polish NGOs had previously received such assistance. Second, Western donors encouraged Polish NGOs to assist other postcommunist countries. Third were reasons of practicality (e.g., geographical proximity, the probability that aid would be well used, their own experience with the transformation process). The fourth category of reasons involved meeting a demand for experience and skills in the recipient countries. Fifth were personal reasons, meaning that NGO activists had material and family reasons for wanting to provide aid. Finally, Polish NGOs perceive their democracy assistance work to be in the service of Poland's national interests.

The most popular reason given for helping Ukrainians and Belarusians was the need to pass on the legacy of Solidarity. As Solidarity made strides, more and more Poles became aware that the fate of their country depended upon them. As expressed by Jacek Michałowski, program director of PAFF, "We wanted to show our friends from Ukraine and Belarus how we took the matter into our hands. . . . We wanted to show our positive experience with transformation—if we managed, they can do this, too!" (FED 2005). Grzegorz Gromadzki of the Stefan Batory Foundation remembered that similar sentiments were expressed even during the First Convention of Solidarity in the fall of 1981, during which the message was sent to the workers in the socialist bloc to struggle for freedom of association. This expression was adopted as a declaration of ideology during those early days of transformation.[30]

The strongest force driving Poland's efforts in Ukraine and Belarus is thus a sense of obligation to share the assistance it received or, in colloquial terms, to "pay it forward." For example, Western social scientists and other experts provided training to political oppositionists. Trainees such as Urszula Doroszewska significantly contributed to Poland's democratization, so these aid recipients then felt strongly about passing their knowledge and experience to Eastern neighbors, according to Katarzyna Bielawska of the Democratic Society East Foundation (DSE).[31] Przemysław Fenrych of the Foundation in Support of Local Democracy (FSLD) remembered these times himself and said that, having received a lot of support from the West during the period of the "Solidarity Carnival" and then during martial law, founders of Polish NGOs feel an obligation and need to help others.[32]

Moreover, in almost every one of these organizations, there can be found some trace of the Solidarity tradition, because many activists in the Polish third sector have roots in the Solidarity movement and the democratic opposition. As the Polish popular newspaper *Rzeczpospolita* (2005) reported, "Underground activists from the 1980s are still active in public life but especially in the nongovernmental organizations (42 percent)." Most people who founded Polish organizations and are working in them today were affiliated with the underground movement and Solidarity. Some organizations, like the Foundation for Young Democracy, were founded by students like Jan Fedirko or Paweł Bobołowicz, who formed an opposition to the Polish communist regime. Later, in the 1990s, these individuals were activists in such groups as the Polish-Ukrainian Youth Forum. Even when the Foundation for Young Democracy was just established, it institutionalized relations with Ukrainian partners. The Center for International Relations is another example of an organization that has been led by the former democratic oppositionists—by Janusz Reiter until 2005, and then by Eugeniusz Smolar. Both figures were affiliated either with the Workers' Defense Committee (KOR) or Solidarity, as well as with other democratic opposition groups in Poland and underground publications.[33]

There are more examples of Polish organizations founded by Polish dissidents, as well as people affiliated with the communist opposition not only in Poland but elsewhere in the region. The Robert Schuman Foundation was established in 1991 by such individuals, including Tadeusz Mazowiecki and Piotr Nowina-Konopka.[34] In the 1990s, the Robert Schuman Foundation, like many Polish NGOs, implemented projects closely associated with the Polish political, social, and economic transition. The organization held meetings, conferences, and workshops that provided forums for discussion of Polish transformation. Later, the foundation shifted its activities toward European integration, in order to prepare Poland for membership in the European Union. Today, the foundation engages in pro-EU activities, working with other countries of the postcommunist region. Another important figure is the economist Leszek Balcerowicz, who together with his wife established the Center for Social and Economic Research (CASE) in 1991 in Warsaw. Balcerowicz was an economics expert in the Solidarity trade union and after 1989 held the positions of deputy prime minister and finance minister of Poland, thus leading the economic transition. As head of a commission of experts to plan and introduce the economic transition in Poland, he was a father of "shock therapy" in Poland—a method for rapid transition from a planned economy to the market economy. CASE scholars and researchers assisted him and other policy makers during the early years of transformation, before turning their attention to other countries and other areas of activity.

It became clear during the fieldwork and in interviews with those many prominent Polish civil society activists and former dissidents that the rise of Solidarity promoted a specific model of democracy assistance. Democracy assistance practitioners call this model of collaborative efforts in the region "cross-border work," an example being Polish-Czechoslovak Solidarity and Charter 77, an informal civic initiative named after the Charter 77 document in Czechoslovakia.[35] This idea of cooperation between civil societies and developing good relations with neighboring countries was promoted by foreign donors as well as many prominent individuals.

Behind the inspiration for the Eastern orientation of Polish NGO activities were many prominent individuals. Persons interviewed for this work pointed out that Polish activists have been inspired by the views and attitudes of individuals like Jerzy Giedroyc and John Paul II, who, before becoming the pope, publicly demanded not only rights for the church in Poland but also human rights for believers and nonbelievers alike.[36] His speeches during his visits in Poland as well as meetings with him gave people a sense of community, solidarity, and responsibility for others. In the 1970s, he became a reference point for a new generation of intellectuals and dissidents, who later, under the banner of the Solidarity movement, began the struggle for democracy, and many of them continued the movement's work in Polish nongovernmental organizations. Giedroyc, however, inspired civil society activists with his conviction that Poland could be an independent democracy only if Ukraine, Belarus, and Lithuania were also independent democracies. He was also persuasive in his view that Poland should do everything possible to promote these countries' independence and democracy as a buffer against Russia, in order to prevent the type of disastrous moments that had occurred in the past. Solidarity proponents believed in Giedroyc's concept, according to NED's Rodger Potocki.[37]

There were also some Polish individuals with links to the West who played an important role in the establishment of Polish nongovernmental organizations. For example, Jan Nowak-Jeziorański, a famous Polish journalist and politician, came back to Poland after living in the United States and founded the College of Eastern Europe in the late 1990s.[38] The institution's mission is to build bridges between the peoples of Central and Eastern Europe and to overcome mistrust between them. Priority recipients of efforts by the organization have always been Ukraine and Belarus. Recently, Russia, Moldova, and the Caucasus countries have also been foci of attention.[39]

Some figures, such as Zbigniew Brzeziński and Nicholas Ray, who were on the board of directors of the Polish-American Freedom Foundation, probably played a greater role than providing financial assistance.[40] From the beginning of its existence, the foundation's goals were to support the development of civil society, democracy, and a market economy in Poland, as well as good relations with its neighbors, and to support transformation processes in other countries of Central and Eastern Europe.[41] Today, the foundation funds many of the activities of Polish NGOs within a program called Region in Transition (RITA).[42] RITA supports the initiatives of different Polish organizations and educational institutions that aim to share the Polish experience of transformation with other CEE countries. Moreover, the foundation finances the Lane Kirkland Scholarship Program, which is implemented by the Polish-US Fulbright Commission.[43] The objective of this program is to help young leaders from the CEE countries learn from the Polish experience regarding systemic transformation.

Another individual having important impact on the engagement of Polish NGOs beyond the eastern border was George Soros. The Soros Foundation was one of the first to bring foreign aid to civil society in Eastern Europe. The foundation was already a prominent supporter of democracy assistance in Central Europe by the mid-1980s. Soros first distributed funds to the underground Solidarity movement in Poland and to Charter 77 in Czechoslovakia. Support from the Soros Foundation represented approximately 30 percent of the total resources provided by all foundations (Quigley 1997, 87; Szabó 2004). It had helped the development of civic engagement with material support and training for activists. The Soros Foundation pursued a model of charitable giving based on the personal, high-profile philanthropy of George Soros. Unlike many of the other foundations operating in Central Europe, the Soros Foundation has local offices with local boards of directors and local staff (Quigley 1997). All the Soros country foundations became linked and informally coordinated by Open Society Institute (OSI) offices in New York and Budapest. Soros hoped to "transform closed societies into open ones and to expand the values of existing open societies" (Soros 1994, 8). He began his efforts to support open society development in Hungary and has applied similar strategies in opening regional offices in other postcommunist countries (Quigley 1997). He established the Soros Foundation Hungary in 1984 and the Stefan Batory Foundation in Poland in 1988 (Szabó 2004; Quigley 1997).

With the Soros funding (approximately $4 million), the Stefan Batory Foundation in Warsaw became the wealthiest grant-giving private foundation in Poland (Siegel and Yancey 1992, 76–77). As a part of the Soros network, the Stefan Batory Foundation financially supported the development of civil society organizations in Poland, thus acting as an investor in civil society. All NGOs in Poland were either partially or fully supported by this foundation at the beginning of the 1990s.[44] For example, the Institute of Public Affairs (IPA) had its origins in the Stefan Batory Foundation. The foundation from the beginning had two main spheres of action—one focused on strengthening civil society and democratic reforms in Poland and a second one focused on the idea of sharing these experiences not only with Ukraine and Belarus but also with Russia and Central Asia.

In the opinion of Grzegorz Gromadzki of the Stefan Batory Foundation, it was an idée fixe of the Soros Foundation to treat the postcommunist region as a separate territory with distinctive features and to encourage contacts within this region.[45] Programs of the Stefan Batory Foundation, founded by Soros, have been based on the idea of an exchange among countries in the postcommunist region. These "East-East projects" suggested by Soros involve financing initiatives of the foundation that incorporate at least two partners from the region to work on joint activities. Other activities were directed specifically toward the Baltic states. However, according to foundation officials, "it turned out that this region [the Baltic states], with regard to expectations regarding assistance, leans closer—culturally, mentally, and geographically—to the Scandinavian states."[46] The governments of the Baltic states looked toward many political and economic reforms in the northern European countries; therefore, after a certain period of time, the Batory Foundation ceased its support to organizations there. At the beginning, Polish NGOs were also active in the other three countries belonging to the Visegrad group (Czech Republic, Hungary, and Slovakia, with Poland being the fourth of the so-called V4), but those countries had their own domestic and Western sources of support.

With funding from OSI, the Stefan Batory Foundation continues to enhance the role of civil society in Poland and Central and Eastern Europe and thus promote civil liberties, rule of law, and democratic changes. The foundation also actively supports Polish NGOs' international cooperation and offers financial opportunities to do so through the East-East Program (subtitled "Partnership beyond Borders"), which is financed by OSI. Polish civil society actors and organizations receive support, if they demonstrate that they seek to engage in cooperation abroad in order to strengthen expertise, share best practices learned in social transformation, create international advocacy coalitions, and work together on solutions to common challenges.[47] Polish NGO projects in the East-East Program can be implemented in Poland or carried out in other countries of the region.

The example of the Stefan Batory Foundation shows that there was strong encouragement from foreign donors—the Soros Foundation, as well as the National Endowment for Democracy, USAID, Canadian International Development Agency (CIDA), the Swedish International Development Cooperation Agency (SIDA)—for Polish organizations to engage in the East. Also, for donor organizations, Polish organizations were the channel through which the societies in Belarus and Ukraine could be reached.[48]

With this Western assistance, many organizations began to operate in Poland. NGOs that had earlier operated underground—such as Polish-Czech-Slovak Solidarity (earlier, Polish-Czechoslovak Solidarity), Karta, and the Helsinki Committee—began to legalize their status and develop initiatives directed toward Eastern neighbors. Eight main organizations paved the way for other organizations in Poland and initiated projects abroad. The Helsinki Foundation for Human Rights gained the status of the most important training center on human rights in Central and Eastern Europe. The Institute for Democracy in Eastern Europe (IDEE) greatly contributed to the promotion of contacts among the organizations of eastern and southern Europe, as well as of the Caucasus region and Central Asia. The Education for Democracy Foundation (FED) focused on building civil society and civil education in Central Europe and Central Asia, and the Polish-Czech-Slovak Solidarity Foundation worked on the establishment of closer links between Polish NGOs, publishers of independent newspapers, and journalists. The Stefan Batory Foundation, as discussed earlier, became the major Polish sponsor of the activities pursued abroad by Polish NGOs. Additionally, the Institute of Eastern Studies Foundation and the Center for Social and Economic Research (CASE) supported economic, social, and political transformations in the countries of the former Eastern bloc through expert services for business and political elites. Finally, a special role was also played by the Polish Robert Schuman Foundation, whose aim was to prepare Poland and its citizens for membership in the European Union.

Along with the Open Society Institute, the bulk of funding to NGOs in Poland was granted by the National Endowment for Democracy (Quigley 1997). NED played a key role in assisting democratic activists and civil society in Central Europe prior to and following the democratic revolutions of 1989.[49] Links established during the periods of communism and transformation persist today, and NED remains a significant Western donor to Polish NGOs' projects in Belarus and Ukraine. The Institute for Democracy in Eastern Europe (IDEE)—an organization based first in Paris, then in Washington—was one of the main recipients of NED money funneled into communist Poland to support underground publishing.[50] After the changes in 1989, IDEE registered the Polish office and was one of the first Polish NGOs to begin working in the East. As the organization began to grow, different people broke off to create their own organizations. The people who today work for the Eastern European Democratic Center (EEDC), such as Paweł Kazanecki, came from IDEE.[51] Kazanecki is an individual who has his roots in the Independent Students' Association (NZS) that supported Solidarity and in a sociocultural association called the Bridge Club. Established at the University of Warsaw, the Bridge Club popularized the idea of anticommunism, and later, after the overthrow of communism, it prepared a team of people familiar with CEE issues to work in the region. He is a well-known activist among the Polish NGOs and an expert on Ukraine and Belarus. His organization, EEDC, is the most determined of all those working in Belarus. As he has said himself, there is no place in Ukraine and Belarus that he has not visited. However, since his activities threatened authoritarian leaders in the postcommunist states, he has no entry rights for Belarus or other members of the Commonwealth of Independent States (CIS) that remain authoritarian.[52]

Moreover, NED financed projects of the American Federation of Teachers, which since the end of the 1980s has trained people like Krzysztof Stanowski and other pro-democratic educators who belonged to Solidarity. As the result of a cooperative effort between Polish and American educators, the Education for Democracy Foundation was founded to carry out programs aimed at teachers, students, and parents in Poland.[53] Stanowski was one of the first people conducting civic education projects across the eastern border of Poland.

NED was also one of the US grantors to the Foundation in Support of Local Democracy.[54] Today, FSLD is one of the oldest and largest NGOs operating in Poland, as well as across Central and Eastern Europe.[55] The founding chairman of FSLD, Jerzy Regulski, and his daughter, Rutgers University professor Joanna Regulska, played an important role in bringing Western funds to this and other organizations.[56] As discussed earlier, FSLD's mission was to promote the idea of civil self-governance by supporting the work of local authorities and nongovernmental organizations in Poland. Today, FSLD promotes the same ideas among civil society groups in the postcommunist region. The foundation began its international activities in 1994 after gaining experience in implementing administrative reform in Poland. Over the years, FSLD has grown to incorporate a network of sixteen regional training centers and four colleges of public administration.

Another example of foreign donors' involvement in the creation of Polish NGOs doing cross-border work is the Poland-America-Ukraine Cooperation Initiative (PAUCI), a project of the governments of three countries, with funding from USAID and a contribution from Freedom House. The condition for getting financial support was the joint cooperation of Ukrainian and Polish partners during the implementation period of projects. After five years of activity, the PAUCI program was transformed into a nongovernmental organization with legal status in Poland and Ukraine, and it changed its name to the Polish-Ukrainian Cooperation Foundation.

Another reason for directing assistance to Ukraine and Belarus is a more pragmatic one. According to Paweł Bobołowicz of the Foundation for Young Democracy, located in Lublin (only one hundred kilometers, or about sixty-two miles, from the border with Ukraine), Poland's geographic proximity to Ukraine undoubtedly determined the organization's choice of recipient country for its activities.[57] Because of this proximity, activities (mainly travel) in Belarus and Ukraine are less costly as compared with activities in more remote regions like Central Asia. Thus, Central Asian countries are in Poland's plans but are not priorities, according to Fenrych of the FSLD.[58] Moreover, Polish NGOs also find cultural and historical proximity important in their decision to direct assistance to Ukraine and Belarus. According to Morawska of the FSLD, it proved to be much easier to communicate the experience of Poland, because its social and political history have much in common with the circumstances of Belarus and Ukraine.[59] Moreover, the language similarities between Ukraine, Belarus, and Poland also facilitate the conduct of activities, because there are no major communication barriers.[60]

Being situated between Western and Eastern Europe, Poland has experiences from both sides, in the opinion of Katarzyna Bielawska of DSE.[61] Current Polish elites and Polish citizens have learned from Poland's regime changes, the democratic transition, and activities undertaken for the democratization of Poland and its later democratic consolidation. With their experience as recipients of aid and knowledge from the West and their ability to adapt it to Polish domestic realities, Polish NGOs can pass this expertise on to Poland's neighbors. With the similarities of their socioeconomic and political systems, Poland can transfer information on their recent experience more easily to countries of the former Soviet Union such as Belarus and Ukraine than to other countries, as every donor wants its aid to be used in the most effective way.[62] When asked why, out of the whole postcommunist region, Ukraine and Belarus are of special focus for Polish NGOs rather than Russia, Gromadzki stated that working in Russia and spreading democratic practices there turned out to be an incredible challenge for Polish organizations, even in a distinctive area such as Kaliningrad oblast, physically separated from but politically part of Russia.[63] Thus, Polish NGOs have chosen to target their efforts where they may bring the best results. As Bielawska stated, "We want our experience to get to the most fertile ground."[64]

Some Polish NGOs have devoted much of their attention to think tank activities, such as public research, advocacy, and analysis. These organizations, like the Institute of Public Affairs, were established to support reform during Poland's transformation. The officials of these organizations believed strongly that they must pass knowledge on to other countries, according to Paweł Kucharczyk.[65] Simply put, "They are doing what they are doing because they like it and know how to do this."[66] Similarly, the Robert Schuman Foundation has since 1991 implemented projects in Poland closely associated with the country's political, social, and economic transition, as well as Polish integration with the EU. Thus, "with such rich experience . . . it is worth sharing it with countries which aspire to a similar process of transformation and integration," said Rafał Dymek, a representative of the foundation.[67] Similarly, the FSLD was founded to implement local government reforms in Poland that had been developed by a group of scholars affiliated with the University of Warsaw, like Regulski himself. The foundation found it appropriate to share its experience with other postcommunist countries by answering, at the same time, calls for assistance.[68]

In addition to the impetus or desire to share the Polish experience, there have been also calls for assistance from Ukrainian and Belarusian civil society groups. In the opinion of Katarzyna Morawska, Poland seems to be, for Ukrainians, the first reasonable choice to emulate. Poland had no regional model to follow and therefore relied on Western examples and adapted Western features to its own circumstances. Ukraine, however, can imitate Poland's model.[69] Morawska gives an example of a study visit of mayors to France and the United States in the early 1990s. During this trip, Polish participants were skeptical about whether what they saw could be achieved in Poland, because the situation in Western countries seemed to be so different from Poland's domestic political, social, and financial conditions. Ukraine and Belarus, however, are in a more advantageous situation than was Poland in its transition because Poland's experience has paved the way for them to follow.

Moreover, for countries like Belarus, whose government does not have good official relations with any democratic governments, Polish NGOs play an important role by spreading democratic ideas and practices in these societies. Knowing that no one other than foreign organizations can create better opportunities for Belarusian people to see a bit of how other societies function, Belarusian students, interns, and representatives of many professional groups make use of Polish NGOs' projects and come to Poland to study, work, and take part in various educational programs.[70]

Additionally, it should be said that staff members of Polish NGOs may also have their own interests in mind when directing activities abroad. When representatives of some organizations, especially those located in the southeastern part of Poland in cities like Lublin, were asked about the reasons for their involvement in Ukraine, many mentioned, in addition to political reasons, personal reasons—family and friends and a passion for Ukrainian culture.[71]

Finally, Polish NGOs perceive their engagement in democracy assistance in Belarus and Ukraine as their contribution to meeting Poland's national interest. Belarus and Ukraine, as neighbors of Poland, are very important for cultural and historical reasons. Poland has had ties with these countries since the Middle Ages—large parts of Ukraine and Belarus belonged to Poland and the Polish-Lithuanian Commonwealth—and many Poles live beyond Poland's borders. As Fenrych has said, Polish civil society activists may have their own selfish motives for having safe and friendly neighbors, just as "everyone wants to have a nice neighbor with whom one can meet for a barbecue or a drink, but one should take care of him and help him when he is in need."[72] Similarly, Jacek Michałowski of PAFF said, "If they [Belarusians and Ukrainians] are better off, better organized, believing in similar values and standards, it will be easier to build a common European space of democracy and prosperity" (FED 2005).

Poland also has a history of many inglorious events with respect to its eastern neighbors. Episodes such as the Khmelnytsky Uprising, the massacres of Poles in Volhynia, and Operation Vistula persist in people's minds, and in order not to allow these memories to dominate relations, a mutual cooperation and partnership should prevail, in the opinion of the FSLD's Fenrych.[73] Otherwise, these countries could grow to fear Poland's former hegemony, in Michalowski's opinion (FED 2005). Therefore, engaging in assistance in these countries may help to heal the wounds of the past. The Poles share their experiences with Ukrainians and Belarusians with full respect for cultural and historical differences and historical memory, in the opinion of Krzysztof Stanowski, former director of the Education for Democracy Foundation (FED 2005).[74]

Activities of Polish NGOs that are directed primarily at Poland's immediate neighbors also help to achieve other national interests. Poland is able to interest Western Europe in Belarus and Ukraine, thus raising Poland's profile in the international arena.[75] The changes occurring in Eastern Europe, especially after the EU enlargement, when Belarus and Ukraine became direct neighbors of the EU, facilitate orientation of Polish policies to these countries. Polish NGOs are perceived as helping to improve EU foreign policy toward these countries and to mitigate difficulties by employing their experience and skills. Because democratic assistance to Belarus and Ukraine is in line with recent foreign policy outlined by the Polish Ministry of Foreign Affairs, Polish NGOs take actions in these states, and since Polish NGOs have experience in these areas, they get involved.[76] It is important to note that projects undertaken by experienced Polish NGOs have a high likelihood of receiving funding, and this funding cannot be ne-

glected as a motivating force behind Polish NGOs' involvement in Belarus
and Ukraine.

funding Polish NGOs' Projects in Belarus and Ukraine

As demonstrated, many Polish NGOs that played an important role during the transformation in Poland and that today are assisting other countries in their democratic endeavors were initially established with Western
funding. Many of these funds came from governmental, semigovernmen-
tal, and private organizations and foundations. Today, some of these entities continue providing funds for Polish cross-border work in Belarus and
Ukraine, but they are not the only sources of funding.

Western Donors and Polish NGOs' Projects

Some Polish NGOs' activities in postcommunist countries are financed
by the Canadian International Development Agency (CIDA), formed by
the Canadian government. CIDA's aims include promoting democratic
governance and human rights, as well as supporting sustainable development. Polish NGOs are able to obtain funding from CIDA because it
works closely with not only Canadian but also many kinds of international
organizations, other donor countries, and, of course, the recipient countries themselves. A similar mechanism of aid provision is promoted by the
Swedish International Development Cooperation Agency (SIDA), which
reports to the Swedish Ministry for Foreign Affairs. SIDA is responsible for
the bulk of Sweden's aid to developing countries, and it channels resources mainly through NGOs, popular movements, universities, and government agencies. Another reason why Polish NGOs receive funds from SIDA
for their projects in the postcommunist region is that one of the Swedish
group's geographic focus areas is Central and Eastern Europe.

In addition to governmental agencies, many Western Europe–based organizations and initiatives actively support Polish NGOs working abroad.
Worth mentioning is the Trialog initiative, which since 2000 has been financed mainly by the European Commission and the Austrian Development Cooperation. The objective is to strengthen development of activities
and cooperation through the integration of NGOs from new EU member
states and accession countries into Concord and other European networks.[77] Some Polish NGOs receive funds from European Solidarity towards Equal Participation of People (EUROSTEP), which is supported by
the EU Presidency Fund, established with financial support from the Irish

and Dutch governments, whose countries jointly held the EU presidency in 2004.[78] EUROSTEP became a network of autonomous European nongovernmental development organizations working to engage and increase the capacity of civil society organizations from the EU's ten new member states in shaping, debating, and advocating EU development policy.

With regard to foreign organizations, German foundations such as the Friedrich Ebert Stiftung, the Robert Bosch Stiftung, and the Konrad Adenauer Stiftung are very active in the sphere of supporting Polish NGOs' projects abroad. Each of these foundations has its preferences regarding the thematic scope of activities funded. Unlike other German foundations, the Friedrich Ebert Foundation has its own office in Poland, opened in 1990. This agency is the largest such office in Central and Eastern Europe in terms of staff and funding. This organization focuses mainly on EU integration and international relations, social and political dialogue, economics and society, labor relations, and social dialogue. Polish NGOs' activities that are in line with these priorities have a chance to be funded. However, the Robert Bosch Stiftung, a foundation associated with a private company, finances a wider range of projects and programs in the fields of science and research, health and humanitarian aid, international relations, and education and society, as well as in society and culture.[79]

The possibility of gaining access to EU funds allocated for NGOs is linked to the entry of Poland into the European Union and its accession to the European Economic Area (EEA). Three countries that are not members of the EU but belong to the European Economic Area—Norway, Iceland, and Liechtenstein—established a form of nonrepayable financial aid for the less affluent countries of the EU so that they could reduce social and economic disparities. These aid recipient countries are the ten new EU members, as well as Greece, Portugal, and Spain. Under the "Agreement on the European Economic Areas (EEA) Enlargement" of October 14, 2003, two support instruments—the EEA Financial Mechanism and the Norwegian Financial Mechanism—were established, and they are managed by the Office of Financial Mechanisms in Brussels. In the opinion of Bobołowicz, of the Foundation for Young Democracy in Lublin, the Norwegian Financial Mechanism is now an important nongovernmental project from which considerable sums can be obtained for activities in Ukraine.[80]

For a long time there was no opportunity for Polish organizations to apply for funds available from the EU, because the EU grants were only for activities in Poland, for Polish matters.[81] However, the role of grants given directly by the European Commission and other funds coming from the EU (from its general budget and from the European Development Fund) has grown and now encompasses financing activities undertaken abroad by Polish NGOs.[82]

Currently, there are a few transborder cooperation funds for which Polish NGOs are eligible to apply. Among the biggest programs are Interreg Poland-Slovakia, Latvia-Poland-Russian Federation Neighborhood Program, and Interreg Poland-Belarus-Ukraine Neighborhood Program, which are funded by the EU and help Europe's regions form partnerships to work together on projects (Zagranica Group 2003). Units that play an important role in administering the programs are Euroregion bureaus.[83]

Within the Interreg Poland-Slovakia program, for example, there is a very popular program called Microprojects. It provides support for initiatives in cultural, recreation, sport, and educational events, as well as local actions aimed at environmental protection and tourism. It also supports the traditions of local communities, organizing trade fairs, exhibitions, conferences, educational cooperation, and youth exchange. By means of the Interreg Poland-Belarus-Ukraine program, organizations can receive financial support for creating new and supporting already-existing Polish-Belarusian and Polish-Ukrainian webs of transborder cooperation among local and regional associations for social, cultural, and educational efforts, as well as business and tourism. The Interreg Poland-Belarus-Ukraine program fund supports direct contacts between the residents of regions situated near the border and creates the basis for preparing projects on a larger scale.

Moreover, there are new EU financial offerings, such as the Poland-Belarus-Ukraine Transborder Cooperation Program or the Poland-Slovakia Transborder Cooperation Program for the years 2007–13, that create new opportunities for Polish nongovernmental organizations working abroad. Within these frameworks, there are opportunities to submit applications in fields other than transborder cooperation—such as human rights. Finally, there are Polish NGO initiatives funded by specific Directorates-General (DG) in the European Commission. For example, DG Education and Culture provides funds for the YOUTH Program, which supports activities addressed to those between the ages of fifteen and twenty-five. This program funds projects that promote the idea of an integrated Europe and projects involving youth in difficult economic and social situations.

Several US foundations have pooled funds to provide assistance, and an example of such an initiative is the Trust for Civil Society in Central and Eastern Europe. The CEE Trust was established by a group of private US foundations, including the Atlantic Philanthropies, the Charles Stewart Mott Foundation, the Ford Foundation, German Marshall Fund of the United States, the Open Society Institute, and the Rockefeller Brothers

Fund. The Trust is an independent public charity that promotes the development of civil societies in Central and Eastern Europe by supporting organizations and their initiatives. Polish NGOs receive financial support from this fund for their cross-border projects.

Despite the diversity of foreign funds, US donors play the major role in assisting Polish NGOs in their efforts. The National Endowment for Democracy is the largest donor to Polish NGO projects in Belarus and Ukraine. NED operates in eighty-six countries around the world with a budget of $110 million, but the budget for the postcommunist region is its largest or second largest among all the regions in which it has worked, according to Rodger Potocki, Europe and Eurasia director at NED.[84] In terms of Eastern Europe and former Soviet countries, Belarus and Ukraine are priorities for NED. The probable reason, according to Potocki, is that NED was successful at supporting the underground and dissident movements in Central Europe, and Ukraine and Belarus are linked to these places. Thus, these countries seem to be natural places for NED to work after the successful democratic consolidation in Central Europe.

Nevertheless, the direct grants aimed at assisting in the democratizing initiatives of recipient groups in Belarus and Ukraine do not tell the whole story of NED grants in these two countries. The agency also provides grants to NGOs based in other Central and Eastern Europe countries, which have their own Ukrainian and Belarusian projects. NED calls these forms of funding "cross-border projects"; in them, Polish NGOs play a major role. Such cross-border projects may also be considered as a way to improve the effectiveness of NED monies spent in the postcommunist region. If one adds up all direct grants and indirect grants to Belarusian and Ukrainian partners through Polish, Czech, Slovak, and Lithuanian NGOs, the overall amount of NED monies going to Ukraine and Belarus rises to 10 percent and the number of projects by 16 percent for the period between 1993 and 2006.[85]

Among all NGOs based in CEE countries, NED started its cross-border work with Polish NGOs almost a decade earlier than other CEE partners. Overall, there were seventy-three cross-border projects in the postcommunist region between 1993 and 2007, and of those, fifty-three went through Polish partners. Polish activities almost always received larger amounts of grant aid than other cross-border projects. To be more precise, more than 75 percent of all NED sums spent on cross-border projects in the former Soviet Union that were implemented by CEE partners between 1993 and 2007 went to Poland.[86] Taking into account only Belarusian and Ukrainian projects, the Polish contribution rises to 85 percent of all grants spent on

NED's cross-border projects. The Czech Republic seems to be NED's second major partner, with 11 percent; the Slovak Republic received 9 percent, and Lithuania, 5 percent of the total amount spent by NED on cross-border projects with CEE countries. Tables 3.1 and 3.2 provide information regarding NED partners from the Czech Republic, Slovakia, Lithuania, and Poland involved in cross-border work.

NED cooperates with Polish NGOs, which can apply for the funds four times a year. Grants are disbursed for a year long program, and grantees have to submit financial and narrative reports every three months. At the end of the project, there is a final report and an evaluation report made by the grantees.[87]

The East European Democratic Center (EEDC) is the major Polish partner in terms of the grants it has received during its fifteen years of cooperation with NED. Also, the EEDC has had the most projects: thirteen projects implemented out of all fifty-three handled by Polish partners. The second major cross-border partner is the Polish-Czech-Slovak Solidarity Foundation, the first organization to undertake NED cross-border projects in Belarus and Ukraine. NED supported the establishment of the foundation, which resulted from cooperation between dissidents from the Solidarity and Charter 77 underground movements. In 1990, the foundation received one of the first grants directed toward Central and Eastern Europe, and, in 1992, the foundation became the first NED grantee to share experiences,

TABLE 3.1. Czech, Slovak, and Lithuanian partners in NED-funded cross-border projects in the former Soviet Union, 1998–2007

NGO	AMOUNT [US$]
Czech Republic	*369,752*
People in Need Foundation	348,193
Civic Initiative "Free Belarus"	21,559
Lithuania	*157,306*
Lithuania Foundation for the Protection of Citizens	20,000
Radio Baltic Waves	50,000
Kaunas Municipal Training Center	39,329
Lithuanian and US Initiatives	47,977
Slovak Republic	*315,101*
Pontis Foundation	154,437
MEMO 98 [Slovak Republic]	61,314
Obcianske Oko [Civic Eye]	50,080
Democratic Initiatives Foundation	49,270

Source: Data received from NED.

TABLE 3.2. NED funding for partnerships with Polish NGOs in cross-border projects in the former Soviet Union, 1993–2007

POLISH NGO	FUNDS (US$)	PERCENTAGE OF TOTAL
Association of Municipalities	24,900	1
Association of Educators	31,203	1
Belarusian Students Association in Poland	16,090	1
Center for Civic Education	104,160	4
East European Democratic Center (IDEE+EEDC)	1,445,025	55
Education for Democracy Foundation	95,014	4
Education Society for Malopolska	32,200	1
International Center for Democratic Development	90,000	3
PAUCI	112,175	4
Polish Euro-Atlantic Association	20,000	1
Polish-Czech-Slovak Solidarity Foundation	315,840	12
Radio Racyja	225,000	9
Solidarity Press Foundation	30,000	1
South-Eastern Research Institute	80,000	3
Stefan Batory Foundation	13,921	1
Total spent on cross-border projects with Polish NGOs	2,635,528	100

Source: Data received from NED.

skills, and program models developed from its work in Central Europe with pro-democracy organizations in the former Soviet Union (NED 2006).

NED's cross-border projects allow Polish NGOs to share their experience in democratic transformation with other postcommunist countries through training, study visits, internships, and other forms of assistance with pro-democratic groups in recipient countries. However, while it is very important to have neighboring countries working in Belarus and Ukraine, most of the democracy-building work should be done by the groups native to these countries, in Potocki's opinion.[88] Therefore, the cross-border work is considered supplementary to NED's direct grants in Belarus and Ukraine, though still a very important aspect of its work.

It should be noted that none of the Western donor organizations exclusively finances activities of Polish NGOs. For example, some Western entities, such as USAID, provided money for the start-up of activities of PAUCI, and today, PAUCI is financially independent of USAID and, like other Polish NGOs, looks for money from different sources.[89] Similarly, until the end of the 1990s, the Stefan Batory Foundation was financed mainly by Soros. As of 2010 the foundation is funded not only by Soros but also the Ford Foundation, the Bosch Foundation, and the Swedish International

TABLE 3.3. Stefan Batory Foundation funding sources and percentage of total donations

FUNDING SOURCE	PERCENTAGE OF TOTAL DONATIONS
Open Society Institute, New York	64.7
Trust for Civil Society in Central and Eastern Europe, Washington	10.5
Robert Bosch Foundation, Stuttgart	5.8
Remembrance, Responsibility, and Future Foundation, Berlin	5.3
Ford Foundation, New York	3.8
1% personal income tax	2.4
Ministry of Foreign Affairs, Warsaw	1.6
Friends of Batory Foundation, Washington [from donations by	
Helen and Peter Maxwell and Taube Foundation for Jewish Life and Culture]	1.1
Agora S.A., Warsaw	1.1
European Economic Area [EEA] Financial Mechanism and Norwegian	
Financial Mechanism	1.1
Commercial Union Poland, Warsaw	0.7
Agora Foundation, Warsaw	0.7
Center for European Policy Studies, Brussels	0.3
Nestlé Poland S.A., Warsaw	0.2
Individual donors from Poland	0.1
Royal Netherlands Embassy, Warsaw	0.04
Open Society Institute, Paris	0.03
Damage fines adjudged by the courts in favor of the foundation	0.01
SPPID Association	0.002
Commercial Bank BH, Warsaw	0.0005
Grants returned	0.6

Source: Stefan Batory Foundation 2007.

Development Cooperation Agency (SIDA).[90] Table 3.3 details the source of funds the Stefan Batory Foundation received for activities abroad (its East-East: Partnership beyond Borders program) based on data provided in its annual report for 2007.

Polish Financial Resources

For many years, the foreign projects of Polish NGOs were financed almost exclusively by foreign donors, and Polish NGOs did not have many opportunities to receive financial support from Polish sources for their activities abroad (Zagranica Group 2003). The possibilities for obtaining funds from semi-Polish sources in the 1990s have arisen mainly because many Polish organizations running their own projects were simultaneously institutions giving grants for other organizations' projects. The Stefan Batory Foundation is an example of such a funding source, especially during the 1990s, as discussed earlier. Today, there is financial support for Polish NGOs' projects from the Polish government, through the Ministry of Foreign Affairs, as discussed in the previous chapter. However, these sources have become available only recently.

At some point there was a need to create permanent cooperation within the group of Polish organizations operating outside the borders of the country to make them aware that even though they work separately, they are united by a shared view of the role they can play in international cooperation as well as in complementing and shaping Polish foreign policy. Tightening cooperation between the organizations began in 2001 during a meeting of all Polish NGOs engaged in cross-border work. In this meeting, the organizations agreed to exchange information and develop relationships with the official institutions formulating foreign policy.[91] As a consequence of this meeting, the Zagranica Group (ZG) was formed as an umbrella organization for Polish nongovernmental organizations working abroad. The Zagranica Group represents the interests of its members, strengthening the position of Polish NGOs vis-à-vis the Polish government. At the same time, "this association is convenient for the government, because it has only one partner to work with, not forty," as Jan Piekło, director of PAUCI, noted.[92]

The members of ZG also played an important role in lobbying the government to establish a governmental aid program. In the opinion of Paweł Kazanecki of the EEDC, representatives of Polish NGOs believed that obtaining aid from Polish sources, rather than relying on Western monies, would make Poland a more credible democracy promoter.[93] This claim was one of the main arguments Polish NGOs used to persuade the Polish government to create Polish Aid. There were many meetings and conferences with Polish ambassadors and representatives of the Polish MFA that served this purpose. In fact, Polish NGOs made Poland, which in the past was the recipient of various kinds of foreign aid, become a donor, as Jakub Boratyński of the Stefan Batory Foundation noted.[94] Later, the EU accelerated pressure on the Polish government to create Polish Aid and determine the amount of funding to be spent on democratic aid activities, as discussed in an earlier chapter.[95]

Moreover, through association with Zagranica Group, Polish NGOs can develop a common position and influence the shape of Polish foreign policy by preparing analyses for the Ministry of Foreign Affairs about relations between Poland and countries receiving Polish aid.[96] Polish NGOs express their opinions regarding Polish and foreign policy during frequent forums with the Development Co-operation Department. The organizations tend to focus on actions that are in line with the MFA focus in foreign policy, yet when the MFA makes its annual call for proposals on aid, their ultimate selection of countries and programs is not random; to some extent, the MFA's focus on particular targets is an effect of nongovernmental organizations' pressure.[97] Polish NGOs also took an important role in reconstructing the Solidarity Fund PL. Krzysztof Stanowski, a former social activist affiliated with Education for Democracy Foundation, the Zagranica Group, and the World Movement for Democracy, became the president of this fund.

Knowing the reasons for Polish NGOs' engagement in cross-border activities in Ukraine and Belarus and the importance of these actions for the Polish government, the question remains why and how Western donors engage Polish NGOs in the field of democracy assistance. The next chapter addresses this question.

The Solidarity movement paved the way for democratic changes in Poland and the development of the civil society sector in Poland. Many founders of nongovernmental organizations that emerged after 1989 made up a major segment of the democratic opposition during communism. As links traced during this study show, those civil society activists who had their roots in the Solidarity movement later initiated cross-border projects to assist other postcommunist countries in their struggle for democracy. Thus, Polish NGOs' engagement in the postcommunist region can be considered a legacy of the Solidarity movement.

There are several reasons for Polish NGOs to engage in democracy assistance to postcommunist countries. First, there is the moral obligation to help other civil societies, because Polish civil society activists received help in breaking down communism and then establishing nongovernmental organizations. Second, Western donors encouraged Polish NGOs to engage in activities in other postcommunist countries. Third, Polish NGOs' activists had a need to share their experience in transforming society with other countries. Polish NGOs were actively involved in the political and economic transition, and they also helped society survive the difficult years of this transformation. They taught participation and civic responsibility and assisted the still weak structure of the young democratic state. Fourth, Polish NGOs have engaged in activities in Ukraine and Belarus because there was a demand for their experience and skills on the recipient side. Fifth, Polish NGO activists often have a personal interest in helping ease postcommunist transitions for material and family reasons. Finally, Polish

NGOs perceive their engagement in democracy assistance in the postcommunist region as their contribution to serving Poland's national interest.

As this chapter has demonstrated, Polish civil society not only played an important role in the democratization of Poland and the region but also, as NGOs, later contributed to democratic consolidation. Having deep contextual understanding of barriers to and opportunities for democracy at the local level, Polish NGOs were lobbying and giving recommendations to decision makers regarding the implementation of political, social, and economic reforms, as well as providing strong socialization and educational impetus. Because of the experience of Polish NGOs as recipients of aid and their involvement in the Polish transformation, Polish NGOs became a natural partner for the Polish government in the provision of democracy assistance to postcommunist countries. NGOs not only are the major partners in the implementation of Polish democracy assistance but also participate in the debate over the targeting of aid, through the Zagranica Group association, and help shape Polish foreign policy. However, it has been clear that Polish NGOs do not act in ways that contradict Polish foreign policy but rather support and complement it.

4

Demystifying
Cross-Border Networks

*Polish NGOs' Civil Society Assistance
in Belarus and Ukraine*

■ The scholarly literature contains very little about cross-border collaborative civil society networks like those established by Polish nongovernmental organizations in Belarus and Ukraine. This chapter fills that void by describing the origin, evolution, and character of these collaborative networks and presenting their potential to diffuse democratic ideas and practices. Initiated before the Polish Ministry of Foreign Affairs started its own aid program, the cross-border efforts of Polish NGOs involved developing different strategies and techniques for reaching civil society in authoritarian Belarus versus democratizing Ukraine. Polish NGOs conceive their programs and projects dealing with civil society assistance differently for authoritarian countries versus in states that are somewhat or newly democratic. Polish NGOs' vision of civil society in Belarus and Ukraine might actually be one of the reasons for successful civil society empowerment. This chapter also analyzes thematically how well Polish NGOs' projects are addressing democracy deficiencies in Ukraine and Belarus.

Cooperating with Civil Society in an Authoritarian Environment

When examining Polish NGOs' cross-border efforts, it is important to have an understanding of the political environment in Belarus and Ukraine, described in chapter 1. To recap briefly, Belarus is an authoritarian state in which political power is concentrated in the hands of the president and where there is no place for democratic institutions or any political opposition. The Belarusian government maintains control with indoctrination through media and the education system, constant surveillance, closure of Belarusian organizations, and harassment of civil society activists. Political and civil rights are subject to ongoing abuse. In such an oppressive regime, civil society cannot freely function, but many organizations continue their activity or work underground. Given the various strengths and weaknesses of civil society in Belarus, as presented in chapter 1, the question is how Polish NGOs find ways to cooperate with Belarusian civil society groups.

Establishing Links with Civil Society under an Authoritarian Regime

Undoubtedly, Polish NGOs have significantly changed their activities in Belarus since Lukashenko assumed the presidency and asserted control. As a result of the situation in Belarus, some Polish organizations that used to work in Belarus, such as the Democratic Society East Foundation (DSE) or the Polish Robert Schuman Foundation, ceased their activities in the country. The Polish Robert Schuman Foundation withdrew from operations in Belarus in 2006 because it had invested considerable financial and human resources in the country and could achieve few results with Belarusian authorities weakening the impact of the NGOs' work. Rafał Dymek of the Schuman Foundation has argued that changes in the organizations' efforts were dictated by practical reasons; the same financial and human resources could produce more results in Ukraine and the Caucasus region.[1] Other representatives of Polish NGOs have indicated that it is difficult to work with Belarusian people because "the majority of the older generation remains silent and passive, whereas the part of young generation that is pro-Western is heavily restricted by the Belarusian regime."[2]

Another obstacle to cooperating with foreign NGOs is that many Belarusians anticipate difficulty in transferring aid money; financial transfers are heavily regulated, and participation in projects funded by nonregistered external sources is considered an illegal act under the criminal code (EEDC 2007). It is a complicated task for donors to support Belarusian nongovernmental organizations that are not registered because such organizations cannot receive foreign aid through the formal registration procedure required by the Belarusian authorities. Lukashenko tightened control over projects implemented by Belarusian organizations in cooperation with Polish organizations, especially after the government crackdown on the Union of Poles in Belarus (ZPB) in 2005. However, Polish NGOs do not use contacts with Polish groups in Belarus to set up projects. Also, it can be difficult to distinguish between civil and uncivil society in Belarus, as well as between authentic and autonomous NGOs and the NGOs that are established by and dependent on the Belarusian government (Raik 2006, 172).

However, despite the complicated political situation in which Belarusian organizations operate, many Polish organizations have not ceased co-operating with them.[3] One member of a democracy assistance organization has claimed that the situation in Belarus makes cooperation difficult but not impossible, that a lot can be done in Belarus, and that there is huge potential there. This individual believed that some Polish NGOs, especially those founded after Lukashenko took power, chose not to work in Belarus because of technical obstacles, such as problems with obtaining visas. More importantly, organizations that want to work in Belarus discover that the environment of conspiracy and suspicion makes it difficult to find a reliable partner and to distinguish good from bad intentions. For organizations that have directed their activities to the East since the beginning of their existence, working in Belarus is not a problem because they have been there since the collapse of communism and have established cooperation, can identify good partners, and know how to operate there.

Polish NGOs' links established in the past with Belarusian partners can still be preserved, even in the more difficult times under Lukashenko. Despite Belarusian authorities' animosity toward them, the NGOs plan to continue operations in Belarus with their Belarusian partners in the future. Moreover, harassment under the Lukashenko regime does not discourage some Polish activists because some of these individuals, as communist oppositionists, were fired from their jobs, persecuted, or even imprisoned. However, the biggest obstacle for the FED, for example, is the disclosure of the names of Belarusian partners required by the donors and the difficulty associated with the financial requirements of this assistance, such as needing to provide a donor with invoices or needing to set up a bank account for the project. However, as one of the representatives of Polish NGOs working in Belarus said, "Even these formal obstacles can be overcome in certain circumstances."

Intensification of repression against Belarusian NGOs (e.g., the outlawing of many organizations, prison penalties for social activity, etc.) created the need to reach other groups—young people, teachers, parents, and so-called leaders in their local communities. These groups were also among the first recipients of assistance in Ukraine when Polish NGOs started their activities there. Outreach directed toward them very quickly "fell on fertile ground" in Ukraine, and therefore Polish NGOs found it important to do the same in Belarus. Thus, the choice of Belarusian teachers, parents, young people, or journalists as target groups is determined by both the situation and the preference of some Polish NGOs.

Other Polish activists strive to make democratic changes in Belarus in a more direct way—by working with outlawed Belarusian groups associated with the opposition. For example, one of the organizations working in Belarus cooperates in projects with informal groups and so-called "young leaders." The informal groups in Belarus with which one of the Polish organizations works are made up of the same people with whom the Polish organization cooperated fifteen years earlier, when Belarusian nongovernmental organizations had not yet been outlawed. The only difference today is that these Belarusian entities now work underground. Since it is illegal to receive assistance from outside groups and recipients can go to jail for doing so, the organization does not publish recipients' names, in order to protect them. However, it must be mentioned that these underground activities belong to the "soft methods" category—raising awareness and a sense of identity and knowledge among the young generation through joint projects, publications in the Belarusian language, and the like. In an interview, one NGO representative expressed his belief that, through such methods, democratic change can ultimately happen in Belarus. He expressed skepticism about financing militias.

One democracy assistance provider has focused on developing and cultivating local elites and leaders who will trigger local society to act for their common good. Organizations identify individuals who demonstrate skill in activating groups of people around specific problems.[4] A Polish NGO organized quarterly meetings with a group of thirty-five leaders from different regions and cities; on the agenda of these meetings was the coordination of activities and long-term planning. For safety reasons, the organization does not provide a list of partners involved in activities in Belarus.

It might be expected that working with so many civil society groups is good, because these activities complement each other and might bring desirable results in the future. However, there are organizations whose representatives argue that it is important to maintain some contact with the Belarusian opposition as well as authorities, not only because isolation is bad but also in order to avoid being associated only with supporters of the opposition or being part of the Belarusian government propaganda. Such an attitude allows the organization to have undisrupted activity with the opposition: "we know that they know what we are doing, but we pretend that we do not know that they know, and thanks to this we can achieve our goals."

The Art of Camouflage

Whereas the choice of Belarusian partners has not changed significantly since the beginning of the 1990s, the nature of cross-border projects has undergone a significant transformation—from those explicitly fostering democracy in Belarus through mobilizing NGOs, to projects working for democratic change in Belarus in an indirect way.[5] Some Polish NGOs try to avoid engaging in projects that might interfere with Lukashenko's regime in a direct way. They declare that their aim is to build civil society, not to organize opposition forces against the current regime. At the same time, however, the NGOs are aware of civil society's potential role in future regime change.[6]

Whereas in the 1990s it was possible for NGOs to implement projects entitled "School of Democracy and Self-Government" and "Creating the Structures for Civil Society in Belarus" or even to organize a conference entitled "From an Authoritarian to a Democratic State—The Character of Political and Economic Reforms in the Republic of Belarus," which focused on strengthening the role of Belarusian NGOs in society, such open collaboration was not possible after the resurgence of authoritarianism under Lukashenko. As the authorities later curtailed efforts by the Belarusian nongovernmental sector, both Belarusian and Polish organizations had to resort to different tactics, which included hiding pro-democratic aspirations (Belarusian organizations have changed their names by removing the word *democratic* during the re-registration process) and altering the nature of their projects. Today, project descriptions omit words that indicate pro-democratic intentions, such as "democracy," "freedom," and "human rights," because they may cause more harm than good. Instead, Polish NGOs sometimes use phrases such as "civic participation," "local activity," or a "personal approach to people," which do not provoke the authorities.

In order to protect Belarusian people, Polish organizations have transferred their efforts to other types of engagement with Belarusian partners that are not overtly political. Training for social activists and representatives of Belarusian NGOs working on civic engagement and democratic change is very rare if not nonexistent. The initiatives that have been planned with Belarusian partners instead focus on improving the instructional skills of young teachers or making school a place for the joint cooperation of teachers, students, and parents.[7] For example, a representative of one Polish NGO working in Belarus argues that projects like "Tourism and Education," which works on improving the amenities of the region to promote tourism, divert Belarusian authorities' attention and allow Belarusian partners to avoid repression. Even concerted actions in the spheres of education, geography, and tourism are believed to integrate small communities. More importantly, as a representative of one Polish NGO pointed out, such projects provide an opportunity for the discussion of other topics and interaction with Belarusian partners who represent pro-democratic forces and are actively engaged in the opposition.

Recognizing the fact that the Belarusian identity, especially the Belarusian language, is neglected by the Belarusian authorities but that opposition forces frequently employ the language, Polish NGOs have responded by working to create conditions in which communities wishing to develop Belarusian culture can operate freely. Polish NGOs focus on publications in the Belarusian language and activities promoting Belarusian culture. For some writers in the Belarusian language, such an undertaking is the only chance for a national literature to exist.[8] In Belarus, conditions favorable for the flourishing of Belarusian language and culture do not exist. Independent Belarusian writers and publishing houses have only a limited ability to publish and present their work within the country. This situation is one reason that publishing is one of the new activities of the Jan Jeziorański College for Eastern Europe in Wrocław. This Polish organization promotes Belarusian culture and language by publishing historical essays, historical monographs, letters of Belarusian emigrants, and a Belarusian-language dictionary. Belarus's limited publishing activity takes place in Grodno, and books about Belarus but written in the Polish language are published in Wrocław at the Jeziorański College.[9] The Jeziorański College undertakes publishing initiatives together with the Center for Civic Education Poland-Belarus in Białystok, the Freedom and Democracy Foundation in Warsaw, and PEN CLUB Belarus in Minsk. In addition to publishing, there are other activities aimed at building Belarusian cultural identity. The Belarusian Culture Festival, held in Wrocław every year and organized by the Jeziorański College, is a broad presentation of independent Belarusian culture by artists, musicians, painters, and photographers.[10] Polish NGOs also aim to promote Belarusian culture through Internet services.

Polish NGOs have made efforts to strengthen independent TV, radio, and other press outlets—an important area of their democracy assistance to Belarus. This form of support is based on the fundamental assumption of Polish NGO activists that freedom of the press and other media is among the most important elements of democracy. The emphasis on cooperation with journalists suggests that Polish NGOs see independent media as essential for an effective civil society, as was true in Poland. These views stem directly from the experience that Polish social activists gained during their own country's transformation. Thus, Polish NGO activists are eager to share their media experience with former Soviet Union countries.[11]

There have been no free, independent media outlets in Belarus since 1996, when the last independent radio station was closed down. Information spread by independent groups is not likely to reach society on a large scale. Recognizing that access to independent information about national and international events is of crucial importance to Belarusian society, the Center for Civic Education Poland-Belarus, which is a Polish NGO, created Radio Racyja, funded by Polish government sources as well as NED funds. This radio station is based in the eastern part of Poland and disseminates objective political, economic, cultural, and educational information and analysis from Belarus and abroad to the citizens of Belarus and eastern Poland. "This radio station is being created for Belarusians living in the free world . . . by Belarusians and for Belarusians"—these words were first broadcast at the beginning of 2006 and became a trademark of the radio station (Belarusian Information Center 2008). The radio station also serves other purposes; it not only supports Belarusian language and culture but also promotes democratic values such as free elections, rule of law, and human rights and informs listeners about the possibility of personal development (e.g., studying and getting a job).[12]

Recognizing that the Internet has become a powerful medium for mass mobilization, as was visible during the protests surrounding the 2006 presidential elections in Belarus, Polish NGOs have responded to this technological trend by offering their support for the development of different websites, blogs, and chat rooms. One such initiative that fostered activism among Belarusians in Poland and supported democratic forces in Belarus was the creation of two websites: www.forbelarus.eu and www.wolnabi alorus.pl (Free Belarus). Polish NGOs have taken the initiative to counter the Belarusian authorities' limitations on Internet development in Belarus. Some Belarusian journalists and local community leaders took part in lectures conducted by experts on electronic media, as well as in study visits to the offices where well-known Polish Internet portals are managed. The aim of activities planned within such a project was to familiarize young Belarusians with the methods of preparing and managing an Internet service. There also are projects attempting to activate Belarusian students through creation of Internet online radio, which serves as a tool for students' communication and facilitates uninterrupted access to the Internet in schools.

In addition to expanding the availability of information in Belarus, these media projects have focused on the development of independent journalists. Belarusian journalists are an important focus for Polish NGOs, despite the difficult situation faced by the media. Polish NGOs are more likely to cooperate with young journalists who are at the beginning of their careers and who work for small local newspapers. The aim is to interest Belarusian journalists in writing about local issues, even if the topic of the article deals with tourism, because these journalists may play an important role in the creation of independent media in Belarus in the future. Also, Polish NGOs have organized study tours for the journalists to visit independent media in Poland, so that they can learn how Polish newspapers operate and how journalists obtain information and improve their writing skills.[13] It is impossible to offer training seminars for independent journalists, so Polish NGOs also give small grants to publishing centers in Belarus. However, there are Polish NGOs that choose not to engage journalists in this way. Przemysław Fenrych of the FSLD pointed out that the effort of working with journalists seemed wasted in the longer term because some journalists begin to cooperate with the authorities or change the focus of their activity in order to survive, whereas those who try to remain independent in their political views go to prison.[14]

Finally, Polish NGOs find it important to contribute to the development of social and human capital at the local level in Belarus by establishing partnerships with some local communities within the parameters of a certain project.[15] The importance of supporting the development of local communities and promoting civil activity at the local level has been emphasized by almost all representatives of NGOs interviewed. Cooperation with local communities is intended to help people change things through their own efforts.[16] Organizations activate Belarusian local communities to improve self-government and to encourage local people to become involved in social issues—even if these relate to such activities as cleaning up neighborhoods, establishing a small local housing council, or improving residential facilities. The idea behind such "activization" is to draw the people's attention to a problem associated with their daily lives; in tackling that problem, they will gain confidence and experience, which may encourage them to take up more complex issues in the future. Such interaction stems from Polish NGOs' supposition that, as was the case in Poland in the 1990s, the development of local and participatory community life in Belarus is one of the greatest needs facing Belarus. Dissidents, dissatisfied students, and other citizens' groups organize themselves, often quite informally, to address particular societal needs. Civil society was built in Poland in just this fashion.[17]

According to many Polish NGO representatives, even when organizations bring a group to Poland to participate in a project rather than organize activities in Belarus, the activities may still have little to do with democratization or civil society building in any overt way, but the visits still offer the opportunity for "cross-border" interactions and might bring desired results in the future. Those Polish NGOs that decide to implement projects in Belarus consult Belarusian partners to ensure that project activities will not endanger their welfare. Other groups choose to initiate projects that, in cooperation with Belarusian partners, focus on a specific final outcome in the form of a book, newspaper, or a policy recommendation. When the Polish representatives work together with Belarusians on publications that consist, for example, of theoretical and practical information about local governance and facilitating local activities, even though the lessons cannot be implemented immediately, the effort may in the future bear fruit if experts eventually do implement administrative reform at any level of government.[18]

The nature of these cross-border projects and the way Polish NGOs establish links with civil society groups show that Polish NGOs tailor activities to political circumstances and understand that the Belarusian people engaged in the activity with Polish partners face possible threats from Lukashenko's regime.

Through Transformation toward Democratic Consolidation

Ukraine presents itself as a postcommunist country that has pursued a convoluted path toward democratic consolidation since 2004, which marked the democratic breakthrough. Prior to the Orange Revolution in that year, Ukraine was considered to have a hybrid regime with power increasingly concentrated in the hands of the president. Although Ukraine presents features of political and civil liberties, the country has encountered many difficulties with commitment to democratic rules and adherence to democratic practices by elites (e.g., increasing power in the hands of the president as well as various oligarchs), unconstitutional activities, lack of transparency during economic transition, unclear lines of accountability, and rent-seeking. These problems, together with the weakness of civil society relative to government and cultural and ideological divisions in society (especially along regional lines), are some of the obstacles Ukraine faces on its path toward democratic consolidation.

For many Polish organizations, cooperation with Ukrainian civil society began in the 1990s and is intensifying today.[19] According to research conducted by the Klon/Jawor Association, in 2002, of the nearly one hundred Polish NGOs declaring that international work was one of their activities, almost all operated in Ukraine.[20]

Although civil society in Ukraine faces fewer restrictions than it does in authoritarian Belarus, Paweł Kazanecki, a Polish NGO activist who has been working in Ukraine since its independence, said that "before the Orange Revolution in Ukraine, it also was difficult for the EEDC to work there . . . and today, Ukraine is blooming, when it comes to the development of civil society."[21] Thus, if both parties have strong faith that their cooperative efforts will yield success, and if both maintain uninterrupted actions aimed at a specific group in one area, sooner or later the progress must be visible. Kazanecki thus expressed optimism about the activities in Belarus.

Most representatives of Polish NGOs interviewed for this study believed that without Polish NGOs' work with particular Ukrainian groups, such as students, teachers, and civil society organizations, the Orange Revolution might not have occurred. Polish NGOs were thus triggering the resurrection of Ukrainian civil society and supporting its revolutionary spirit before and during the Orange Revolution.[22] Polish NGOs could not predict the moment of the revolution but knew that pro-democratic forces with whom they had contact in Ukraine sooner or later would speak up. The real breakthrough and origin of the changes was the association of nongovernmental organizations known as Pora. The group activated and mobilized young people, and without Pora, the Orange Revolution would not have been possible. Jan Fedirko of the Foundation for Young Democracy said that "one could have expected that some changes would come, but that these changes would be in the form of the Orange Revolution, one could not."[23] To assess the pre-revolutionary engagement of Polish NGOs, it would be instructive to trace links between members of Pora and Polish NGOs.

The efforts of Polish people during the ten-year period prior to the Orange Revolution contributed to some extent to the changes in Ukraine. Discussions about freedom and patriotism among Ukrainian and Polish intellectuals, such as Bogumiła Berdychowska and Jerzy Giedroyc, facilitated the efforts of Polish NGOs.[24] However, just as it is difficult to assess whether Polish NGOs' actions contributed to democratization in the recipient country (in this case, Ukraine), it is difficult to evaluate definitively which factor had the most significant effect on the Orange Revolution. Probably one factor could not be singled out as having a particular effect, but many different factors taken together produced results. As the Robert Schuman Foundation's director put it, "The activities of all NGOs have some degree of impact on what happened in 2004 in Ukraine, but it is hard to tell for sure."[25] However, the important thing is that "we [Polish NGOs] in our small scale create an environment from which others can learn, if they want" (Michałowski 2005).

While the Polish government's involvement during the Orange Revolution has been well acknowledged in the literature and mass media, it is worth highlighting here the remarkable role of Polish civil society during the Orange Revolution (Maddox 2004). Some activists with Polish organizations, such as Jan Fedirko of the Foundation for Young Democracy in Lublin, took an active role in the Orange Revolution.[26] He assisted Ukrainian opposition forces and civil society activists with everything from communicating their message to supporters to the logistics of staging a street protest (e.g., placing orange decorations). He helped thousands of people traveling from other cities to Kiev in obtaining housing and food. He also gave speeches and joined demonstrators in singing and protesting. Also, having experience with public protests, he knew that it was difficult to keep social emotions at a steady level; therefore, he helped to introduce new activities. In notes that he shared during an interview, he described an overwhelming faith among people gathered that their protests would bring desired changes, and with such hope these people filled the Maidan Nezalezhnosti (Independence Square) in Kiev: "It is an amazing feeling of brotherly love and joy, even toward the opponents of the revolution, which comes from the confidence of having the truth. This gives strength and determination in the pursuit of justice. Thus, even if the current crisis has not ended as millions of people wish, no one or nothing will prevent the success of the national awakening of consciousness and sudden explosion of civil society."[27] Whereas the whole world was seeing Kiev as a center of major events, Fedirko noticed that "there were hundreds of Maidans like in Kiev across the whole of Ukraine, but few noticed them."[28] Ukrainians seemed to be pleased with the overwhelming help coming from the neighbors. It is worth quoting another fragment of Fedirko's memoir, written during his stay in Ukraine:

> Residents are particularly happy with the arrival of guests, especially from abroad. I think that Ukrainians will remember for a long time our words of support, solidarity, and recognition for their behavior. Perhaps these symbolic oranges and mandarins [fruits] that we distributed to children, who came with their parents in the cold weather for the demonstration of support for Yushchenko, will be remembered better than the white-red [Polish] flags among the numerous Ukrainian banners and orange pennants. Although the participation of Polish politicians is highly valued in Ukraine, I think that the consolidation of friendly relations between the Poles and Ukrainians has been achieved more by the visits of people reach-

ing out to [Ukraine]. The mere fact of being with these people gives them huge encouragement and assures them in the belief that they are fighting for the right thing.[29]

The activity of students from Warsaw University also was particularly noticeable. At some point after the 2004 elections, students established an association called Free Ukraine, consisting of all those Polish students at Warsaw University who were actively involved in the Orange Revolution. Also, students from other Polish universities followed the actions of their counterparts from Warsaw University. For young Polish people, a visit to Ukraine during the elections and being involved in the struggle for democracy was like the experience their parents had had as members of Solidarity (Michałowski 2005).[30]

Whereas some Polish NGOs were actively involved in the Orange Revolution, others—although very active before the event—preferred to step aside during the revolution, arguing that it was the Ukrainians' national struggle and that foreigners should not interfere.[31] Nevertheless, taking into account the experience with the Orange Revolution, it became clear that it was necessary to strengthen not only political but, above all, interpersonal contacts: "Through the strengthening of contacts we show what democracy is" (Boratyński 2005). The Orange Revolution provided people with the opportunity to have such contact.

Although the civil society resurgence in Ukraine during the Orange Revolution has strengthened its role in building democracy, Ukrainian civil society remains polarized and weak vis-à-vis the government, as presented in chapter 1. After the Orange Revolution, civil society grew, especially in terms of the number of organizations that emerged. However, civil society has not played a dominant role since then. NGOs still have a low public profile and weak links with their constituencies overall, as the NGO Sustainability Index reports. This weakness of Ukrainian civil society in the postrevolutionary political environment stems from divisions in Ukrainian society with respect to the democratic transition (Laverty 2008). Geopolitical, historical, and economic divisions between western and eastern Ukraine play a role in this polarization. Political elites, however, instead of mitigating disparities among groups, regularly pursue polarizing strategies.

The weakness of civil society and problems with political culture contribute to the uncertainty around democratic consolidation in Ukraine. Given these weaknesses, the question is how Polish NGOs address these deficiencies in their projects with Ukrainian counterparts. On the question about plans for the future, many Polish NGO activists admitted in interviews that there is still a lot to be accomplished in Ukraine in the next ten years, as new challenges and opportunities for cooperation emerged after the Orange Revolution. Some even argued that the Orange Revolution and the mass support of the Poles for a democratic transition in Ukraine created a unique climate for the establishment of new sustainable initiatives between Polish and Ukrainian NGOs.[32]

Guaranteeing Democracy's Survival

Civil society is connected with the durability and quality of democracy, and an organized civil society often determines how quickly democratic practices are absorbed into the new political system. There are several different factors that determine the speed with which the consolidation of democratic institutions takes place (Diuk 2006, 70). Scholars seem to agree that in the framework of a functioning democracy, it is important to activate citizens' participation in society, because it "inculcates skills of cooperation as well as a sense of shared responsibility for collective endeavors" (Putnam 1994, 90), "quickens political awareness" (89), and "dispels isolation and mutual distrust" (138). Civil society offers the opportunity for citizens to participate in public debates beyond elections. Since civil society acts as a channel for protecting and promoting personal values and interests, NGOs and civic groups provide public authorities with valuable information and expertise on the problems and needs of the society.

Taking into account the weakness of civil society in Ukraine, especially its polarization, many Polish NGOs also find it important to work on the geographical expansion of the civil society sector, networking between organizations and increasing the capacity of the Ukrainian nongovernmental sector. After the collapse of the Soviet Union, the development of Ukrainian NGOs was limited to larger cities in the western part of Ukraine. The western region is not only geographically but also historically and culturally closer to Poland. Thus, it should not be surprising that there have been many Polish NGO projects with western Ukrainian partners. However, today, many Polish NGOs are recognizing both the needs of localities in eastern Ukraine and the fact that emerging organizations in eastern Ukraine are small, nonprofessional, isolated, and often antidemocratic. Hence, Polish NGOs are shifting their focus there. They are cooperating with organizations from Kharkiv, Donetsk, and Berdyansk, and in the oblast of Odessa, located in southern Ukraine. However, contacts with entities from Volynsk oblast and L'viv oblast, which are easier to maintain because of their geographical proximity, still dominate.

One of the projects that focused on strengthening civil society in the eastern part of Ukraine was funded by the Stefan Batory Foundation and implemented by the FSLD in cooperation with Ukrainian partners in Donetsk in 2003. The goal of the project was to create a coalition of NGOs in the Donetsk region, so that they could work together on local problems and strengthen their role vis-à-vis local government. Ukrainian organizations from the Donetsk region could engage with representatives of Polish NGOs, as well as learn from the Polish example, during their training and visits to Poland.[33] Eastern Ukrainian organizations can also receive support through grants from the Stefan Batory Foundation.

Also worth mentioning is a project implemented by the EEDC: "From the Local Initiative to Civic Activity: Support for the Young People's Initiative in Ukraine" (EEDC 2008). This project aimed to contribute to the creation of a network of regional nongovernmental youth organizations in Ukraine. Featuring organized visits to Poland, the project allowed forty-seven participants from different regions in Ukraine to become familiar with various forms of cooperation among Polish NGOs. However, the majority of project activities took place in various oblasts in Ukraine: Chernihiv, Sumy, Zaporizhia, Odessa, Kherson, Ternopil', Poltava, and Kharkiv. Organizations from these regions could meet and learn about advantages resulting from networking. The organization also distributed nineteen mini-grants within the call-for-proposal mode.[34]

A common methodology is for Polish NGOs to work with western Ukrainian partners on a project and then try to include eastern partners in that project. The inclusion of the long-term western partners in the project also increases chances that the project with eastern Ukrainian organizations will succeed. It is natural that organizations prefer working with "partners with whom there are long-established relations and whom they can trust, since mutual trust is very important in project work."[35]

An example of a project in which there are two Ukrainian partners—one from the western region and one from the eastern—is the 2007–8 project initiated by FSLD Krakow and funded by the European Initiative for Democracy and Human Rights with monies disbursed by the delegation of the European Commission in Kiev. One of the Ukrainian partners was an NGO from Ivano-Frankivsk, in western Ukraine, and the other from Donetsk, in the far eastern part of the country. The project, "I Am a Citizen: Shaping Citizens' Attitudes among Young People in Ukraine," aimed at facilitating interest in and spreading awareness of social issues and local problems among the young people in Donetsk through improvement in civic, social, and political education at schools.[36]

In working to strengthen Ukrainian civil society, Polish NGOs seem to recognize that it is also important to strengthen its links with media. Some projects' activities focus on training journalists and organizing a variety of workshops on how to report activities of Ukrainian civil society organizations and how journalists' work can contribute to civil society empowerment in Ukraine. Some projects include large grants for the development of media; the EEDC, for example, provides grants of ten thousand to fifteen thousand dollars to newspapers.[37] Other Polish NGOs' work with Ukrainian journalists involves cooperation on more specific topics, such as projects implemented by the Democratic Society East Foundation that aimed to train journalists on how to report and present elections on television. In one such project, Ukrainian journalists from public and private, national and regional television stations came to Poland during the Polish presidential elections, participated in seminars, and prepared reports on the election in Poland for their own media outlets.[38] The seminars also raised the issue of the Polish experience as state television shifted into private hands.

Polish NGOs seem to recognize that divisions in Ukrainian society with respect to democratic transition translate into the weakness of civil society that undermines democratic consolidation; therefore, Polish NGOs recognize the need to strengthen links between civil society groups and with the media in different parts of Ukraine.

Strengthening Civil Society's Role

A strong and organized civil society represents an important element of democratic consolidation (Bermeo 2003; Biekart 1999; Diamond 1999; Putnam 1994; Putnam et al. 1983; Rose-Ackerman 2007; Tilly 2007). Polish NGO elites seem to acknowledge the fact that a healthy and strong civil society in Ukraine needs a well-functioning state, a state that creates favorable conditions for civil society to flourish and to fulfill its functions. They seem to agree that the best avenue to follow in pursuit of that goal is to strengthen local governance.

One means of strengthening local governance is by decentralizing power. Undoubtedly, the Polish preference for facilitating a devolution of political and administrative power is motivated by Poland's successful experience with local government reform, which is considered one of the well-implemented reforms in Central and Eastern Europe and one of the most successful Polish administrative reforms. Polish activists feel strongly enough to share their experiences with Ukrainian counterparts and local authorities. Particularly active in this field is the Foundation in Support of Local Democracy, or FSLD. The foundation was involved in the preparation and implementation of Polish administrative reform in 1999. Having had this involvement, FSLD undertook efforts to transfer its experience to Ukraine, where local government reform is under discussion or on the public agenda. FSLD support for the development of local governance has ranged from training organized for recipient countries' public employees and political parties to translating and publishing the act of the Polish administrative reform law into several languages commonly used in countries formerly controlled by the Soviet Union.[39]

Many representatives of Polish NGOs expressed in interviews their view that administrative decentralization would be a key to furthering Ukraine's democratization. In the opinion of Jan Piekło of PAUCI, decision making should not be concentrated in Kiev because it has been ineffective.[40] The interest of Polish NGOs in local government reform in Ukraine has been facilitated by changes in the Ukrainian political situation that make implementation of the administrative reform more visible. Since the Orange Revolution, projects that involve the idea of local governance have become particularly popular. However, representatives of Polish NGOs observe problems with the implementation of local government reform in Ukraine. Paweł Kazanecki of EEDC points out that the ability of Ukraine to begin undertaking more rapid administrative reform following the Orange Revolution was overestimated.[41] Even though particular politicians speak of devolution as a positive and indispensable reform, there is no one in the political arena who wants to deal with this type of change. It has been shown that Ukrainian elites are afraid that giving more powers to local-level units will divide the country. Moreover, authorities might be less willing to take on responsibility for this reform, because bringing about change leads to social costs and loss of popularity and elections.

Polish NGOs take a bottom-up strategy in strengthening state capacity and facilitating political reforms by targeting local authorities (e.g., mayors of cities) in a direct way. Jan Fedirko points out that he was impressed by the behavior of local leaders during the Orange Revolution: despite being uncertain about the consequences of revolution, they risked their own careers and the futures of their families by supporting Viktor Yushchenko.[42] In small towns—for example, in Horokhiv—where most residents know one another, if the central authority targeted local authorities, they would have little chance of changing jobs or leaving town. Organizations like

FSLD directly cooperate with institutions from Donetsk and Luhansk—regions where hints of secession were apparent during the Orange Revolution (Karatnycky 2005, 48).[43] Also, many Polish NGOs' projects organized by the Stefan Batory Foundation, the College of Eastern Europe, FSLD, and others focus on study visits and internships in Poland for Ukrainian representatives of local administration from Donetsk and Luhansk.

However, the majority of Polish NGO projects regarding local governance are still implemented in partnership with civil society organizations in Ukraine, which constitute an important element of social control over processes that are taking place at the administrative level. For example, Polish organizations arrange training seminars for local representatives of NGOs at the district level in Ukraine (especially from the central and eastern regions) and workshops for local youth organizations' leaders. The projects focus on the issues important for the development and sustainability of local NGOs and their ability to work with local media and local governments and follow the patterns described below.

Initiatives incorporating Ukrainian local authorities and NGOs focus on a wider spectrum of issues pertaining to local governance, like the project entitled "Establishing a Client-Friendly Office—Quality in Administrative Work," funded by PAFF. This project was implemented by the Foundation for Young Democracy in Lublin along with its expert partner, the Training Center for Local Administration (CSSA), which has experience in implementing international standards for quality management (under the auspices of the International Standards Organization, or ISO) in the Lublin region. Their partners are the south-central Ukrainian organization European Road in Berdyansk and the municipal government of Berdyansk, in the Zaporizhia oblast. The aim of this project was to improve the city's customer service, the qualifications and competence of employees, the organizational structure, and the flow of information. As a result of these changes, the Berdyansk city hall was able to meet the international standard (ISO 9001) for quality management. The successful implementation of this project in Berdyansk encouraged authorities from municipalities in other Ukrainian regions to introduce changes in their city hall offices as well (FED 2005).

The majority of project activities aimed at strengthening local governance includes training for Ukrainian local government officials and representatives of nongovernmental organizations or exchanges (Stefan Batory Foundation 2007).[44] Less common but still used by some organizations are small grants to Polish and Ukrainian NGOs for reform programs targeting local government, NGOs, and media. PAUCI offered small grant programs of this type, thus allowing local NGOs to monitor local governments for transparency and accountability and to educate journalists about the standards of good governance.

Projects bringing together NGOs and local authorities serve another purpose: they facilitate cooperation and thus make the Ukrainian nongovernmental sector an important player in local public life so that Ukrainian authorities can better meet the specific needs of the local population and presumably its wishes—or what Easton (1975, 438) would call "demands."[45] The creation of partnerships in Ukraine between public and civil society sectors, in the opinion of Paweł Bobołowicz, stems from the belief, based on Polish experience, that such projects allow nongovernmental organizations to become advocates of the local community's interests and to strengthen their position vis-à-vis local authorities.[46]

Such close cooperation of Ukrainian NGOs with governments at the local level not only can accelerate democratic consolidation by means of civil society empowerment but also can improve the image of local institutions and make them more accessible to citizens. According to Linz and Stepan (1996, 7), the development of a free and lively civil society is one of the main conditions a democracy needs in order to be consolidated. Moreover, the authors mention that democratic consolidation must involve political society and must entail cooperation and complementarity between civil society and political society (Linz and Stepan 1996, 8–10). However, in Ukraine, especially in the eastern oblasts, there are still a lot of prejudices lingering from Soviet times and causing division between citizens and political leadership. The involvement of local authorities in projects helps them to be accessible and more "human" in the local community's eyes, in Bobołowicz's opinion.[47] Finally, working with local authorities also is useful in that it helps redirect their thinking about the building of local governance, away from an emphasis on infrastructure toward a focus on investing in human capital.[48] According to officials of the Stefan Batory Foundation, "Institutions were established and reforms are being implemented, but Ukrainian citizens do not know how to operate in new circumstances; therefore, the aim is to invest in social capital."[49]

Securing Democracy in Ukraine

Shortly after the Orange Revolution, Polish NGOs responded to President Yushchenko's interest in integration with the West. Interest in closer ties with Brussels, which at some stage would lead to Ukraine's membership in the EU, facilitated Polish NGOs' activities with Ukrainian organizations regarding European integration.

Because Ukraine is the largest Polish neighbor and, contrary to Belarus, has demonstrated democratic progress, Polish NGO activists are interested in having Ukraine in the European Union, as stated by Jan Piekło: "Ukraine offers the opportunity to widen the Euro-democratic civilization, up to Kiev, Luhansk, Donetsk, and it would be beautiful."[50] Also, it should be stressed that Polish NGOs' activities in this area are compatible with the Polish government's long-term goal of promoting the membership of Ukraine in the structures of the European Union (Polish Ministry of Foreign Affairs 2007a).

Moreover, based on the Polish example, it seems that Polish NGOs consider close integration with the European community to be very important for postcommunist countries' democratization—a way to safeguard democracy and to secure it in the country.[51] Also, Polish NGOs find it appealing to share their knowledge and experience regarding European and transatlantic integration, since they helped prepare Polish society for membership in Western communities.[52] Some organizations even made sharing the Polish experience in Euro-Atlantic integration the core purpose of their activity. One such example is the PAUCI organization. It was originally created in 1999 to share the best practices of Poland's successful transition from a centrally planned economy to a liberal, market-oriented democracy. However, facing new challenges and recognizing the changing needs of Ukrainian society, the PAUCI program not only changed its name to the Polish-Ukrainian Cooperation Foundation but also changed its mission to building the capacity of Ukraine to integrate more closely with European and Euro-Atlantic structures through the application of Polish and European experiences.[53]

Polish NGOs are becoming actively involved in facilitating Ukraine's membership in the EU in two ways: by raising awareness and facilitating knowledge about European integration and by helping Ukraine to fulfill the requirements for membership in the EU.

Whereas some European projects in Ukraine were under way before the Orange Revolution, many Polish NGOs began to understand the importance of these projects after this event.[54] Although it was the aspiration of the Yushchenko administration to join the EU and NATO, many Ukrainian elites in the government, as well as many citizens, especially from the eastern oblasts, are not very interested. Therefore, Polish NGOs find it important to disseminate information about Euro-Atlantic integration. Many projects organized with Ukrainian NGOs on the topic of EU and transatlantic integration are oriented toward Ukrainian elites and representatives of different professional groups. PAUCI, for example, organizes the Transatlantic Forum, an annual conference in Kiev. According to Piekło of PAUCI, "The aim of this forum is to create a platform for public debate on what NATO is and to explain that NATO is not a war machine but an important political organization dealing not only with military matters but also with international cooperation, peace, and security in the world."[55] Similarly, the Stefan Batory Foundation has implemented a nationwide campaign to inform and engage the Ukrainian public about the democratic values involved in Euro-Atlantic integration. Together with central European experts, the foundation plans to hold a series of public hearings and roundtables in Kiev, Donetsk, Kharkiv, and Odessa—four cities that have a plurality of residents who tend to oppose Western-oriented reform.[56]

Within projects are organized debates, meetings, and discussions on topics such as European integration, the consequences of the EU eastward enlargement, EU and NATO policy toward post-Soviet countries, the Polish role in shaping EU policy toward Ukraine, European security and justice, and relations between Poland and former Soviet states. Also, recognizing that interest in EU issues is evinced primarily among western Ukrainians and that much has already been done in raising their knowledge about the European integration, Polish NGOs find it is important now to transfer knowledge and experience to eastern Ukraine.[57] Polish nongovernmental organizations have shifted their efforts to eastern Ukrainian regions along the Russian-Ukrainian border for another reason as well—"there is the need to create a counterbalance to Russian quasi-NGOs that are present there and that spread negative opinions about NATO and the EU," according to an official with the Foundation for Young Democracy in Lublin.[58]

When spreading knowledge about the EU, Polish and Ukrainian NGOs target the most import group: young people. Polish NGOs try to share the Polish experience about European School Clubs—informal organizations established in Polish schools that bring together students and teachers interested in European integration. One example of a project inspiring the development of European School Clubs in Ukraine is "Together in Europe," implemented by the Polish Robert Schuman Foundation in 2008. The program was intended to increase Ukrainian students' and teachers' interest in European issues. As part of this effort, Polish teenagers who are active in European School Clubs and their teachers visited Ukraine; Ukrainian groups later visited their Polish partners. Rafał Dymek of the Polish Robert Schuman Foundation has described these European School Clubs as "sometimes the only centers of pro-European activity in local communities and an important place to learn the mechanics of democracy and civic society."[59] Another interesting project aimed at bringing European democratic values closer to young people in Ukraine was a project initiated by the Casimir Pulaski Foundation but organized by young people, for young people, in form of the "Eurobus." For three weeks, young people from different European countries traveled on board a bus in Ukraine, from L'viv to Donetsk, and activists organized the happenings, demonstrating how multicultural Europe is and how Ukraine could be an integral part of the Union. These events were organized in small towns in Ukraine in particular and were accompanied by the meetings organized in Ukrainian schools and universities.[60]

With respect to helping Ukraine meet and adjust to EU political and economic requirements, PAUCI, for instance, works to prepare civil service employees for the changes associated with EU membership. PAUCI organizes training for Ukrainians who, in turn, train and instruct civil servants at the central and local administration levels in their country. The project is very popular in Ukraine, and the Delegation of the European Commission to Ukraine in Kiev strongly supports this initiative.[61] Moreover, the projects help Ukraine to adjust to the new circumstances existing after the EU eastern enlargement. Since Ukraine is the raison d'être of the European Neighborhood Policy Instrument (ENPI)—the EU initiative aimed at promoting democratic and economic changes in Ukraine—many NGO projects aim to explain the advantages of this mechanism, especially how to use funds granted within ENPI. Also, the projects focus on the consequences of the Schengen Zone, because Poland's accession to this zone caused major dissatisfaction and resentment among Ukrainians and made Ukrainians' attitudes toward EU assistance more negative, as some Polish NGOs' representatives claim.[62] Because cross-border trade is not possible anymore and visas are expensive and short term, many Ukrainian people relying financially on cross-border work were left without sufficient money to live.[63]

Finally, some Polish think-tank organizations work with Ukrainian counterparts in order to conduct research and engage in advocacy as well as to advise the European Commission on any shortcomings associated with EU policies toward Ukraine and other neighboring states. The aim of this initiative is to guarantee that all of the various EU initiatives will meet with positive reaction from the Ukrainian people. For example, the Center for International Relations (CIR) prepared, in cooperation with similar institutions in Ukraine and other countries, publications (periodicals, reports, books) on the economic aspects of the ENPI (analyses of the flow of people, capital, services, and goods) and also held roundtables, meetings, and conferences both in Ukraine and abroad.[64] Another example is the project "Friendly EU Border," initiated by the Stefan Batory Foundation and conducted with the goal of reforming Polish and EU visa regimes, improving the quality of services at EU border crossings, and raising public awareness of the need to implement friendly border control mechanisms for EU eastern neighbors. In addition to meetings and training of border guards, there were projects by the Batory Foundation about the consequences of the Polish participation in the Schengen Zone in terms of passenger traffic and the introduction of visas for those traveling to Ukraine, Belarus, and Moldova.[65] Some analyses related to the European integration are also being presented in the Directorates General for Enlargement in the European Commission, as well as in the DG for External Relations.[66]

The projects described above show how civil society can improve cross-border democracy assistance to make it more in tune with the domestic political realities of recipient countries. However, there are certain types of projects that may be implemented regardless of circumstances in the recipient country.

Democratic Education

Whereas many projects of Polish NGOs are crafted to address deficiencies in Belarusian and Ukrainian civil society, the so-called civic education or democratic education projects—that is, activities for teaching citizens of recipient countries basic values, knowledge, and skills relating to democracy—are implemented in both countries regardless of political circumstances. Also, the fact that they are implemented in different post-communist countries emphasizes the universal character of these projects. A common target group in these projects is young people, because they can be influenced more easily than people whose opinions are already set.[67] Many programs targeted toward young people aim to educate them and, at the same time, to activate them to be more socially responsible for their local community, region, and country.

The most popular forms of democratic education projects are study tours, internships, scholarships, and exchange programs organized by Polish NGOs for young people from Ukraine and Belarus and other postcommunist countries, including Russia (i.e., Kaliningrad oblast), Moldova, and Georgia. One of the projects that aim to educate young people is the large-scale Study Tours to Poland program (STP).[68] STP allows students and young professionals—local government administrators, journalists, NGO officials, economic experts, or school headmasters from the post-Soviet area—to get accustomed to the functioning of democracy and organizations of civil society in Poland. This program is important for sharing the

Polish experience not only with democratization but also with systemic/
economic transformation and the experience of traveling the "Polish road"
to membership in the European Union. Another example of internship
projects is the "Wrocław Solidarity Bridge," organized by the College of
Eastern Europe to allow young trainees from postcommunist countries to
come to Poland for internships in many institutions. The main components
of the study visits and internships include meetings with Polish leaders and
many prominent Polish social activists and politicians, like Lech Wałęsa;
visits to public institutions and agencies, newspaper editorial offices, radio
and TV stations; and meetings with university administrators, professors,
students, journalists, and NGO representatives.

Of course, the situation of partner countries is reflected in the number as well as the types of participants coming to Poland for internships.
For example, in STP in 2007, there were 218 participants from Ukraine
and only 40 from Belarus. There are also significant differences in intern
profiles by country. Whereas Ukrainian participants have been employees
of local government administrations, economic experts, journalists, and
members of NGOs, from Belarus the only representatives of professional
groups are school headmasters.[69] During internships, participants have a
chance to work on specific projects of interest that relate to the situation
in their country, such as cooperation of nongovernmental organizations
with government administration, and they can look for some solutions in
Poland, but, according to Jan Andrzej Dąbrowski of the College of Eastern
Europe, "they are not told which ones are good or bad: we also show them
Polish mistakes; we simply give them a chance to evaluate and think about
these issues."[70]

Another group of democracy education programs for young people
consists of scholarship programs, in which scholars can, for example, spend
months conducting research at Polish institutions of higher education and
working with a mentor on a doctoral-level project. In this vein, there are
different kinds of summer or winter schools, like those organized in a joint
initiative by the College of Eastern Europe and the Center for East European Studies of Warsaw University since 2004. Such schools are aimed at
graduate students (mainly those from countries of the former Soviet Union
but also from other postcommunist countries) who are working on their
master's theses in history or political science on topics related to Central
and Eastern Europe. The school experience consists of lectures given by
international experts, seminars, visits to research institutions and libraries
of Wrocław, and participation in cultural life.

However, the most popular educational grant aimed at young people is the Lane Kirkland Scholarship Program, implemented by the Polish-US Fulbright Commission and funded by the Polish-American Freedom Foundation.[71] The objective of this initiative is to help young leaders from the postcommunist countries learn from Polish experiences in economic, social, and political transformation.[72] Kirkland scholars are young leaders from public administration, academia, business, media, or politics. The program is implemented in Polish universities and tailored to the individual needs of each researcher. Such a scholarship offers a monthly stipend and also covers university fees plus the cost of accommodations, insurance, travel, public transportation, and research material.[73] Participants in the program take courses and do research in areas such as economics, management, public administration, business administration, law, social sciences, and political science. The program offers a two-semester supplementary study program for MA degree holders in Polish schools of higher education and two to four professional internships in governmental and private institutions. Each fellow has the opportunity to learn and work with specialists in the field, meet with politicians, participate in conferences, and so forth.

An educational program like the Kirkland Scholarship very much resembles the role that the Fulbright program has played, especially before and during the democratic transformation in Poland, when many prominent Polish intellectuals were granted Fulbright scholarships to study and work at American universities. The Kirkland program seems especially important for students from Belarus, who, during thirteen years under the Lukashenko regime, have been subject to unusually strong indoctrination in schools and universities. Moreover, this scholarship program not only allows participants to continue their education at universities in Poland but also aims to support the leaders who come to Poland, establish relationships with the people, and later maintain this contact, simply "the same of what the United States has done for the whole world," as Renata Koźlicka-Glińska of PAFF said.[74]

In addition to offering scholarships and internships, many Polish NGOs organize exchange programs between young people from Poland and those from other postcommunist countries. On a larger scale than others is the RAZOM project of PAUCI. This exchange program with Ukrainian young people has been financed by the MFA from the beginning of the Polish governmental aid program. Every year within the RAZOM framework, young people from both countries get together and work on shared projects.[75] Within this initiative, young people from Ukrainian and Polish partner schools are engaged in joint activities of different kinds, from soccer games to protecting the common cultural heritage. As Jan Piekło of PAUCI stated, these are perhaps not ambitious projects, but they mobilize young people to do something together, learn about each other, and get teachers interested in some initiatives, as well.[76]

However, in order to reach young people, many Polish NGO projects are targeted to groups that have an immediate impact on young people, such as teachers and parents, so that they can transfer their knowledge about democratic ideas to their students and children. Recognizing the importance of schools and teachers as a medium for the dissemination of democratic ideas and behaviors, Polish NGOs very early on decided to direct their activities at teachers. One of the first Polish NGO projects in Ukraine directed at teachers was initiated by the Institute for Democracy in Eastern Europe (which later changed its name to the East European Democracy Center) and directed at Crimean Tatars in southern Ukraine.[77] Urszula Doroszewska, Krzysztof Stanowski, and Paweł Kazanecki, Polish activists and leaders of three Polish NGOs—the Democratic Society East Foundation, the Education for Democracy Foundation, and EEDC, respectively—were on the team that headed south to the Crimean region.[78] These Polish activists began to help set up schools for the returned Tatars and began to work with teachers and parents, creating schools as local community centers for the Crimean Tatars.[79] The NED funded these organizations' projects for the promotion of civil society in Crimea and school reforms in this region.

Many civic education projects teach civil society organizations about the importance of school in shaping and diffusing democratic values and practices. Some projects that brought together both teachers and parents led to the creation of parents' councils, students' clubs, educational councils, European School Clubs, school newspapers, school sports clubs, and special interest circles (PAUCI 2007b). Moreover, the schools collaborate with nongovernmental organizations and other school-affiliated social organizations and institutions, in both Ukraine and Poland, making the diffusion of democratic ideas more likely.[80]

Of course, in authoritarian regimes like that of Belarus, cooperation with schools is not without obstacles. Since official cooperation with schools is not possible in Belarus, Polish partners establish links with individual teachers and school administrators. The reason for targeting this group is that, since teachers interact with young people every day, the activists have the possibility of influencing young people through their teachers. Young people are subject to unusually strong indoctrination in schools and universities, and Belarusian teachers often have to hide their out-of-school activities and take off from work in order to participate in events organized by Polish NGOs, such as training and workshops. Meetings in Belarus take on an aura of conspiracy as they are held in restaurants and other places that do not draw Belarusian authorities' attention. Therefore, some organizations, when it is possible, bring Belarusian teachers to Poland and thus implement the projects in the safety of Poland. During their stay in Poland, teachers from Belarus can participate in workshops and learn how to prepare similar workshops in Belarus. However, other Polish organizations, taking into account the complicated situation in Belarus, prefer to choose projects with young people, teachers, and parents that are neutral. One such project focused on creating educational clubs in Belarusian schools to provide cultural, tourist, and historical information about a given region.

The Polish citizenry's experience as recipients of democracy assistance from the West, as well the role that Polish civil society played in the democratic transformation in Poland, is reflected in Polish NGOs' engagement in the postcommunist region. While implementing projects in Belarus and Ukraine, Polish NGOs have cooperated with civil society groups, recognizing that civil society plays an important role in bringing democracy, as well as in buffering the societal shocks and disorder that are associated with political, economic, and social transitions. Polish NGOs recognize the importance of civil society in both democratic breakthrough and democratic consolidation. However, because civil societies display varying needs in different regimes and have different functions to perform, there is differential emphasis put on various aspects of assistance associated with civil society development in Belarus and Ukraine. Projects are tailored to the needs of recipient countries' third sectors, and projects also address political obstacles to change.

As discussed in this chapter, Polish NGOs acknowledge that different regimes offer different space for the civil society groups; therefore, what is called civil society may vary from country to country. Under the conditions imposed by an authoritarian regime, like that of Belarus, where democracy and civic freedoms do not exist or are severely restricted, there is limited space, if any, for independent civil society. Therefore, the choice is whether to comply with the requirements of a legal (undemocratic) system and to cooperate with organizations that are approved by the state (but not supporting it) or to cooperate with local organizations that have been banned by the system and thus work in the underground. Polish organizations have found both ways to be good strategies for building democratic civil society in Belarus. Both methods complement each other and serve common goals: activating Belarusian society and exposing its members to values, norms, and behaviors related to democracy, even if in an indirect way. Regardless of the methods of reaching civil society, there is a consensus among Polish NGO activists that civil society needs to be built in Belarus. Thus, Polish NGOs mainly focus on the development of social and human capital through activization of people and through democratic education. Such a strategy will help to plant the seeds of civil society and cultivate it to be ready for democratic changes in Belarus.

Whereas in Belarus the emphasis is on building civil society, in Ukraine today Polish NGOs work to make civil society a more powerful actor; thus, activities focus on strengthening links between different civil society groups (especially those of different regions) and strengthening civil society's role vis-à-vis the state. Polish NGOs try to support a relationship with the state through cooperation with local governments—the level of government at which citizens are most likely to take an active role. Engaging local governments in projects can help citizens communicate their needs and demands much more directly and reinforce civil society's position vis-à-vis local authorities. Finally, Polish NGOs help Ukrainian NGOs find their new role by introducing them to topics such as European integration and political reforms, as well as administrative reform and other reforms regarding local governance.

Polish NGOs' democracy assistance described in this chapter does not automatically speak for the effectiveness of Polish efforts in assisting democratic tendencies in Belarus and Ukraine. The question still remains as to whether Polish NGOs' cross-border work has the potential to successfully diffuse democratic ideas and practices in Belarus and Ukraine; the next chapter presents an attempt to evaluate this cross-border work.

5 | Why Polish Democracy Assistance Matters

■ Polish democracy assistance relies extensively on Polish NGOs' efforts, which may be analyzed through different prisms: the literature on democracy assistance, Polish NGOs' own opinions and evaluation of the results of their efforts, and the opinions of Western donors about Polish practices. Are Polish NGOs' efforts in delivering assistance really so different from those criticized in the literature? If so, how are such strategies different? In addition to addressing those questions, this chapter demonstrates how Polish NGOs view their work and how they assess the outcomes of their projects in Belarus and Ukraine.

The diffusion literature suggests that the greater the similarity between the transmitters and the prospective adopters on one or more sociocultural dimensions, the greater the chance of successful diffusion (Bunce and Wolchik 2006; Lahusen 1999; Snow and Benford 1999). Thus, taking into account a special relationship, as well as strong historical, cultural, and societal connections between Poland, Ukraine, and Belarus, one should expect democratic diffusion through democracy assistance offered by Polish donors to work better and produce more substantial results, compared with programs from countries that are less familiar with each other. Do Polish NGOs believe they have the potential to be more effective in delivering democracy assistance to neighboring states than other (more distant) actors? If so, why? Do close cultural and historical relations automatically translate into the success of the diffusion of democracy? Why do Western donors, such as NED, decide to cooperate with Polish NGOs and finance their projects in Belarus and Ukraine?

This is not to argue that cross-border democracy assistance is superior to other forms of assistance; the point is to evaluate these efforts and to demonstrate that, because of Polish NGOs' knowledge, skills, strategies, and close geographical and cultural links with civil society in the region,

Polish NGOs can play a very important role in transnational advocacy networks of democracy assistance to postcommunist countries. It sends the broader message that the inclusion of civil society organizations from young democracies in transnational networks may improve the effectiveness of democracy assistance to other, more authoritarian states or to fledgling democracies in the region.

Polish NGOs' Efforts and Common Critical Evaluations

Despite the enormous interest and goodwill of foreign assistance donors, as well as their overall role in fostering democratization in recipient countries, scholars have criticized donor strategies that resulted in failure, limited results, or—in some cases—even negative effects. The majority of research on the impact of democracy assistance and on civil society development and democratization in recipient countries refers to Western assistance—governmental and nongovernmental aid from the United States, Britain, Germany, and elsewhere in Western Europe—provided in the 1990s to Central and Eastern European countries (Ballentine 2002; Boone 1996; Quigley 2000; Siegel and Yancey 1992; Wedel 2001) and more recently to Russia (Henderson 2000, 2003; McMahon 2002, 2004; Mendelson 2001; Richter 2002).

Based on the criticism in the democracy assistance literature regarding some practices of Western donors, Wilde (2002, 433) gives some recommendations on how to improve the delivery of aid. She suggests that donors should (1) continue funding programs that promote democracy but consider adding social projects to their assistance strategy; (2) maintain continuity by supporting organizations that have achieved a measure of success; (3) create micro-grant programs that support grassroots initiatives and develop local organizations; (4) reach a wider audience; (5) improve the technical capacity of all forms of communication; and (6) encourage networking and partnering, both internally and externally. These recommendations, together with criticism in the democracy assistance literature, may be used to evaluate Polish NGOs' democracy assistance efforts.

Responding to Domestic Circumstances and Needs

One of the most frequent critiques in research on democracy assistance is that donors have done little to adapt projects to local circumstances (Carothers 1999, 2004; Ottaway and Chung 1999; Quigley 2000, 192; Siegel and Yancey 1992, 57–58). Scholars argue that Western practitioners acted with little knowledge of regions, neglecting historical, cultural, and institutional legacies (Aksartova 2005; Grugel 1999; Mendelson and Glenn 2002, 66; Narozhna 2004; Quigley 2000). They tried to impose their Western practices without considering the target country's domestic needs and local conditions (Henderson 2002, 155; Siegel and Yancey 1992, 58).

Critics have argued that donor-driven building of NGOs was undertaken without considering the state of the political environment, norms, beliefs, and practices in the recipient country and also did not encourage local ideas and strategies while promoting civil society (Henderson 2000, 2003; McMahon 2002, 2004; Mendelson and Glenn 2002; Sundstrom 2006). In other words, Western organizational and cultural models are assumed to be superior to local models, and many donors have overlooked the fact that civil society is about citizens' interests, domestic politics, and local culture (McMahon 2004, 251). With respect to African or Asian countries, US civil society assistance has also received criticism for ignoring the specificity of the society in recipient countries—the many layers of clans, castes, village associations, ethnic organizations, and the like (Carothers 1999, 249). Therefore, scholars argue that in order for the promotion of civil society to be successful, the internal conditions that influence civic groups should always be taken into consideration (Hadenius and Uggla 1998).

Moreover, scholars point out how little most aid providers know about democratic transformations and how they try to apply the same democracy assistance patterns in each country in which they intervene (Hadenius and Uggla 1998; Mendelson and Glenn 2002, 4; Ottaway 2003; Ottaway and Chung 1999). They push assistance recipient countries to adopt the same political institutions and the same path of transformation, regardless of prevailing conditions. Programs developed in Western capitals failed to acknowledge the distinctiveness of each country's domestic political situation, which determines what is both desirable and possible. Thus, scholars have come to the conclusion that, just as democratization is a different experience in different states and regions, democracy assistance should show different patterns and be more relevant to the recipient country.

The analysis in the previous chapter has shown that Polish organizations have focused resources on a variety of issues important to democratization in Belarus and Ukraine. In the case of Belarus, cooperation has focused on the creation and development of a sphere independent of government control, thus, in an indirect way, preparing the ground for the breakdown of authoritarianism. In the case of Ukraine, Polish NGOs help Ukraine build state capacity, develop local governance, and spread information about European integration, and they assist Ukrainian authorities with political and economic reforms. Thus, Polish NGOs' projects respond to current opportunities and challenges in recipient countries. Since Polish organizations tailor their work in Ukraine and Belarus according to the political situation in these countries, the complaint regarding the Western efforts does not apply to Polish NGOs' assistance. Also, the nature of projects demonstrates the acceptance by Belarusian and Ukrainian partners of the values of Polish NGOs and, by inference, an understanding of recipients' values.[1]

Before starting assistance activities, many Polish organizations find it important to assess the needs of the recipients by asking them, "How can we help you? What can we do for you?" because their own past experience as assistance recipients taught them to do this.[2] Then these needs are transformed into a project, and then the project is transformed into a proposal to be submitted to a funding institution. Polish NGOs also get a sense of needs, as well as ideas for present and future projects, through their officials' travels.

The fact that Polish NGOs tailor their activities to the political situation in recipient countries can be shown by changes in the organizations' approach toward their work in Belarus and Ukraine, as presented in the previous chapter. In Ukraine, funds are now allocated to support activities that focus on political and economic reforms, on efforts to show local governments how to be more responsive, and on strengthening civil society and its position vis-à-vis government. In Belarus, the particular focus is on politically oriented civil society groups, supporting Belarusians' contacts with foreign groups, civic education assistance, and the development of Belarusian cultural identity.

In the mid-1990s, donors began to sponsor programs labeled as "strengthening civil society" across the developing and postcommunist world, with the assumption that civil society is crucial in the transition to and consolidation of democracy (Carothers 1999, 209; Bernhard 1993; Bernard et al. 1998; Blair 1998; Cohen and Arato 1997; Dahl 1989; Deutsch 1961; Diamond 1994, 1996; Linz and Stepan 1996; Ottaway and Carothers 2000; Putnam 1994).[3] However, when Western donors provided "civil society assistance," they were usually referring specifically to their support for nongovernmental organizations (Carothers 1999, 210; Hadenius and Uggla 1998; Mitlin 1998; Raik 2006, 175; USAID Mission to Poland, Europe, and Eurasia n.d.). NGOs are a vital part of civil society, because the NGOs help citizens solve community and social problems, lobby government on behalf of citizens' rights and concerns, promote awareness, and press for transparency in government and business. Nevertheless, one cannot automatically equate civil society with NGOs in each recipient country (Carothers 2004;

Henderson 2000, 2003; Rose-Ackerman 2007). In authoritarian countries that repress the emergence of NGOs, equating civil society with NGOs may be especially an inaccurate assumption (Carothers 2004).

Polish NGOs work with Belarusian and Ukrainian civil society groups according to the scheme represented in the figure above. Many examples of projects that are conducted according to this scheme were mentioned in an earlier chapter. However, it should be said that Polish NGOs' approach to selecting civil society groups in Belarus and Ukraine for assistance demonstrates that Polish NGOs recognize that civil society in authoritarian and new democratic countries may comprise different actors. Their approach offers further evidence of how Polish organizations tailor their projects to the political circumstances in the recipient country. Their strategy also responds to the criticism about equating civil society with NGOs.

In the case of Belarus—where, as a result of the conditions imposed by the authoritarian regime, civic freedoms do not exist or are severely restricted—Polish NGOs' cross-border projects recognize that civil society entails different combinations of politically oriented individuals and groups. The Polish groups avoid working with many Belarusian NGOs because they are tied to the government. Instead, Belarusian partners selected for assistance include autonomous individuals, dissident groups, educators, women or youth, and organizations working underground, as discussed in the previous chapter. The cooperative efforts also avoid contact with and attention from local political elites, because even though some municipal commissioners are opposed to Lukashenko, the possibility of their working with Polish NGOs, not to mention generating any meaningful change, is small if not nonexistent.[4] Instead, recognizing the importance of schools and teachers as a medium for dispersing democratic ideas and behaviors, Polish NGOs very early decided to direct their activities at teachers. The programs of Polish NGOs are flexible, to allow some funds to be disbursed secretly to informal groups.

Since the political situation is different in Ukraine, there is no need to look for and to support opposition groups. Civil society recipients consist of interest groups, nongovernmental organizations, volunteers, trade union associations, professional organizations, free media, and the like. Some projects might concern supporting cooperation between civil society groups with specific social groups—political scientists, sociologists, and journalists and other experts or intellectuals, as well as local authorities. Such cooperation with other groups within projects is often facilitated by the partner organization, usually NGOs, in Ukraine.

Support for Grassroots Initiatives and Development of Local Organizations

Polish NGOs' projects are designed and implemented to fit the needs, habits, and demands of local communities and realities, but "local owner-ship" of projects is also a common practice. Scholars evaluating Western assistance have observed that "local ownership" of the aid projects, mean-ing that ideas and funds are shared by aid providers and recipients or that they remain fully in the hands of recipients, translates to the greater suc-cess of aid provision (Carothers 1999; Quigley 2000). For Western donors, the local grants method requires the establishment of local foundations, as George Soros has done, or direct grants, which NED uses.

A few Polish NGOs have, like the Soros Foundation, established orga-nizations in recipient countries. Some of the impetus for establishing new organizations in the post-Soviet republics also resulted from the Polish as-sociations' long-term activity and frequent work with civil society groups there. For example, as a result of links established with teachers, young people, and their parents in the northeastern part of Belarus, one of the organizations included in this study established an organization there that is similar to a Polish partner organization and plays an important role in long-term cooperation between Belarusian and Polish partners. Likewise, from the beginning of its existence, FSLD found it important to establish long-term links with Ukrainian partners with whom long-term interaction on projects would be possible. For this reason, FSLD created independent centers or organizations in different places in Ukraine, such as Cherkasy, L'viv, Kherson, Donetsk, and Kharkiv. These entities later became perma-nent partners of FSLD. The FSLD, together with these Ukrainian centers, implemented projects that aimed to share Polish experience regarding the functioning of Polish local government (Stefan Batory Foundation 2003). The centers have also been concerned with the development of local democracy through activities directed to different groups, such as teachers, youth, journalists, and nongovernmental organizations.[5] Despite those examples, establishing counterpart organizations in foreign countries is not a common activity of Polish NGOs.

With respect to the grants method, it is generally the larger Polish organizations that hold the status of "foundation" and have better access to large amounts of funding. The Stefan Batory Foundation, for example, provides assistance through two main channels: (1) grant-giving, in which monies are given directly to organizations (10–15 percent for administrative activities), and then the foundation simply approves activities and monitors the implementation of the project; and (2) operations, in which the foundation is involved in the organization of conferences, meetings, and various types of activities through partnerships.[6]

When there is re-granting, the funds that Polish NGOs obtain from their donors are distributed to a selected partner, usually by means of a call for proposals. There can be observed two different re-granting schemes in Polish cooperation with Ukraine and Belarus. The first pattern is seen when Polish NGOs directly receive money from their donor and then make a regrant to a smaller group in Belarus and Ukraine. Some of these sub-grants are made to individual NGOs, some to newspapers, and some to what are called "civic initiatives." The figure below illustrates this procedure.

For example, one Polish organization carried out projects in which small grants were distributed to independent organizations and civil society groups' meetings were organized to improve cross-border democracy-building programs. Within the program supporting the development of civil society, the organization offered micro-grants to Belarusian civil society groups. For the purposes of the program, an anonymous Belarusian-language website was created; on it, an individual or a group of people could upload a proposal for any small project with a budget of no more than five hundred dollars. For security reasons, the organization does not provide the names of these grant recipients. The impetus for such micro-grants emerged after the 2006 presidential elections in Belarus, when there was a rapid increase in the number of small activities undertaken by pro-democratic young leaders. The micro-grant project was created in order to support these activities and facilitate their development in the future.

The second scheme, as shown in the figure below, includes further re-granting, and such projects are more popular in Ukraine. In other words, the Ukrainian recipient of a Polish grant distributes this money to other grassroots initiatives and local organizations within Ukraine.

The Stefan Batory Foundation's grant-making program offers an ex-ample of such double re-granting. The program is financed by the Ford Foundation and aims to support democratic changes and the development of civil society in postcommunist countries. This program offers grants for civil society groups that support grassroots initiatives, engage in building partnerships with public administration sectors, and undertake civic edu-cation activities. As Grzegorz Gromadzki and Agnieszka Komorowska of the Stefan Batory Foundation argue, "Ukrainian organizations receive funds so that they can finance others—it is very important because they know best what needs to be done."[7] They may undertake further re-granting to other local organizations. The grants are distributed on the basis of open competitions, thus creating an equal opportunity for all organizations in recipient countries, which plan to organize activities that fall within the grant's theme—legal education and legal counseling for citizens, protection of civic rights, civic education for young people, establishing local civic ac-tivity centers, securing transparency of governance and access to informa-tion, and development of philanthropy.[8] As expressed by Gromadzki, "An open competition, which is the foundation's rule, opposes the strategy that the German Marshall Fund uses by funding only partners with which it has long-established relations. Since the foundation also aims at supporting civil society, the rule is that all organizations should have an equal chance to receive assistance."[9]

Carothers (1999, 271–72) points out that the grant method has many advantages (for example, money goes directly into the recipient society), but such a mechanism involves difficulties and limitations as well, because it calls for an in-depth understanding of the recipient societies. Polish NGOs give grants to organizations that have knowledge about local conditions and have a vested interest in local issues in Belarus and Ukraine. By financing those organizations, Polish NGOs hope to support democratic changes and the development of civil society in small communities. For small communities, the small grants from Polish NGOs may be the only chance to receive foreign funding, as Belarusian and Ukrainian local organizations do not have access to funds from Western donors, who usually require big, institutionalized organizations and lack the managerial capacity to redistribute small grants. As Jarábik (2006, 91) notes, the funding from Polish NGOs, even though modest as compared to that provided by Western donors, has been more effective in addressing local civil society groups' needs.

Distribution of micro-grants is difficult especially in Belarus. Due to the political situation in Belarus, some organizations do not give grants, preferring instead to cooperate with Belarusian partners. Before 1999, there were no restrictions on foreign assistance; Polish NGOs, together with their donors, could freely cooperate with Belarusian organizations on the projects.[10] After the return of authoritarianism, any transfer of money from abroad had to be approved by Belarusian authorities, so Polish NGOs cannot transfer monies directly into the bank accounts of their Belarusian partners. Many Polish organizations find it impossible to track their support money because the political situation forces them to transfer funds to private individuals' bank accounts or to deliver funding in cash.

In Ukraine, those Polish NGO activists who favor re-granting as a method of cooperation with Ukrainian entities are in the minority. The majority of Polish NGOs still believe that transferring funds directly to Ukrainians, who then implement the project, is less effective. Despite the fact that Ukraine has progressed further on the democratic trajectory than Belarus, some of the project partners in that country still need the guidance, knowledge, and experience that Polish partners have regarding democracy.[11] Thus, the EEDC, for example, offers re-granting only for the development of newspapers and has otherwise stopped redistributing money to organizations in Ukraine.

Merits of Partnering with Civil Society Groups

In addition to giving grants and helping recipients to establish local foundations, Polish NGOs offer a third method of pursuing localism. They work through close partnerships, and this method is not the exception but the rule. All Polish NGO representatives interviewed mentioned that the most common form of assisting groups in Ukraine and Belarus is through joint projects. Establishing a joint initiative for so-called cross-border projects is the primary form of cooperation with civil society groups in Belarus and Ukraine and is the legacy of the Solidarity movement. For all cross-border projects, the organizations involved must have a partner on the other side—sometimes two partners, depending on the specificity of the project or the geographic extent of it. Even though building relations with civil society groups in Belarus has been difficult as compared to Ukraine, each cross-border project has had a Belarusian partner. Before starting any assistance activities, many organizations find it important to assess the needs of their partners, because their own experience as assistance recipients in the past taught them to do this. Then these needs are transformed into the "project" and then the project into the proposal to be submitted to a funding institution.

This form of cooperation stands in contrast to the "Marriott Brigade," the Western model used in Eastern Europe at the beginning of the 1990s. According to longtime Polish activist Paweł Bobołowicz, of the Foundation for Young Democracy, "Western specialists . . . were coming to Poland at the beginning of the 1990s to conduct training at the Hotel Marriott and talk about changes that should be carried out while never going out to the streets of Warsaw and seeing real life." Polish NGOs, he continued, "acknowledge the importance of knowing the domestic context in which recipients operate and engaging partners in projects."[12] As Bobołowicz stated, Polish NGOs always try to analyze the needs of their partners and discuss with them the project outline before applying for the grant.[13] Therefore, amid the differences between Belarusian and Ukrainian projects, there is one firm commonality in all Polish NGO cross-border projects: partnership with civil society groups, thus contributing to the development of the third sector in both countries. In other words, no matter whether a country is authoritarian or going through the democratic transition, supporting civil society is of great importance.

It is not just the Polish experience as a recipient of democratic assistance that is behind this strategy; partnering is required by the Polish government, as discussed earlier.[14] Other donors to Polish NGO aid projects stress the importance of partnership.[15] The National Endowment for Democracy, which is one of the major donors funding Polish democratic assistance in Eastern Europe, gives priority to projects that demonstrate partnership between Polish and civil society groups in recipient countries;

such projects are more likely to receive funding from NED. As indicated by Joanna Rohozińska of the National Endowment for Democracy, "The bonus is if there is interaction with other groups, if there is a kind of networking together in the project submitted for grant."[16]

Having partnership with Ukrainians or Belarusians means that Polish NGOs assist rather than act and that rather than assuming the lead, they share responsibility and decision making in project implementation. Project implementation is thus 100 percent collaborative, with Polish NGOs and recipient partners complementing each other, cooperating, and developing the project together. In the case of Ukraine today, Polish NGOs are not sole initiators of action; many Ukrainian organizations develop ideas for projects and then contact Polish NGOs for assistance. The partners in the recipient county undertake responsibilities for the project according to their capacity to do so, while Polish NGOs help with the remaining areas of effort. For example, the Polish partner provides the so-called "know-how," and a partner in Belarus or Ukraine is responsible for the organization of events.[17]

Polish NGOs recognize that assessing needs and dealing with matters in which assistance providers have knowledge and experience are important, but even more essential is sustaining long-term partnerships.[18] Whereas some Western donors may have difficulty identifying appropriate local partners, Polish NGOs have partnerships with Ukrainian nongovernmental organizations and Belarusian civil society groups that have lasted for years. Some Polish activists frequently travel to Ukraine and have built personal ties there.

The merits of partnering have been acknowledged by many social scientists, who point out that coalition networks offer more chances for civil society to take hold and persist (Keck and Sikkink 1998; Smith et al. 1997; Tarrow 1998, 2005). Magdziak-Miszewska (2002) implies that cooperation between democratically oriented nongovernmental groups on both sides of the Belarus-Poland border may be the most realistic means of providing democracy assistance. Other researchers also recognize that civil society assistance in the postcommunist region can be effective only with the participation of individuals and organizations in the recipient country (Bunce and Wolchik 2006; Jacoby 2006).

Scholars also recognize that building sustainable civil society requires continuity, particularly long-term funding (Henderson 2003, 153; Jarábik 2006, 86; Ottaway and Chung 1999; Quigley 2000; Siegel and Yancey 1992). As Tudoroiu (2007, 340) argues, short-term foreign financial aid can help develop NGOs, but that type of short relationship is "not enough to ensure the large-scale diffusion of democratic values within the population and civil society's associated rapid development."

Reaching a Wider Audience and Encouraging Networking Internally

Scholars find that, in addition to external partnering, fostering internal networking with citizens and organizations is crucial for both building and strengthening civil society (Henderson 2002; McMahon 2000, 253; Richter 2002; Wilde 2002, 433). One of the critiques of Western civil society assistance is that it does not typically include networking; rather than facilitating networks among groups, Western foreign aid favored those NGOs that already had connections with the West. The lack of networking strengthened the division of the civic community between "the haves and the have-nots" (Henderson 2003, 10; Narozhna 2004, 248). In other words, rather than fostering networks between different civil society groups, Western aid contributed to the emergence of isolated (although well-funded) civic groups. Scholars point out that lack of networking may prevent small groups from developing trust, a sense of solidarity, and the ability to cooperate effectively with other assistance resistance organizations. It may also lead to the marginalization of civil society groups.

Polish NGOs facilitate the development of links between different groups by reaching out to new civil society groups in new places and making connections between their new and long-term partners. The scheme of such cooperation is illustrated in the above figure. Engaging partners from eastern Ukraine can be difficult, however. To combat this problem, the EEDC employs Ukrainians who have a better understanding of the situation in that part of Ukraine.[19] The Education for Democracy Foundation (FED) prefers to work with its partners in L'viv on projects that address activities for communities in Dnipropetrovsk. There are three purposes for such cooperation. First, western Ukrainian organizations may have better access to communities in eastern Ukraine than do Polish agencies. In addition, through such cooperation, western Ukrainian and Polish NGOs are able to find other Ukrainian partners. Finally, eastern Ukrainian organizations are more likely to enter into partnerships when they see the results achieved through Polish and western Ukrainian organizations' cooperation and how organizations from the West work.[20]

In the case of Belarus, the strategy of aid providers is to avoid working in big cities like Minsk, Grodno, or Vitebsk and to reach out to small communities instead; it is also possible to reach smaller communities through prior contacts with long-term Belarusian partners. Moreover, for reasons of security, Belarusian groups sometimes prefer their aid contact to be Belarusian rather than Polish. Interestingly, one Belarusian organization facilitates the creation of networks with other groups in Belarus, as well as with Polish entities. This organization has activists in many regions of Belarus, and, through them, the Polish NGOs are able to reach out to local communities. There are between 130 and 150 leaders in Belarus who share the same ideas and vision and who are very active in some regions. Sometimes these leaders are in charge of informal groups, groups of friends, civic groups, and so forth. Through this linkage, Polish NGOs are also able to reach these grassroots groups.[21]

Another opportunity for Polish NGOs to look for partners to the network is during the meetings or conferences they organize, as well as international forums. An example is the Warsaw Regional Congress of NGOs, which brings together under the auspices of the Council of Europe representatives of two hundred NGOs from Central and Eastern Europe.[22] Another example is the Forum of Central and Eastern Europe, which brings together many NGOs from the region each September in Krynica, Poland.[23] This forum is a platform for the exchange of views, ideas, and contacts among politicians, business leaders, and NGO regional activists, and it provides the opportunity to meet potential aid partners. The Regional NGO Congress of the Council of Europe is an annual meeting with the goal of initiating dialogue with national nongovernmental organizations from the forty-seven member countries of the Council of Europe. In 2006, the congress was held in Warsaw and, in 2007, in Kiev; both meetings brought together more than two hundred NGO representatives from Central and Eastern Europe.[24]

Networking among nongovernmental organizations is also facilitated by communication platforms, such as www.non-gov.org or www.tri.net.pl. The latter website has been run by the Polish Robert Schuman Foundation and the PAUCI Foundation since 2006, and its content is addressed to NGOs in Germany, Poland, and Ukraine that might be interested in tri- or bilateral cooperation.[25] This virtual Ukrainian-Polish-German forum provides a communication tool for NGOs and up-to-date information on

trilateral projects. In May 2007, thanks to the support of the Bosch Foundation, the first NGO forum attended by groups from all three countries gathered in Warsaw and brought together fifty NGOs. Participants exchanged
information on how to improve civil society cooperation in Central and
Eastern Europe in the areas of civic education, ecology, youth empowerment, local government support, and migration (PAUCI 2007a).

An initiative of the FSLD led to the creation of an international network
of independent civic organizations operating in the sphere of civic education: the Education for Democracy International Network, or EDIT-Net
(www.editnet.org). The network includes organizations from eight countries (Poland, Belarus, Ukraine, Russia, Azerbaijan, Tajikistan, Uzbekistan,
and Mongolia) and is a platform for cooperation and exchange of experiences and ideas between organizations that build their programs on a foundation of local culture and traditions. Member organizations of this network
organize hundreds of workshops each year in Eastern Europe and Central
Asia, and several thousand NGO leaders, teachers, representatives of local
administrations, and local educational authorities attend (FSLD 2007).

Different Forms of Communication

Polish NGOs engage in diverse activities for their cross-border projects
with Belarusian and Ukrainian partners. Those activities fall into two categories: (1) information dissemination through exchange, seminars, conferences, visitation, fellowships, and internships; and (2) training.

Most activities undertaken belong to the first category, and data show
that workshops, seminars, and conferences were the most prevalent form
of information-dissemination activity in 2007. Study tours were the next
most popular form of activity. The Stefan Batory Foundation's East-East
program, launched in 1991 by the Open Society Institute, has a strong
emphasis on the exchange of opinions and ideas, and it supports projects implemented by Polish organizations in cooperation with at least one
partner organization from Central or Eastern Europe, Central Asia, or the
Caucasus region. The Batory Foundation also offers the Citizens in Action
program, financed by the Ford Foundation to support democratic change
and the development of civil society in Belarus and Ukraine. The Region in
Transition program, administered by the Education of Democracy Foundation, supports democratic and free-market changes in Eastern Europe,
primarily through study tours.

Some of those forms of cooperation are implemented in Poland and
some in the recipient country. Although partnership is the main principle

guiding cooperation of Polish NGOs with Belarusian and Ukrainian partners, NGOs are divided on the issue of whether activities within projects should take place in Poland or in a recipient country. The advantage of organizing activities in Poland is that participants are exposed to the culture, experience, and practices of the nonprofit sector in Poland. The disadvantage is that most of the money for these activities is spent primarily by Polish NGOs in Poland. Paweł Kazanecki of the EEDC is a strong advocate of undertaking aid activities in the recipient country: "the aid makes sense when money is spent in Belarus, not in Poland."[26] If the money is spent in Poland rather than in Belarus, then Polish NGOs are no different from the "Marriott Brigade." Similarly, Przemysław Fenrych of the FSLD expressed a belief that the visits of Belarusian people to Poland do not translate into visible changes in Belarus.[27]

As for the other primary area of communication between partners, training for civil society groups exposes people who live under authoritarian regimes to the real world of democracy, according to Katarzyna Bielawska of the Democratic Society East Foundation.[28] Many Belarusians know little about life in the neighboring democratic countries, and once they see how much better off people are in Poland, they may be encouraged to act as advocates of pro-democratic changes Belarus. However, organizing activities in Poland for Belarusians is not an easy undertaking, as many Polish NGOs' representatives acknowledge, because sometimes Belarusians who come or plan to come for NGO events are harassed, threatened, or prevented from crossing the border. In some cases, participants in events organized in Poland did not want to return home, because they found out from family members that Belarusian police officers were waiting for them at their residences. Some Polish NGO activists still firmly believe that bringing a group of potential beneficiaries for training in Poland is more promising than sending money or sending Polish experts across the border, because the political situation in Belarus might complicate successful implementation of a project in Belarus.[29]

Taking into account the pluses and minuses of activities organized in Poland and abroad, Polish NGOs do not restrict their projects to only one form of communication. Very often within a given project there is a marriage of methods.

Results of Polish NGOs' Activities

Representatives of Polish NGOs claim that their democracy assistance efforts have resulted in many achievements. However, it is still difficult to assess the impact of these efforts in the recipient countries. In interviews, the representatives of Polish NGOs tended to divide the results into the tangible (measurable) results and results that are difficult to gauge.

In evaluating the short-term results, Polish NGOs look for things that are specific, straightforward, and easy to measure. Among the "touchable results" Polish NGO activists mentioned are a parents' council established in a school, a customer service unit set up in a city hall, and the organization of European School Clubs, for example (Stanowski 2005a). The NGOs individually report on some specific areas in which something has changed in a particular school, the village, town, or city. For example, Paweł Bobołowicz of the Foundation for Young Democracy said that, based on his observation and opinions gathered from Ukrainian partners, the quality management ISO 9001 project in which the foundation was involved in the city of Berdyansk, located on the Sea of Azov in eastern Ukraine, has contributed to better cooperation between civil servants and people. The project upgraded procedures of the city and made public institutions more accessible to citizens through, for example, the installation of a stand with informative handouts in the city hall. The city officials were in the process of earning a certificate of quality (based on ISO 9001 requirements) for improved communication among public officials. The new level of communication changed citizens' views about governmental entities.[30] Appendix 5, based on data from PAUCI, shows examples of how Polish NGOs typically report the results of their projects.

Another way to evaluate results is to look at the overall organizational capacity of partners involved in projects, that is, whether NGOs grow and develop their structure, staff, and equipment. In the opinion of Grzegorz Gromadzki and Agnieszka Komorowska of the Stefan Batory Foundation, the NGOs in Ukraine are "growing like mushrooms after rain," and Polish NGOs have actively been working to help establish some of them.[31] Some projects are so successful that they become institutionalized and registered as organizations. Bobołowicz gave two examples of such organizations: the Polish-Ukrainian Education Center and the Association of Quality Cities in Ukraine.[32] However, measuring the success of Polish NGO projects on these terms is problematic in Belarus because the number of civil society organizations operating without government oversight or control is declining rather than increasing, as the result of repression by the Lukashenko regime.

Thus, whereas some results can be measured immediately, others can be better assessed after ten years or so have elapsed, especially if the activities within the project focused on spreading information, establishing contacts, and offering scholarships, internships, training, and the like. In such instances, the common practice among Polish NGOs is to base their decision about the continuation or termination of projects on surveys conducted among participants of specific projects. Recently, Polish organizations in Crimea, an autonomous republic of Ukraine, passed the ten-year mark of their work in that region, so some evaluations of the impact of Polish activities can be made. The work was a long, gradual process that started with helping Tatars regain their identity; the project presented the Polish Kashubians as an example of a people recapturing a sense of their group identity.[33] Later, Tatars received financial assistance for the construction of school buildings, and there was a training period for teachers, as well as local authorities, to learn how these schools should operate within the region. Over several years, in close cooperation with the Crimean Tatars, Polish NGOs built several schools providing education in the Tatar language.[34] The Crimean Tatars thus were able to strengthen their ethnic identity and culture that had been repressed for so long. Today, Crimean Tatars frequently contact Polish NGOs when they are developing an idea for a project. With many Tatars studying at Polish universities, Polish NGO representatives are waiting to "see how they will make use of their knowledge and experience" when they return to Crimea.[35]

Scholars suggest that the results of democratizing projects can be captured not only by searching for the effects on institutions (organizational capacity or improved advocacy and service provision) but also by observing changes in society and people's lives (Quigley 1997; Richter 2002, 56). In other words, it is easier to observe the impact on particular participants.[36] Polish NGOs' activists give numerous examples of changes in their Belarusian or Ukrainian partners' behaviors. The fact that some Ukrainian civil society activists with whom Polish organizations had cooperated joined Yushchenko's supporters before the Orange Revolution and later held high official positions in the government can be attributed to Polish NGO activity.[37]

Taking into account the suppressed state of civil society in Belarus, one might argue that there has been no visible progress in changing Belarusians' behaviors. However, the fact that Polish NGOs are finding ways to maintain contact with Belarusian groups that want their country to be free, as well as the fact that Poles and Belarusians work together on various projects, shows that something is changing, in the opinion of Marta Pejda, of the Zagranica Group.[38] Moreover, she argued that, whereas the impact on democratization is harder to prove since investments and results are difficult to assess right now, it is easier to demonstrate that certain civil society

groups were exposed to new ideas and approaches through their participation in projects. It might take longer to see visible results, but it might
be more promising simply to invest in people. Thus, rather than targeting
the opposition in Belarus, the majority of Polish NGOs aim to influence
the behaviors and opinions of people. An important objective is to show
postcommunist societies that, in their struggle for a democratic state, other
methods can be used in order to bring about desired change.

Indeed, Polish civil society activists are able to trace the links between
their assistance and changes in specific civil society groups in Belarus or
Ukraine. There are some examples of journalists who, after training, visits
to Poland, and close cooperation with Polish journalists, have started to
write articles about local issues.[39] Also, people who participated in FED's
civic education projects at school in Ukraine became pro-democratic activists and hold high positions in the government.[40] Many youth organization
leaders who took part in training programs now work in administration
and facilitate cooperation between governments, local media, and local
NGOs. They took on such roles as presidents of city councils, governors,
and advisers of former president Viktor Yushchenko.[41]

Indeed, especially receptive to Polish NGO activities are young people,
who participate in youth exchange programs, scholarships, and internships.
According to Jan Piekło, the project known as RAZOM, directed at young
people, has shown dramatic results. This initiative helps fight negative ste-
reotypes and shapes the open, tolerant, democratic attitudes of the younger
generation of Poles and Ukrainians. Another fact that speaks to the success
of this initiative is that RAZOM has been evaluated positively by the Ministry of Foreign Affairs, which continues to provide funding every year.[42]
Moreover, this initiative may gain a more institutionalized character. There
are talks and initial plans with the Germans to join this project and make it
a tripartite Polish-Ukrainian-German exchange program. Similarly, in the
opinion of Urszula Sobiecka, of the Polish-American Fulbright Commission, the Lane Kirkland Scholarship program demonstrates a strong impact on young people from postcommunist countries.[43] About 50 percent
of scholarship recipients represent academia, and upon returning home,
they write and publish works based on the experience they gained during
their stay in Poland.

Some scholarship recipients and participants in exchange programs
and internships actively work on pro-democratic initiatives upon return to
their home country. One resident of the Ukrainian city of Berdyansk who
was a participant in the 2001–2 Lane Kirkland Scholarship program chose
to study the topic of decentralization and local governance; she established

many contacts with Polish NGOs that had experience in this area.[44] Upon returning home, she undertook many initiatives to interest Polish and Ukrainian NGOs, as well as local authorities, in implementing the ISO 9001 quality management system in Berdyansk. She also later established an organization called the European Road, which promoted knowledge about the European Union. This organization, together with others in Ukraine, organized European Day in Berdyansk's schools. Participants' actions and efforts to make changes in their own countries are the best evidence of the success of a project.

Polish NGOs involved in scholarships and internships find ways to stay in touch with participants, which allows the organizations to get updates on their situations. The Lane Kirkland program, for example, has organized conferences every three years for all current and past participants. During these meetings, the scholars complete surveys about their current occupations and career development since their program participation.[45] In the opinion of Jan Andrzej Dąbrowski, of the College of Eastern Europe, there is huge potential in education programs in Poland—internships, scholarships, and schools; there are plans to create an association of people involved in internships, scholarships, and schools and to provide a similar follow-up mechanism that would allow Polish organizers to monitor the development of participants or the participants to contact each other.[46]

The opinions of Ukrainian or Belarusian participants who were exposed to new ideas and approaches through educational programs also speak for the way in which involvement in exchange programs, scholarships, or internships affected individuals' lives. One young participant, Lyudmila Kuzminova, today chief of the Department for Youth Policy of the Donetsk oblast government in eastern Ukraine, said, "The main thing that I realized is not to be passive but to act, and that we have many things to learn. The most impressive thing was that Polish local government focuses on the protection of every person in the region" (PAUCI 2005). Maria Shibneva, from Ternopil, in western Ukraine, took part in a program that offered young Ukrainian lawyers brief internships in Poland. She reported that "this one-month internship contributed a lot to my professional growth and improvement. I attended a program at the School of Polish and European law, where I learned about Poland's system of practical legal implementation" (PAUCI 2005).

In evaluating Polish NGOs' efforts, one should also remember, as many interviewees pointed out, that the opportunities that Polish NGOs provide also depend on the recipients themselves—how much they absorb in their experiences, which circles they represent, and also from which country they come.[47] In the opinion of Sobiecka, coordinator of the Kirkland program, one can observe that the same opportunity may be differently used by Ukrainian and Belarusian participants.[48] For example, Ukrainians who finish their studies in Poland and defend their theses or dissertations successfully return to their home country and generally experience rapid growth in their careers within a short period. Some Belarusians have to extend their educational work beyond the usual duration. After returning to their country, they hide the fact that they participated in the program because the press sometimes reports that the Kirkland program is training members of the Belarusian opposition. Thus, in contrast to the experience of Ukrainians, participation in the program harms Belarusians' careers, and about 10 percent of Belarusian participants in the program decide to stay in Poland.[49]

It often happens that Ukrainians approach Polish NGOs and invite their collaboration on an initiative of their own devising; they learn very fast, and when the project ends, they set out to organize similar initiatives in other parts of Ukraine, as Aleksandra Kujawska of the FED reported.[50] For example, Ukrainian teachers came to Poland for a project that offered training for conducting an anticorruption campaign; upon returning to Ukraine, they set up their own anticorruption training campaign. Moreover, in Ukraine activities proceed faster than in Belarus; results of some projects are visible in as little as two months in Ukraine, but in Belarus it may be as long as two years, as Paweł Kazanecki of the EEDC has noted.[51]

Finally, there is a significant divergence in Ukrainians' and Belarusians' attitudes, which explains why projects in Ukraine have been producing more substantial results. As Kazanecki said, "Belarusian society is in despair—only a minority of Belarusians support Polish efforts; they do not know which way they want to go, and even a democratic opposition sometimes is inconsistent in its behavior. Therefore, it has been difficult to work there." Despite all efforts, Kazanecki has, after fifteen years of activity, a sense of failure in Belarus, like "tilting at windmills," because the impact of the programs is so difficult to gauge. He would be more satisfied with the results if he saw that Belarusian opposition leaders had gained a better understanding of their actions against the Belarusian government. He criticizes the Belarusian opposition for passiveness and indecisiveness. In his opinion, the opposition forces are weak, threatened, and not ready to take responsibility for their actions. At the same time, Kazanecki stated, before the Orange Revolution in Ukraine, it also was difficult for the EEDC to work; today, however, Ukraine is blooming with respect to the development of civil society.[52] Thus, the most important thing is to sustain contacts, and sooner or later progress may be visible.

In sum, Polish NGOs are aware that democratization is a process that must occur simultaneously across a political landscape. As an official of the Polish Robert Schuman Foundation noted, "It is like a pyramid—there cannot be a single narrow foundation, because it will collapse."[53] Thus, even though Polish NGOs take different approaches and, at first glance, their actions might not seem to have a direct connection with democratization in the recipient countries, all Polish NGOs strive to achieve that goal. It is difficult to say which activities are more effective, because each of them in some way contributes to democratization. The projects targeting the media are important, because the media influence public opinion, but it is pointless to say that there are more or less important methods to use in democratization, because "it is like trying to decide what is more important—brain or stomach—without both one cannot live."[54] All interviewees also agreed that they take an action not only because they believe that it will be useful and have a positive effect on the local community in the recipient country, but organizations also are more likely to focus on activities at which they are good and in which they specialize. Moreover, the Polish NGO experience as recipients of aid from the West has shaped the nature of their projects with Belarusian and Ukrainian partners.

The Importance of Experience and Geographical and Cultural Proximity

Polish NGOs' democracy assistance in Belarus and Ukraine is not only about the benefits that stem from partnering and networking between civil society groups; it is also about the experience that neighboring partners can share. This experience, as well as the knowledge that comes with it, seems to be more relevant just across the border than in geographically distant countries, often because of the history and culture that neighbors share.[55] It is argued here that, because of this proximity, Polish NGOs have the potential to play an important role in democratic diffusion to neighboring states and thus should be included in the transnational democracy assistance network. Some Polish NGO officials are of the opinion that Western donors should be calling on them to provide expertise for the West's efforts to bring democratic change to the region.

Representatives of Polish NGOs believe that such factors as cultural, historical, and geographic proximity mean that someone from Poland will have greater expertise than an outsider in the region; it is "natural that the Poles have more knowledge about Ukraine and Belarus, just as the Portuguese know more about Morocco or Algeria."[56] Arkadiusz Goliński of the St. Maximilian Kolbe House (DMK) added that, historically, Poland has always been the bridge between the East and the West and that today Polish NGOs may perform this function very effectively. Polish NGOs are more likely to be familiar with local groups as well as the situation on the ground in Belarus and Ukraine, as suggested by officials of the Stefan Batory Foundation: "The Poles have a better understanding of what is happening in Eastern Europe. It is just easier for Poland than for the Western countries to understand postcommunist countries' affairs, and it is easier to work in these countries because of close cultural and historical links."[57] Because of this better understanding of the internal conditions, social norms, and the political situation, it is easier for Polish NGOs to work there, too.[58] Moreover, the geographical and cultural proximity facilitates faster and easier sharing of democratic norms and practices.[59] Frequent contacts between civil society groups are more feasible, which means that Polish NGO activists have more direct knowledge about political and social conditions in neighboring states. Also, the absence of cultural barriers facilitates those contacts.

Another factor contributing to the effectiveness of Polish democracy assistance in Belarus and Ukraine, in the opinion of Polish NGOs, is language. Polish assistance providers find few language barriers—the similarity between Slavic languages makes communication easy. Even if the Poles do not know these languages fluently, these aid providers can still communicate with Belarusian and Ukrainian partners. It is natural that during the meetings between the Poles and Ukrainians, participants speak in their own languages, and everybody understands one another (Stanowski 2005a). In the case of Belarusian partners, many Polish NGO workers are able to communicate with them in Russian. As Katarzyna Morawska, of the FSLD, said, "The only positive aspect of the Soviet Union is that the whole region speaks Russian, although it has been changing in countries like Armenia, Georgia, and Azerbaijan."[60] There has also been a renaissance of the Russian language in Poland, and many young people again want to learn this language.[61] Moreover, many Polish NGOs hire employees who speak many languages—Ukrainian, Tatar, Russian, German, Belarusian, Estonian, and Lithuanian—making communication even easier. Language skills are very important if an organization wants to reach small local civil society groups, and a person with fluency in a partner's language is in a better position to recognize if that partner is reliable.[62] In addition to language fluency, communication style is also very important in regional partner relations. The style people from the West use is very different from that of Eastern peoples; this difference in style could impede communication (Stanowski 2005a). Use of an interpreter in the conversation only hinders contact, because instead of listening to the partner one focuses on what the interpreter is saying, and direct contact between persons is very important in assistance work (Michałowski 2005).

However, as one Polish NGO activist said, "The geographical and cultural proximity does not give you the right to know; you have to engage yourself in order to know."[63] Many Polish NGO activists have Belarusian or Ukrainian roots or are fascinated with these countries and want to work there (Stanowski 2005a). It becomes clear to anyone who spends a significant amount of time with representatives of Polish NGOs that these are energetic people who know a lot about the region. A lot of goodwill, enthusiasm, and interest in the East is another advantage of Polish NGOs. Also, as one EEDC official noted, the driving force behind some of the Polish NGO activists is their personal commitment due to Belarusian or Ukrainian heritage.[64]

It also has become popular among young people in Poland to expand their knowledge about Eastern Europe, and this trend was already visible before the Orange Revolution (Michałowski 2005). It explains why the number of people with significant knowledge about Belarus and Ukraine is increasing. There are multiple centers in places such as Poznan, Warsaw, Wrocław, and other academic cities that educate about Eastern issues. Such programs combine different disciplines, such as political science, history, economics, anthropology, and philology, to offer a broad-based education about countries that emerged from the territory of the former Soviet Union. From the Center for East European Studies, led by Professor Jan Malicki at Warsaw University, have emerged many prominent figures who today help shape foreign policy in direct and indirect ways.[65] In contrast, in Western Europe, especially in Germany, which used to have many experts on East European issues, there is an observable retreat in interest in Eastern matters, as indicated by the closure of many departments and institutes at universities that were once centers of Eastern European knowledge.[66]

Another reason for the effectiveness of Polish democracy assistance is that Poland, with its outreach experience and successful postcommunist transformation, can serve as an example to its neighbors that share the Soviet legacy and want to move in the same direction as Poland. Thus, Poland may be better at sharing its experience with democracy and free-market reforms than other exemplars, such as Switzerland. However, as one NGO official summarized the situation, "It is not the model that is important but the road itself, and Polish experience with some more and less successful aspects of transformation can be very helpful."[67]

Polish NGO representatives also frequently mentioned in interviews that they have a deep understanding of the political reality in Eastern Europe, as well as of the social norms and practices that continue to exist as the legacies of communism. Having this more detailed, nuanced knowledge about local conditions in postcommunist societies, Polish NGOs are more likely to know how to act in order to achieve planned results. Paweł Bobołowicz of the Foundation for Young Democracy gave an example: because of problems with project implementation in an eastern region of Ukraine, the foundation decided to contact local authorities there in order to get support. "Because we knew that the mayor of the city in the eastern part of Ukraine is treated like a tsar," he said, "we contacted him and he said to the Ukrainian people involved in the project that if anybody created obstacles during the project implementation, he or she would be dismissed. In this way, through an undemocratic tactic, we were able to realize a democratic project."[68]

Having engaged in underground political activities themselves, Polish NGO representatives feel well equipped to work in Belarus and deal with obstacles generated by the Belarusian regime. Some leaders of Polish NGOs mentioned during interviews that, because they were part of the opposition forces in Poland not so long ago, none of the Lukashenko regime's techniques of repression and KGB provocations would discourage them from working in Belarus. Moreover, some interviewees pointed out that an important factor in providing democracy assistance to authoritarian countries is to know the people; Western donors typically do not have access to such people. One anonymous Polish NGO representative working in Belarus said that "five to six employees were refused entry to Belarus, but still money is being delivered, and workshops are being organized in Belarus by means of reliable partners and channels that were established over many years." He said that he personally knew about fifteen thousand people; thus, even if one person cannot perform work or is not able to leave Belarus, others will do it.

Moreover, Polish NGO assistance providers believe that their more forgiving attitude regarding logistical aspects of the project is very important in dealing with partners from authoritarian or democratizing countries. Western donors "are very much concerned about getting invoices and receipts, and do not understand problems with bank transfers and other issues that arise due to the situation in which recipient organizations operate. Sometimes it negatively influences their decision to finish a project."[69] Similarly, Arkadiusz Goliński from the DMK stated that Western democracy aid providers cannot finish a project in the space of two months due to their pragmatism and the careful structuring and systematic planning of each step of their activity. "Sometimes things simply cannot be achieved in the desired manner and pace," he remarked.[70]

All representatives of Polish NGOs interviewed agreed that their activities are important, because Polish government officials act sometimes too harshly toward Belarus by threatening sanctions, for example. The NGOs' activities also complement the Polish government's assistance efforts.[71] In fact, Polish NGOs make the Polish government programs possible, in the opinion of Magdalena Dębkowska of the EEDC.[72] Polish NGOs generally function well, which is reflected in journalist and politician Jan Nowak-Jeziorański's statement that a treaty can "be signed within a few minutes; changes in the mentality shaped through centuries by historical experience cannot be undone from one day to the next. It requires time and deliberate effort. It is the desire of the Polish state to support social initiatives, which aim at close and mutual understanding between people. Only through direct knowledge of the Poles and Germans, Poles and Russians, Ukrainians, Belarusians, Lithuanians, Czechs, and Slovaks can one build a lasting foundation for the agreements concluded at the government level."[73]

Since Polish experience is applicable to the situations in Belarus and Ukraine, cooperation between Western donors and Polish NGOs benefits each party. Transnational networks that include Western donors, who provide funding, and Polish NGOs, which provide their expertise, are more likely to contribute to the diffusion of values, norms, and practices. According to an official of the FSLD, "The creation of the Polish-America-Ukraine Cooperation Initiative, in which Americans gave money and Poles their know-how, gave evidence that the US recognizes the cultural distance between the people of America and Ukraine and that people closer [to the region and its circumstances] could do something in a more efficient way using foreign resources."[74] Katarzyna Morawska offered as an example of this approach a USAID project in which Polish NGOs were involved in assisting members of the Armenian parliament who wanted to establish an office that would provide analytical services for budgets, government programs, and the like.[75] The project was funded by the USAID, but Polish NGOs arranged to bring Armenian politicians to Poland to visit a similar office, because it was already well developed and because this model was more applicable in postcommunist Armenia than were Western models developed in a very different type of environment. Another example is the Dutch-Polish-Ukrainian project that developed the framework for the Matra Program, created by the Dutch Ministry of Foreign Affairs to promote the development of democracy, grounded in the rule of law, with room for dialogue between government and civil society in Ukraine. In this initiative, which ended once Poland joined the EU, Poland served as regional expert and the Dutch provided money and the Netherlands' example of governance.[76]

Given the views of Polish NGO officials on their cross-border work, one might ask what the donors think about this type of assistance. NED representatives pointed to the importance of links with Polish NGOs that today translate into cooperation with Western donors in Belarus and Ukraine. Other reasons for the endowment's work with Polish NGOs in the postcommunist region were given by Joanna Rohozińska, who responded that "they understand the situation better. . . . It is not just empathy and sympathy but they also understand how things work a little bit better, so NED finds them more effective than other groups." Rodger Potocki, head of NED's programs for Europe and Eurasia, added that "there are lot of reasons why it [cooperation between CEE and Belarusian and Ukrainian partners] works—similar language, and a common experience of living under communist dictatorship."[77]

Potocki and Rohozińska gave several reasons for Polish NGOs' major role in cross-border work, and they also discussed how NED evaluates the work of Polish NGOs in Belarus and Ukraine. Polish NGOs dominate cross-border cooperation because, since 1992, they have been the most interested in going into these places. As Potocki stated, "The Poles were the first who came to us [NED] and wanted to do this cross-border work, and we always have been an organization that responded to what our partners think is the best thing to do. So we started with the Poles; then we added the Czechs, the Slovaks, and the Lithuanians."[78] In other words, cooperation was mutually beneficial: organizations like the Polish-Czech-Slovak Solidarity Foundation asked NED for assistance, and NED helped to spur the activities of this organization. Thanks in large part to the Polish-Czech-Slovak Solidarity Foundation's ground-breaking programs, NED became a pioneer and has steadily increased its budget for cross-border democracy-building work (NED 2006). At the same time, cooperation with NED "has helped Polish and other Central European NGOs to survive and develop new capabilities" (NED 2006). After twenty years of cooperation, NED has a network of partners that continues to grow. Polish organizations spread information to other organizations, to other donors and embassies, and to the Polish government.

NED's cooperation with Polish NGOs also stems from links established during the time of communism. Many activists from Polish NGOs used to be NED grantees during the underground period. Potocki gave the example of the Institute for Democracy in Eastern Europe (IDEE), a group that was based first in Paris and then in Washington and was the main recipient of NED money funneled into communist Poland to support underground publishing. After the regime change in 1989, the IDEE registered a branch office in Poland, and Paweł Kazanecki, in communist times a student activist and later a political activist, worked in this office. As the IDEE began to get bigger and bigger, different people left the group to create their own organizations. The people who are in the Eastern European Democratic Center today came from IDEE. Thus, links between Polish organizations stem from these times.

Almost all the older individuals among leaders of Polish NGOs who have been involved in this cross-border work were originally in the Solidarity underground. One person active in this cross-border work early on was Jarosław Szostakowski from the Polish-Czech-Slovak Solidarity Foundation. Others were Zbigniew Janas and Zbigniew Bujak, who started non-governmental organizations and facilitated the activity of the civil society in Poland. All the people with whom NED worked had ties to Solidarity. There is also an entire generation of young people, even the children of some of those who were active in Solidarity times, who are in the Wolna Białoruś (Free Belarus) organization in Warsaw.

Potocki gave many other examples demonstrating that current partners of NED in cross-border projects were recipients of NED assistance during the communist era and the transformation period. There is a straight line from the core group of people originally trained in communist times to today's leaders in democracy assistance. Krzysztof Stanowski was originally trained by the American Federation of Teachers in a program conducted in Poland by Americans. He became one of the first to travel eastward and carry out education projects for the Education for Democracy Foundation (FED). Stanowski was the undersecretary of state in the Polish Ministry of National Education and in the Polish Ministry of Foreign Affairs and in 2011 became President of Solidarity Fund PL. As Potocki said, "Kazanecki was one of the original people who believed in working in Belarus, and he took both of us [Potocki and Rohozińska] there from the beginning."[79] Another direct line is Senator Jerzy Regulski, who together with his daughter, Professor Joanna Regulska, were grantees of NED, which gave the first grants for the development of local government in Poland to the Foundation in Support of Local Democracy, the Polish organization of which Regulski was a founding chairman. The FSLD is now an active promoter of the development of local governance in Belarus and Ukraine, as well as elsewhere in the postcommunist region.

Potocki and Rohozińska noted additional connections between groups that used to be recipients of NED assistance in the 1980s and Polish NGOs that today are active in Belarus and Ukraine. The current chair of the board of the Stefan Batory Foundation, Aleksander Smolar, was a grantee of NED when he was working in the democratic underground before the Open Society Institute decided to establish the foundation as one of its regional organizations. As Rohozińska pointed out, "It is not difficult to trace these links; you just have to know who was who back then . . . you might want to look at groups that are in the Zagranica Group; if you focus on them, then you have got a direct line to almost all of them."[80]

According to NED representatives, every Polish organization with which NED is cooperating has its own niche and does specific work. For example, in Potocki's opinion, Paweł Kazanecki's group is expert at promoting local media—newspapers particularly—because his organization has assisted with this kind of activity in Poland and contributed to the successful development of independent media in Poland when the underground press became mainstream in 1989. Today, as Potocki emphasized in the interview, Kazanecki's EEDC does this work in Belarus and Ukraine.[81] Another example of Polish NGOs that do specific work is Krzysztof Stanowski's FED. That organization specialized in civic education and leadership training in Poland and today is transferring its knowledge to other postcommunist countries. Regulski's FSLD has been doing local government work.

Moreover, the importance of cooperation with Polish NGOs, especially in Belarus, stems from more practical reasons: because of the difficult political situation in Belarus, Potocki and Rohozińska cannot get visas; they must go to Vilnius, Kiev, or Warsaw to meet with Belarusian groups. Still, Polish NGOs have established long-term links with groups in Belarus, and many employees are able travel there. Polish NGOs thus serve as a conduit of information about the situation in Belarus. They also find new groups and recommend NED as a donor or give small Belarusian organizations grants to help them grow. When Belarusian organizations are big enough, they can apply to NED for a direct grant.

When it comes to evaluating Polish NGOs' work, Potocki pointed out that it is a very difficult process. For example, in the case of newspapers, one can see improvement in quality or circulation, or other activities, and one can see that some organizations have managed to expand to cover different regions. Yet, sometimes, effects are less observable. It is hard to evaluate, for example, whether some programs with youth groups have been successful or not, because in Belarus the government represses youth groups with particular force, and young people often get put in jail. Therefore, it is almost impossible to say whether these projects contributed to the development of youth groups' activities. Thus, as Potocki pointed out, it is also important to adopt different kinds of evaluation criteria for different fields of endeavor. In general, every Polish group is doing something unique, and NED decides to cooperate with them based on a group's particular expertise that might be useful on the other side of the border: "We think that each Polish group brings special skills, they have a lot of experience, including that transition experience of doing something first in the underground and then in an open and legal way. . . . Poland has a unique comparative advantage in different things: independent media, local government, and think tanks." When asked whether NED finds Polish NGOs to have greater expertise in civil society assistance than other organizations in Central and Eastern Europe, Potocki wanted to avoid saying that Poland is any better in civil society assistance. He suggested that Polish NGOs are more active in civil society assistance because Poland had a much longer underground period, a much bigger underground, and a much more successful transition than most other countries. Moreover, Poland has a particularly strong number of models for successful transformations, such as local government, civic education, and local press. The school reforms in civic education work have been handled better in Poland than anywhere else in the region. Moreover, the local government in Poland serves as a model for CEE countries; the local independent press is also a success story. Nevertheless, the Czech Republic, Slovakia, and Lithuania have also made achievements. Civil society, in terms of democracy building, is very strong in Slovakia because "they had [Prime Minister Vladimir] Meciar during the 1990s, and Slovak NGOs had to be political for a much longer time than in Poland," in the opinion of Potocki.[82]

Polish expertise in the fields mentioned above is reflected in the fact that almost 70 percent of NED's funding for Polish NGO projects in Belarus is spent on the development of media and publishing, while about 23 percent is spent on democratic education in Belarus.[83] Like the cross-border projects in Belarus, Ukrainian projects implemented by Polish NGOs also have focused on independent media and democratic education. However, some Ukrainian projects focus on local government reforms such as improving transparency by implementing anticorruption programs. Cross-border projects with Polish NGOs aimed at developing the Ukrainian third sector have focused on training seminars for local representatives of NGOs at the district levels in Ukraine (especially from the central and eastern regions) and workshops for local youth organization leaders.[84]

Of NED's other cross-border projects implemented by Czech, Slovak, and Lithuanian partners, the dominant emphasis is on undertakings directed toward the whole CEE region (with Ukraine and Belarus being only two of the recipients). A Czech organization, the People in Need Foundation, is a pioneer in this type of activity. Since 1998, the foundation has been offering training, study tours, material support, and networking activities to groups of journalists, economists, and political science students in the former Soviet Union. Lithuanian organizations implemented projects that aimed at supporting an independent radio station, assisting local NGOs and independent newspapers, and facilitating the activities of local government officials from democratizing countries through public meetings, training workshops, roundtables, and study visits to Lithuania. Slovak organizations seem to have been specializing in election-monitoring projects. These efforts focused on strengthening domestic media monitoring programs prior to key elections, developing media reform strategies, and facilitating networking among election-monitoring NGOs from Eastern Europe and Eurasia. In particular, one of the Slovak organizations, the Pontis Foundation, aimed to strengthen voter education and mobilization prior to the summer 2006 presidential elections in Belarus by organizing an informal coalition of Belarusian NGOs and think tanks to analyze public opinion polls in order to craft an effective "get-out-the-vote" campaign.[85]

There is one more thing that Potocki and Rohozińska considered unique about Polish NGOs' work, something that is a bit of a phenomenon in the CEE region: Poland is the only CEE country in which NGOs doing cross-border work are based not only in the capital city, Warsaw, but also in other regions of Poland. In terms of NGOs implementing projects abroad, there is a network that includes Szczecin, Lublin, Wrocław, Gdańsk, and Krakow. In the Czech Republic there are groups based in Prague and a single group based in Brno; in Slovakia, NGOs are based only in Bratislava; and in Lithuania there are a few groups based in Kaunas, but the majority are in Vilnius. Rohozińska thinks that since regions in Poland are diverse themselves, regional NGOs can use their region-specific knowledge to adapt reforms to the particular area, and thus they can demonstrate that there is a "local way of doing reform; there is no cookie-cutter formula."[86]

Whereas Polish NGOs offer grants and establish organizations just like Western donors, the primary method of their democracy assistance to recipient countries is based on partnership with civil society groups in these countries. Cross-national work is what dominates and defines Polish democracy assistance to Belarus and Ukraine. Although Western democracy assistance practices face particular obstacles, Polish NGO projects almost always function with a partner from the recipient country, and such partnerships increase the likelihood that programs will be well tailored to the local context of the recipient country. Furthermore, Polish NGOs' projects foster links between civil society groups by bringing other groups into projects, thus contributing to the networking and geographical expansion of the sector in the recipient country. Polish NGO projects pursue long-term relations and do not equate civil society with NGOs. Such features of democracy assistance enhance civil society in Belarus and Ukraine and make diffusion of democratic ideas and practices to groups in Belarus and Ukraine more likely.

The results reported by Polish NGOs show that some activities in Belarus and Ukraine have tangible impacts that are easy to measure and that NGOs can report some specific changes, for example, in a particular school, village, town, or city. More frequently, however, it is difficult to gauge the tangible results, especially if the project activities focused on establishing contacts and offering scholarships, internships, training, and so forth. Polish NGO activists point out that the success of civil society assistance should be measured not only in terms of organizational capacity but also in terms of changes in the behaviors of Belarusian and Ukrainian partners.

Activists working in Polish NGOs play an important role in assisting democracy in Belarus and Ukraine. Interviewees pointed out many advantages of Polish democracy assistance, such as: (1) the Polish officials having a thorough understanding of the internal conditions, norms, and political situation in the recipient country due to their shared history; (2) the Polish experience with political and economic transformation, which is more relevant to neighboring countries; (3) the geographic and cultural proximity of these nations, which facilitates certain activities that otherwise would not be possible; (4) the Polish NGOs' greater flexibility with regard to program changes; (5) the Polish NGOs' ability to target civil society groups other donors may not be able to reach; and (6) the enthusiasm and interest of Polish NGOs' activists for working in Belarus and Ukraine.

Western donors, such as the National Endowment for Democracy, acknowledge the Polish NGOs' facility in democracy assistance and financially support their endeavors. Although NED cooperates with associations from other countries in the region, Polish NGOs are NED's dominant CEE grantees for cross-border work in postcommunist countries. The links established during the Solidarity times made Polish NGOs trustworthy and reliable partners. Moreover, representatives of the National Endowment for Democracy interviewed for this study find Polish organizations an important partner in democracy assistance because: (1) they have skills and knowledge in specific fields; (2) they have links with Belarusian and Ukrainian partners and the ability to reach new civil society groups; (3) Poland has a large number of models of successful transformation, in areas such as local government, civic education, and local media; and (4) Polish cross-border projects demonstrate adaptability and flexibility in implementing reforms.

It has been suggested in this chapter that Polish NGOs are important partners in transnational democracy assistance networks because of their knowledge and experience with democratization. It sends the broader message that a transnational network comprising geographically, historically, and culturally proximate states may offer better opportunities for the successful diffusion of democracy.

6 | Implications for Theory and Practice

■ This book has taken a detailed look at a particular example of democracy assistance efforts provided by a young democracy, something that has not been studied before.

This book makes some contributions to research on democracy assistance, which motivated the questions addressed in this study. However, this book also participates in important debates about democratization and democratic consolidation, the role of external actors in these processes, and regional diffusion of democracy. Findings from the Polish case permit an assessment of the implications of these findings for the fields of comparative politics and international relations, as well as for the practice of democracy assistance.

Findings from the Polish Case

Without the Solidarity activists and all who contributed to the success of the movement, the remarkable growth of Polish nongovernmental organizations and their involvement in democracy assistance would not have been possible. In almost every Polish organization engaged in democracy assistance, there can be found some trace of the Solidarity tradition. Inspired by the Solidarity spirit, activists of that period and their political heirs found it natural and important for Polish NGOs to form partnerships with civil society groups abroad and to help them in their struggle for democracy.

Polish NGOs were the first to take on important social issues during the transformation; they built bridges between the state and public sector; supported many political, social, and economic reforms; and lobbied the government to introduce institutional changes in the third sector. These activities helped Poland move toward democracy and then toward the consolidation of democracy, and they inspired Polish NGOs to share this experience beyond Poland's borders and to lobby the government to establish an aid program.

Whereas the Polish government's involvement in aid provision stems partly from Poland's membership in international organizations, the decision to provide aid for democratizing purposes originated domestically, not only from the desire to "pay it forward" after receiving assistance in its own democratic transition. The Polish government also considers democracy assistance to Poland's neighbors important because of the belief that democracy is crucial for sustainable economic development and for political and strategic reasons. Polish elites perceive democratization of neighboring states to be a means of safeguarding Polish international and political interests because of the belief that Poland cannot be truly secure without democratic neighbors. Moreover, by helping other countries in the post-communist space, the Polish government demonstrates that taking the lead in making the eastern border safe strengthens Poland's position in the European Union.

A significant finding of this work is that the Polish government's approach to democracy assistance in Belarus and Ukraine is not exclusively political or developmental. Polish programs have features of both approaches and thus are adapted to the different situations in each recipient country. Support for civil society remains a high priority in Polish democracy assistance to both countries, and it has been demonstrated that with Poland's accession to the European Union, the government and NGOs of Poland have been changing the EU's outlook on democracy assistance to Belarus and Ukraine.

The political situations in democratizing Ukraine and authoritarian Belarus are reflected in the approaches and strategies used in reaching out to civil society groups. In the case of Belarus, aid activities focus on promoting independent culture and the Belarusian language, as well as on initiatives aimed at activating civil society. Cross-border projects have established a radio station, a television channel, and websites in order to provide access to credible information about Belarusian history, literature, and the social and political situation in Belarus, as well as about international events. Since Alexander Lukashenko became president and Belarus moved toward authoritarianism, projects in Belarus have changed from those directly fostering democracy to projects working for democratic change in an indirect way. As the result of repression against Belarusian nongovernmental organizations, Polish NGOs' cross-border projects in Belarus are implemented with individuals—young people, teachers, and parents in local communities—as well as with informal groups working underground. Many programs targeted at these groups aim to educate and activate citizens to be more socially responsible for their local community, region, and country.

Projects in Ukraine show more variety than those in Belarus. The Polish government-funded programs focus on the state's capacity to enforce decisions associated with complex political (especially local governance), economic, and social reforms as well as on Ukraine's integration into the European Union. In order to achieve these goals, the Polish government cooperates not only with Polish NGOs but also with local and central entities in Poland. However, Polish NGOs are still the major recipients of Polish government assistance funds. Although Polish NGOs' projects in Ukraine have evolved from those aimed only at training people to participate in public life to projects focused on cooperation with Ukrainian local authorities, Ukrainian civil society actors are still major partners of Polish NGOs in working to strengthen links between Western and Eastern civil society groups, to strengthen the role of civil society organizations in relation to local governments, and to facilitate cooperation between organizations and media outlets (through the training of journalists and raising their awareness of local issues). There is a strong emphasis on democratic education projects in both Belarus and Ukraine; such projects teach citizens of recipient countries about democratic values, institutions, and practices. These projects are directed toward young people, as well as teachers, parents, NGOs, and administrative officials.

Polish organizations engage in assisting civil society groups in other countries for ideological reasons—to help others break down the communist legacy and achieve the same transformation that Poland did. Members of Polish organizations may also feel a personal obligation to help their counterparts across the border; some have roots or family members in Ukraine or Belarus or simply wish to help improve their neighbors' lives. Also, Polish NGOs perceive their engagement in democracy assistance as their contribution to meeting Poland's foreign policy goals of healing the wounds of the past between Poles and Ukrainians and Belarusians; increasing security in the region in order to protect Polish democracy; and raising Poland's international profile, especially in the European Union.

The demonstrated ability of Polish NGOs to reach civil society groups makes their cross-border activities important for Poland's democracy assistance. The NGOs also participate in debates over how and where to provide government aid and are major partners in implementing the government's democracy assistance. The Polish Ministry of Foreign Affairs delegates a considerable share of its funds to the postcommunist countries through

Polish NGOs, with the largest amount of money earmarked for projects in Belarus and Ukraine.

Moreover, the Ministry of Foreign Affairs considers the NGOs to be consultants with respect to foreign aid provision. Consultations regarding where, how, and to whom to provide aid allow the MFA to design its assistance for a recipient country. Moreover, as subgrantees of Polish governmental aid, NGOs also are aware of the drawbacks of the annual funding process, such as short-term funding or a long waiting period for funds, and therefore organizations actively work to make this process more efficient so that funds can be disbursed in a quick and efficient manner.

It is essential for the Polish government to work with NGOs because the government is not able to reach and cooperate with civil society in recipient countries and is not authorized to send funds directly to these groups. The Polish NGOs provide not only the "added value" represented by their detailed knowledge of conditions in specific countries but also, and more importantly, the ability to work with civil society groups and local communities when authorities from the recipient countries are hostile to democracy.

As the research for this book has shown, many of the connections between Western donors and Polish NGOs stem from links established during the communist regime. American assistance to CEE countries largely targeted Poland, and much of that aid, coming chiefly from the US government and private foundations, focused on human rights, freedom of the press, and citizens' participation. Today, the bulk of funding to NGOs in Poland comes from the National Endowment for Democracy, and it is one of the major donors to Polish NGOs' cross-border projects. The leaders of some Polish NGOs fostered the idea of cooperation with other civil society groups in the region, and Polish NGOs, with their demonstrated capability in adapting initiatives to different environments, have been the major recipients of NED funding for cross-border projects since 1992.

The findings of this study have potential policy-making implications for assistance providers such as the European Union. A major obstacle to the success of EU assistance efforts is that Union policies envision cooperation with governments, rather than directing assistance efforts at society. Although the EU's approach has begun to change, it still does not sufficiently take into account the importance of civil society, especially with regard to democracy assistance to Belarus and Ukraine. The EU should, like NED, develop long-term partnerships with local nongovernmental organizations, thus making its assistance more relevant to the specific conditions of a recipient country and making civil society a more important priority in its assistance efforts.

The scholarly literature is replete with critiques of Western efforts to support civil society in CEE countries, but Polish NGOs do not engage in the strategies that have attracted such criticism. The absence of these faults in Polish NGOs' projects puts these organizations in a better light in terms of their potential to exert a positive influence. These organizations adapt their programs to political conditions, identify the strengths that Belarusians and Ukrainians already have, and combine these propensities with the donors' skills and insights of Polish organizations. Polish NGOs' activists do not believe in a donor-driven mentality; they believe that ideas should come from recipient groups and that the majority of resources should go to groups inside these countries. Toward that end, Polish NGOs create microgrant programs that support grassroots initiatives and help local organizations to develop.

Moreover, Polish NGOs do not perceive NGOs as the only possible recipients of civil society assistance. Polish agencies actively attempt to reach a wider audience of civil society groups in the recipient countries and to improve all forms of communication with those groups. Polish NGOs also seek to establish long-term relationships with Belarusian and Ukrainian partners, believing that these ties are more likely to contribute to the development of these societies, and they encourage networking and partnering both internally and externally. Partnerships increase the likelihood that programs will be well tailored to the local context of the recipient country. Moreover, coalitions with Polish NGOs help to sustain civil society in Belarus and Ukraine, thus improving the chances that democratic ideas and practices will take root in those countries.

Polish NGOs believe that the advantages of a regional actor—lack of language and cultural barriers; greater familiarity with local actors and perhaps personal ties; in-depth understanding of internal conditions, social or cultural norms, and the political situation; and a keen vested interest in the recipient countries—make neighboring democracies better engineers of democracy than more distant countries. Moreover, Polish NGO activists believe that through their ability to form linkages between civil society groups and their willingness to cooperate with these groups on an equal footing, their actions contribute to the "activization" of societies in recipient countries and thus to positive change in those countries. The officials of Polish NGOs are of the opinion that without their work with particular Ukrainian groups, such as students, teachers, and civil society organizations, the Orange Revolution of 2004 in Ukraine would have been less likely to occur.

Civil Society and Democratization

The findings of this study have some important implications concerning both theory on civil society and democratization and practice with regard to providing democracy assistance to postcommunist countries.

Polish democracy assistance strongly emphasizes civil society development, regardless of the recipient country's political situation. However, this assistance takes into account the different roles civil society plays within the context of an authoritarian regime versus a new democracy. In order for civil society to play a major role in undermining an authoritarian regime and facilitating the establishment of democratic rule, it has to overcome certain obstacles. To initiate the transition to democracy in Belarus, Polish NGO activists have focused on the "education" of civil society activists about their role in and responsibility for social and political actions, as well as about democratic values and practices. They encourage the activization of Belarusian society and cooperation between civil society groups to help them both overcome passiveness and facilitate linkages. Later, these groups can organize themselves into a united opposition front that is able to mobilize the masses. As Ukraine's Orange Revolution demonstrated, a civil society–based opposition was considered a real alternative to the regime, and the regime got the sense that the nation did not accept it and that people were ready to take action to fight for their freedom. Similarly, in Belarus such a signal may facilitate the collapse of the regime, in addition to other possible ways of ending authoritarianism.

Polish groups are in many cases nurturing the seeds of civil society where its formation is impeded; in the case of Belarus, external influences appear to be an important factor in building and strengthening civil society. Financial and moral support for pro-democratic groups is also important for developing social capital and stimulating civil society–based opposition toward an authoritarian regime. The cooperation of Belarusian civil society groups with Polish NGOs demonstrates that even an authoritarian regime cannot completely isolate civil society groups from external influences.

However, in the case of an authoritarian country, it is important to make a distinction between civil and uncivil society, since some nongovernmental organizations may be supported and financed by antidemocratic governments. Therefore, it also is crucial to recognize that civil society includes a range of people—women's groups, young people, teachers, and journalists—who can either mobilize a "popular upsurge" and delegitimize a regime or compel it to be more responsive to its citizens.

Ukrainian civil society shows that it may be feasible to strengthen civil society's role vis-à-vis the government, so that it counterbalances and disperses state power and acts as a bridge between citizens and governments, as well as a watchdog for citizens' interests. A strong, robust civil society that is capable of generating political alternatives is an important factor in solidifying democratic tendencies in the country, as scholars argue. On the question of why projects regarding Ukrainian local governance are conducted in partnership with civil society organizations in Ukraine, Polish NGOs respond that such projects prepare Ukrainian organizations to become an important source of social control over processes that are taking place at the local administration level. Moreover, since nongovernmental organizations act as advocates of the local community's interests, such cooperation makes civil society a partner in resolving problems of democratic governance and thus may contribute to good, effective, and responsive government.

Finally, Ukraine's case shows that clear geographical divisions with respect to democracy weaken civil society's overall role in this process. Instead of applying consociational strategies, Ukrainian leaders have polarized society in order to use those divisions in their struggle for political power. Therefore, Polish NGO activists recognize that achieving a consensus among civil society groups and people regarding democracy in their country is an important challenge for Ukraine. According to the scholarly literature, one of the criteria for successful democratic consolidation is the existence of a strong majority who subscribe to a belief that democratic procedures and institutions are the most appropriate (Dahl 1997; Huntington 1991; Inglehart 1988; Linz and Stepan 1996; O'Donnell 1988; Putnam et al. 1983). To deal with this problem of civil society polarization, Polish organizations foster the creation of networks between civil society groups in Ukraine through, for example, projects in which there are two Ukrainian partners—one from the western region and another from the eastern region.

In sum, strategies of reaching out to and working with civil society groups are different when implemented in authoritarian countries versus those that are newly democratic states. Such findings give reason to argue that such tailored democracy assistance has a high chance of success in diffusing democratic ideas and practices.

Implications for Democracy Assistance Literature and Policies

Scholars have in the past suggested that democracy assistance efforts are either political or developmental. It has been demonstrated that the inclusion of young democracies in the democracy assistance "industry" changed the quality of democracy assistance. As this study has shown, the new, "third-wave" democracy that is Poland and an erstwhile recipient of democracy assistance now offers a type of assistance that does not fall neatly into the dichotomy suggested by scholars. Poland offers aid that is neither strictly political nor solely developmental. Instead, it adapts aid strategies to the particular situation in the recipient country.

The tailoring of assistance to different political circumstances in recipient countries shows that the Polish approach to democracy assistance is complex. The scholarly literature on democracy assistance should now reflect this new view, in which context-driven democracy assistance gives priority to those kinds of aid that would produce the greatest results in a particular situation and that could be tailored to the specific social and political features of recipient countries. In other words, such an approach responds to both challenges and to opportunities for aid provision.

For example, if democracy assistance providers are working in an authoritarian country like Belarus, it might be more appropriate to target civil society and encourage overall social mobilization instead of focusing on developmental aid, since this type of support is usually channeled through the governments of recipient countries. Whereas it is difficult, if not impossible, to cooperate with a government that is hostile to democracy, in the case of a country that is a new democracy, it may be suitable to support not only civil society groups but also other entities. In such a case, it would be reasonable to direct assistance to the government in order to aid in the building of democratic institutions, to improve state capacity to implement political and economic reforms, and to support political society (political parties, lobbying groups, and the like).

Another contribution of this work to the theory and practice of democracy assistance is the idea that civil society plays an important role both as a provider and as a recipient of democracy assistance. Whereas there is a significant amount of literature referring to nongovernmental organizations being recipients of Western aid, this study is the first to investigate in depth the role of NGOs as transmitters of democracy assistance to other civil society groups across the border—a relatively new phenomenon.

As this study shows, governments that want to provide democracy assistance may find many reasons to work with NGOs: their experience with aid and democratization, their ability to reach civil society groups in recipient countries through links established in the past, and their detailed knowledge about local needs. The Polish government has relied heavily on the democracy work of civil society organizations, and the Polish model of democracy assistance is a likely presence in other third-wave democracies that emerged by means of civil society resurgence.

By engaging NGOs in democracy assistance, young democracies demonstrate that there might be another strategy of delivering democracy assistance besides the well-known strategies of direct grants or opening local organizations. This new strategy is based on assisting democracy through the collaborative work of actors from various countries in the region—what might be termed "civil society–to–civil society work" or, in the terminology of some practitioners, "cross-border work." This study suggests that such cross-border work as a democracy assistance strategy may complement other methods.

Analysis of the merits of civil society–to–civil society work yields the conclusion that this strategy has the potential to influence the diffusion of democratic ideas and behaviors for several reasons. The democracy assistance literature describes the pitfalls of strategies employed by other donors, such as failing to take into account the situation of civil society groups in recipient countries, neglecting local circumstances, providing short-term funding only for large organizations rather than small local groups, equating civil society with nongovernmental organizations, and failing to create networks among civil society groups in the recipient country. However, cross-border cooperation engages civil society groups in neighboring states and actively involves them in implementing projects. Moreover, such cooperation facilitates certain activities that otherwise would not be possible and allows for flexibility and quick adaptation to the local context. Furthermore, long-term cross-border cooperation increases the possibility of influencing groups in the neighboring society. Finally, cross-border work has the capability of fostering links between civil society groups and contributing to the geographic expansion of the third sector in the recipient country.

Therefore, the engagement of various organizations in democracy assistance is important for not only the authorities but also Western donors. The Polish democracy assistance also provides the message to foreign democracy assistance donors that, instead of providing direct grants to recipient countries, it might be more feasible for Western donors to take advantage of the knowledge and skills of regional NGOs and finance their cross-border projects. For donors interested in the postcommunist region, Polish NGOs' projects could be the channel through which the final beneficiaries in Belarus and Ukraine could be reached, with the National Endowment for Democracy work providing an example of this strategy.

The Diffusion of Democracy and Impact of Transnational Actors

By examining the transnational interactions of civil society activists across the borders between Poland, Belarus, and Ukraine, this study suggests that such networks may be associated with both democratic transition and consolidation. NGOs embarking on democracy assistance across national borders may have long-term, well-established connections with civil society groups, in-depth knowledge about the local context, and the desire to share their own experience in democratization. Therefore, engaging neighboring NGOs in a transnational democracy assistance network may improve the ability of such networks to spread democracy, pressure domestic elites, and raise the costs of antidemocratic behavior in a democratizing country. In other words, such networks can better facilitate transitions to democracy, as well as guarantee its survival.

Different modes of analysis—scholarly literature, as well as documents and opinions of Polish NGOs and Western donors—yield strong arguments and lead to the same conclusion: that NGOs' cross-border work with civil society groups has the potential to play an important role in democratization. These findings also suggest that the obstacles to democratization or democratic consolidation can be mitigated with targeted democracy assistance undertaken by NGOs from neighboring democracies—which might also be an underlying reason for the mass mobilizations and regional democratic diffusion observed in the region. It is up to future research to determine the long-term outcomes of third-wave democracy assistance.

Appendix 1 *Interviews Conducted*

POLAND

Polish Nongovernmental Organizations

Casimir Pulaski Foundation, Warsaw. Zbigniew Pisarski, president of the board, July 14, 2008.

Center for International Relations (CIR), Warsaw. Andrzej Bobiński, program coordinator, July 15, 2008.

Center for Social and Economic Research (CASE), Warsaw. Artur Radziwiłł, vice president of the board, July 1, 2008.

College of Eastern Europe, Wrocław. Jan Andrzej Dąbrowski, president of the board, June 18, 2008.

Democratic Society East Foundation (DSE), Warsaw. Katarzyna Bielawska, member of the board, June 27, 2008.

East European Democratic Center (EEDC), Warsaw. Magda Dębkowska, director, June 5, 2008; Paweł Kazanecki, president of the board, July 14, 2008.

Education for Democracy Foundation (FED), Warsaw. Aleksandra Kujawska, program coordinator, July 15, 2008.

Foundation for Young Democracy, Lublin. Jan Fedirko, program coordinator, June 6, 2008; Paweł Bobołowicz, president of the board, June 6, 2008.

Foundation in Support of Local Democracy (FSLD), Szczecin. Przemysław Fenrych, program coordinator, July 22, 2008; Katarzyna Morawska, project specialist, management office, June 5, 2008.

Institute of Public Affairs (IPA), Warsaw. Paweł Kucharczyk, president of the executive board, June 30, 2008.

Poland-Ukrainian Cooperation Foundation (PAUCI), Warsaw. Jan Piekło, director, June 30, 2008.

Polish-American Freedom Foundation (PAFF), Warsaw. Renata Koźlicka-Glińska, program officer, June 12, 2008.

Polish-American Fulbright Commission, Warsaw. Urszula Sobiecka, coordinator of the Lane Kirkland Scholarship Program, July 1, 2008.

Polish Robert Schuman Foundation, Warsaw. Rafał Dymek, general director, July 14, 2008.

St. Maximilian Kolbe House for Meetings and Reconciliation (DMK), Gdańsk. Arkadiusz Goliński, vice-director, July 2, 2008.

Stefan Batory Foundation, Warsaw. Grzegorz Gromadzki, director of the International

Cooperation Program; Agnieszka Komorowska, coordinator of the Civil Initiatives in Eastern Europe Program, June 12, 2008.

Zagranica Group, Warsaw. Marta Pejda, executive secretary, June 27, 2008.

Polish Ministry of Foreign Affairs

Development Cooperation Department. Mirosław Sycz, vice-director; Agata Czaplinska, head of the Implementation of Development Assistance Program, June 27, 2008.

UNITED STATES

National Endowment for Democracy (NED), Washington, DC. Rodger Potocki, director for Europe and Eurasia; Joanna Rohozińska, program officer for Europe and Eurasia, November 20, 2008.

Appendix 2 *Interview Questions*

Questions for Polish Nongovernmental Organizations

1. Is democracy promotion in Ukraine and Belarus one of the main goals of your organization in relation to other goals?
2. What is the reason for your organization's engagement in democracy promotion in Ukraine and Belarus?
3. How does your organization promote democracy in Ukraine and Belarus?
4. How would you say your organization is different from others, such as [name], that do similar work in Ukraine and Belarus in regard to democracy promotion?
5. Which of these activities are most effective in promoting democracy?
   (a) democratic institution building
   (b) monitoring of human rights
   (c) education development
   (d) supporting free media
   (e) civil society development
   (f) direct financial support
   (g) rule of law development
   (h) others
6. In which form of democracy assistance is your organization involved and why?
7. (Depending on above answer) Why does your organization emphasize (not emphasize) development of civil society? What does the organization view as being the role of civil society and NGOs in the promoting of democratic states?
8. How do you look for recipients of your democracy assistance activities? What criteria are being used in the decision to grant either financial or nonfinancial assistance?
9. How does your organization look upon the idea of projects aimed at facilitating the development and increasing the involvement in politics of Ukrainian and Belarusian NGOs?
11. Do you have any such programs? Please describe their nature and process.
12. Which of the following activities were initiated by your organizations?
    (a) building NGO networks in Ukraine/Belarus
    (b) creating websites or other information sources
    (c) organizing conferences, travel opportunities
    (d) organizing training, internships, etc.
13. How does the organization go about funding these projects?
14. Does the organization engage Ukrainian and Belarusian NGOs in projects?

15. How do you select Ukrainian and Belarusian NGOs for project partners? What criteria are being used?

16. Do you have any informational brochures about these projects? Are there any reports following up from projects that I could have?

17. Do you have a list of organizations and projects funded by your organization with dates, locations, and amounts of the assistance? Could I have a copy of this information?

18. Has the cooperation with Ukrainian and Belarusian NGOs been efficient? Have you encountered any problems/obstacles from Ukrainian and Belarusian sites that withheld or delayed some activities?

19. Is your organization a partner in multilateral events/projects promoting democracy that have been initiated by different institutions and organizations, such as the Polish Ministry of Foreign Affairs or European Commission? If yes, please describe.

20. What impact do you see your organization having on democracy development in Ukraine and Belarus? To what extent would you say your organization's activities in supporting democracy/civil society are effective? Are the results of your activities observable? Please provide support for your argument. How could these activities be improved?

21. Have your organization's goals, strategy, or decision making regarding democracy promotion activities in Ukraine and Belarus changed? If yes, why and how? What are the future plans of the organization?

Questions for Government Officials from the Polish Ministry of Foreign Affairs

1. From the MFA website we can find out about different types of foreign assistance activities that MFA provides within the Polish Aid initiative. How important is democracy assistance compared to other forms of assistance offered by the MFA?

2. Is Poland obliged to secure part of its budget for foreign assistance or does it do so on a voluntary basis? Does the membership in the European Union (EU) obligate Poland to provide assistance to nonmember neighboring states? Please explain.

3. If the EU has influence on the decision to provide foreign assistance, does it also influence what form it takes and where Polish assistance should go?

4. Do Polish democracy assistance activities complement EU efforts to influence democratization in nonmember states? If yes, in what sense?

5. When did Poland begin supporting democracy in Ukraine and Belarus?

6. Can you tell me about the total amount of the assistance to Ukraine and Belarus that Polish governments have disbursed so far? Do you have detailed information on how monies were used?

7. Would you say that Polish activities aimed at democracy promotion in Ukraine and Belarus are more effective than the EU ones? If yes, why?

8. To what extent could the following make Polish democratic assistance more effective than EU assistance? Please explain.

(a) better understanding of social and cultural factors in Ukraine and Belarus

(b) close political cooperation

(c) nature of projects themselves

(d) involvement of Ukrainian and Belarusian partners

(e) cooperation with Polish NGOs

(f) no language barrier

(g) others

9. What is the reason for the government's involvement in democracy promotion in Ukraine and Belarus?

10. To what extent did the following factors influence the decision to promote democracy in Ukraine and Belarus? Please evaluate each.

(a) security concerns beyond Polish eastern border

(b) historical and cultural ties with Ukraine and Belarus

(c) close economic cooperation

(d) geographic proximity

(e) balancing the influence of Russia on the political and economic situation in Ukraine and Belarus

11. Which of these factors would you say have the strongest impact on the decision to promote democracy in Ukraine and Belarus?

12. What in your opinion is the role of NGOs in building a democratic state? Are Ukrainian and Belarusian NGOs increasing their ability to influence public opinion and politics in their countries?

13. Please explain MFA activities aimed at promoting democracy.

14. Which of the following actions does the MFA find to be the most important in promoting democracy? Why?

(a) democratic institution building

(b) monitoring of human rights

(c) education development

(d) supporting free media

(e) civil society development

(f) direct financial support

(g) rule of law development

(h) others

15. Does your ministry interact at all with Polish NGOs when promoting democracy in Ukraine and Belarus? What does this cooperation look like?

16. Does the MFA initiate projects and encourage Polish NGOs to participate in them? How does the ministry offer cooperative opportunities and decide about the project partners?

17. Can you list the [titles] of these joint projects with the dates and names of Polish NGOs involved in these democracy assistance initiatives in Ukraine and Belarus?

18. Do Polish NGOs have the same idea of democracy promotion initiatives as MFA? Are there any disagreements?

19. Do you have any mechanism for communicating to NGOs the MFA ideas about the ways of promoting democracy?

20. To what extent do the NGO democracy assistance activities complement the ministry activities?
21. Would you say that the cooperation with the NGOs is satisfactory and fruitful? What are the benefits and drawbacks that result from such work with NGOs? How could cooperation be improved?
22. Have you encountered any problems/obstacles during project implementation? Was/is it the MFA, Polish NGOs, or the Ukrainian and Belarusian parties that contributed to the failure of the project? Have Ukrainian and Belarusian parties ever blocked or delayed some Polish activities?
23. What is your opinion about the current political situation in Ukraine and Belarus? Has it changed for better or for worse? Why?

Questions for Foreign Donors to Polish NGOs' Projects

1. Is democracy promotion in Ukraine and Belarus one of the main goals of your organization?
2. What is the reason for your organization's engagement in democracy promotion in Ukraine and Belarus?
3. How is your organization promoting democracy in Ukraine and Belarus?
4. Why is the organization assisting Polish NGOs in their democracy promotion efforts in Ukraine and Belarus?
5. When did the organization begin providing funds for projects by Polish NGOs in Ukraine and Belarus?
6. Does the organization have other partners with whom it cooperates on democracy assistance projects in Ukraine and Belarus? Who are they?
7. Do you have a list of organizations funded by your organization with amounts of the assistance? Could I have a copy of this information?
8. How important is the cooperation with Polish NGOs in relation to cooperation with other partners?
9. Does the organization's assistance to Polish NGOs' projects stem from the established links developed in the communist period? What was the nature of linkages between the organization and Polish NGOs in the past?
10. Has the cooperation with Polish NGOs been efficient?
11. To what extent would you say Polish NGOs' activities in supporting democracy/ civil society in Ukraine and Belarus are effective?
12. Do you have any democracy assistance programs/projects in which your organization is the only initiator of activities in Ukraine and Belarus? Please describe the nature and process of these projects.
13. If the answer to question 12 is "NO": Why does the organization provide assistance through other partners?
14. If the answer to question 12 is "YES":
    (a) Why is the organization engaging in projects by itself?
    (b) Does the organization engage Ukrainian and Belarusian NGOs in projects?

(c) How do you select Ukrainian and Belarusian NGOs for project partners? What criteria are being used?

(d) Does the organization build links between recipient countries' NGOs?

(e) Do you have any informational brochures about these projects? Are there any reports following up from projects that I could have? To what extent would you say your organization's activities in supporting democracy/civil societies are effective? Are the results of your activities observable? Please provide support for your argument.

Appendix 3 *Polish Ministry of Foreign Affairs' Assistance Data*

TABLE A3.1. Allocation of Polish Ministry of Foreign Affairs bilateral funds in 2008 (millions of Polish złoty [PLN])

	NGOs	CENTRAL ADMINISTRATION	LOCAL ADMINISTRATION	POLISH EMBASSIES	TOTAL
Belarus	4.5	2.5	0.5	0.5	8
Ukraine	8	6.5	1	0.5	16
Afghanistan	1	6	1	0.5	8.5
Moldova	2	1.5	0.5	0.5	4.5
Central Asia and Southern Caucasus	1	0.5	0.5	1.5	3.5
Western Balkans	0.5	1	0	0.5	2
Georgia	2	1.5	0.5	0.5	4.5
Others	6	2	0	7	15
Total	*25*	*21.5*	*4*	*11.5*	*62**

Source: Based on "Polish Aid Program Administered by the Ministry of Foreign Affairs of the Republic of Poland," issued by the Polish Ministry of Foreign Affairs (MFA) in 2008.

*Total bilateral MFA assistance in 2008 equals PLN 62 million plus PLN 18 million (allocated directly from the MFA budget to TV BELARUS), for a total of PLN 80 million.

TABLE A3.2. Number of Polish NGOs' projects financed by the Polish Ministry of Foreign Affairs in 2008

	NUMBER OF PROJECTS IMPLEMENTED BY POLISH NGOS
Belarus	12
Ukraine	34
Afghanistan	3
Moldova	9
Central Asia and Southern Caucasus	8
Western Balkans	3
Georgia	10
Others	19
Total	*98*

Source: Based on the list of Polish NGOs' projects financed by the Ministry of Foreign Affairs (MFA) within its 2008 call for proposals, obtained during an interview with MFA officials, June 27, 2008.

Appendix 4 *NED Data on Cross-Border Work*

TABLE A4.1. Funding amounts provided by NED for cross-border projects with partners from Central and Eastern European countries in the postcommunist region, 1993–2007 (in US dollars)

YEAR	POLAND	CZECH REPUBLIC	SLOVAKIA	LITHUANIA	TOTAL
1993	50,000	0	0	0	50,000
1994	50,000	0	0	0	50,000
1995	20,000	0	0	0	20,000
1996	129,952	0	0	0	129,952
1997	200,737	0	0	0	200,737
1998	157,500	34,650	0	0	192,150
1999	430,210	29,690	0	0	459,900
2000	433,921	50,000	0	70,000	553,921
2001	60,000	0	0	0	60,000
2002	100,000	0	0	0	100,000
2003	244,010	24,744	52,000	66,673	387,427
2004	209,543	65,000	126,814	20,633	421,990
2005	65,000	69,109	87,017	0	221,126
2006	211,500	75,000	49,270	0	335,770
2007	273,155	21,559	0	0	294,714
Total	2,635,528	369,752	315,101	157,306	3,477,687

Source: Data obtained from the National Endowment for Democracy.

Appendix 5 *Typical Polish NGO Project Summaries*

SKILLS FOR THE FUTURE: THE SCHOOL OF UKRAINIAN YOUNG GOVERNMENT LEADERS

This project, begun in 2001 and repeated in 2003 and 2004, involved improving the knowledge and skills of young Ukrainian deputies serving on local councils by transferring Polish experience in selected aspects of local governance. Participants worked in groups according to their personal interests, in areas such as education, social policy, communal property, service management and local finances, and economic transformation of rural areas. Methods included workshops in Ukraine, study tours to Poland, and a final conference. The program created a network of 150 young Ukrainian local council deputies who have been trained in Poland and who maintain close relationships with Polish counterparts to share information, ideas, and practices. Other activities included the development of statutes for several Ukrainian cities; the creation of local development agencies, based on Polish models, in the Ukrainian cities of Kobelyaki and Izaslav; and the preparation of local development strategies for several cities.

REFERENDUM ISSUES AND PUBLIC AWARENESS OF THE EUROPEAN UNION

This program shared Poland's experience with the European Union referendum process and aimed to support the pro-European community in Volyn oblast in Ukraine. The program was implemented by the Foundation Nowy Staw (a Polish NGO) and the Ukrainian Center for Public Youth Organizations of Volyn oblast. Twenty-five young Ukrainians from Volyn, including fifteen journalists, participated in a four-day workshop and six-day study visit to Poland during the Polish EU referendum. Participants observed how advocates and opponents of Polish EU accession ran their campaigns, and participants discussed how to improve debate in Ukraine regarding the EU. Volyn regional media produced more than eighty EU-referendum-related articles. Participants initiated new Polish-Ukrainian cross-border programs and launched a new regional cooperation website, www.euromixbug.org. Volyn residents also created several European School Clubs.

ENCOURAGING PRO-EUROPEAN VALUES THROUGH SOCIAL AND YOUTH POLICY AWARENESS

This project introduced more than 170 local government officials from Donetsk, Kharkiv, and Sumy oblasts to European standards for social and youth policies. The program was implemented by the Institute of Public Information (Gdynia, Poland) and the Youth Debate Center (Donetsk, Ukraine). The study visits included seminars on EU standards for social and youth policies, the EU legislative process, the Copenhagen Criteria, and the Polish model of adapting EU standards for use at the local level. Ukrainian officials met with a number of officials from Gdańsk and Sopot in Poland. The project created a group of pro-European professionals in eastern Ukraine willing to introduce reform at the local level.

Source: Based on PAUCI 2005.

Notes

Introduction

1. The terms "third-wave democracies" and "young democracies" refer to a group of countries that underwent successful democratic transitions during the widespread international push toward democracy, called the "third wave of democratization" (Huntington 1991), that occurred in the late twentieth century. In contrast to the long-established "old democracies" of the West, these countries are new but successfully consolidated democracies, in regions such as southern Europe, Latin America, eastern Asia, Southeast Asia, Central and Eastern Europe, and sub-Saharan Africa.

2. Analyzing the transitions from authoritarian rule in southern Europe, Schmitter (1986, 5) concludes that the "external factors tended to play an indirect and usually marginal role" in democratization. However, his findings tend to clash with some obvious facts surrounding the transitions that have occurred in Central and Eastern Europe. After the rapid political transitions in Eastern Europe, followed by the collapse of the Soviet Union, Schmitter (1996, 27) has admitted that "perhaps it is time to reconsider the impact of the international context upon regime change."

3. For more about democratic transformations in CEE states, see Crawford and Lijphart 1995; Ekiert 2003; Kopstein and Reilly 2000; Pridham et al. 1997; Rose and Haerpfer 1995; and Whitehead 1996.

4. Since 2000 there have been four mass mobilizations in the postcommunist region, including the "Bulldozer Revolution" in the Federal Republic of Yugoslavia (in former Serbia and Montenegro) in 2000, the "Rose Revolution" in Georgia in 2003, the "Orange Revolution" in Ukraine in 2004, and the "Tulip Revolution" in Kyrgyzstan in 2005. The common term for these events is "Color Revolutions," and these events were characterized by massive street protests that followed disputed elections and led to the resignation or overthrow of political authorities considered to be authoritarian and the rise of new power elites who favored democracy. For more about revolutions in the postcommunist region, see Fairbanks 2004; Karatnycky 2005; Thompson 2004; and special issues on the Orange Revolution in Problems of Post-Communism, March–April 2005, and in the *Journal of Democracy*, April 2005. Outside Europe there was the so-called "Cedar Revolution" in Lebanon.

5. Democracy is defined here and elsewhere as a form of government with: (1) regular elections that are free, fair, and competitive and that put in office public officials taking responsibility on behalf of the citizens; (2) authorities accountable to the citizens; (3) rule of law; and (4) civil liberties and political rights guaranteed by law. The most common mechanism that fosters accountability is elections (Schumpeter 1947). However, O'Donnell et al. (2004, 32) and Rose-Ackerman (2007) see civil

society as providing mechanisms of accountability as well. Democratic consolidation, however, is defined as a process of building a democracy following the collapse of an authoritarian regime and continuing to stabilize the democratic regime so that it survives. Scholars tend to consider democratic consolidation as a process by which the rules, institutions, and constraints of democracy come to constitute "the only game in town," the one legitimate framework for seeking and exercising political power (Diamond 1997, xviii; Linz and Stepan 1996; Przeworski 1991, 26).

6. The concept of civil society is incorporated in the definition of liberal democracy with which scholars prefer to work. The concept of liberal democracy devotes more attention to human rights secured through constitutional, limited government, the rule of law, and freedom of speech, press, organization, and association than does that of electoral democracy (Bunce and Wolchik 2006; Diamond 1999; Pateman 1970; Tilly 2007). In Dahl's (1971, 1989) understanding, what makes countries truly democratic is the dependence of officials' decisions upon the expressions of preferences by the citizenry, as well as citizens' chances to express their interests and values by means not only of parties and elections but also of the independent associations that individuals have the freedom to establish and join. In Dahl's opinion, civil rights are essential for the exercise of political rights. Specifically, Dahl (1989, 233) argues that in a democracy, which he defines as "polyarchy," citizens have an effectively enforced right to form and join autonomous associations, including political associations such as political parties and interest groups, that attempt to influence the government by competing in elections and by other peaceful means.

7. Detailed discussions about the role of civil society during transitions from authoritarianism to democracy in these regions are in Bernhard 1993; Diamond 1994, 1996; Diamond and Plattner 2001; Freres 1999; Ekiert 2003; Hadenius and Uggla 1998; Henderson 2003; Lehning 1998; O'Donnell and Schmitter 1986; and Linz and Stepan 1996.

8. This definition is widely used by Biekart (1999), Carothers (1999), Cohen and Arato (1997), Dahl (1989), Deutsch (1961), Putnam (1994); Linz and Stepan (1996), and White (1994). By "political society" Linz and Stepan (1996, 8) mean political parties, elections, electoral rules, political leadership, interparty alliances, and legislatures, which they describe as an arena in which the polity specifically arranges itself to contest the right to exercise control over public power and the state apparatus.

9. Some scholars, such as Payne (2000) and Keane (1998, 115), distinguish between civil and uncivil society based on the use of violence in that society. Here, usage of terms follows Whitehead 1997, as well as Shils's (1992) definition of organizations or groups with a lack of democratic ideas or with antidemocratic components. Shils (1992) argues that only certain organizations qualify as part of civil society, namely those that support and embrace liberal democratic values and institutions. Berman (1997) argues that the term civil society is vague, and she implies that in fact this concept may refer sometimes to uncivil society. Whitehead (1997, 107–8) points out that uncivil society negatively influences the quality and stability of the democracy

as a whole, and whereas uncivil society may also be well established in Western democracies, in new democracies such uncivil society occupies a much larger social space, often more than that occupied by the emerging civil society itself.

10. For more about the role of civil society see, among others, Bermeo 2003, 9–11; Bernhard 1993; Biekart 1999, 34, 46; Cohen and Rogers 1992; Dahl 1971; Diamond 1994, 1999, 239–50; Diamond et al. 1989, 35; Linz 2000; Putnam 1994; Putnam et al. 1983; Rose-Ackerman 2007; Rueschemeyer et al. 1992; Taylor 1990; Tilly 2007; and Walzer 1991, 300.

11. Even though the terms democracy assistance and democracy promotion are used interchangeably, this research emphasizes the difference between these terms and defines democracy assistance as one of the instruments of democracy promotion, following Quigley (1997) and Azpuru et al. (2008). Contrary to other measures aimed at establishing or strengthening democracy, such as diplomatic pressure, conditionality on aid (including conditionality for joining organizations like the European Union), economic sanctions, or even military intervention, the term democracy assistance suggests that the impetus for democratic development in a given country is internal, not external. In other words, by providing foreign aid in the form of direct grants or technical assistance to a recipient country in which domestic actors are working to facilitate conditions that could lead to democracy's rise, democracy assistance recognizes that the principal responsibility for developing democracy rests with the actors in recipient countries.

12. In Schumpeter's (1947, 269) conception, democracy is defined as elite competition: "the democratic method is the institutional arrangement for arriving at political decisions in which individuals acquire the power to decide by means of competitive struggle for the people's vote." Thus, according to Schumpeter, democracy means that the people have the opportunity of selecting, through a competitive electoral process, those who will represent their interests. Even though scholars agree that a system for choosing the government through free, fair, and competitive elections organized at regular intervals with universal suffrage is an essential feature of democracy, many experts and practitioners believe that elections are not enough to make a state democratic. Thus, a "minimalist" definition of electoral democracy proposed by Schumpeter—although still employed today (e.g., Cheibub et al. 1996)—is rather rare among scholars. However, O'Donnell (2001, 9) points out that Schumpeter (1947, 271) realizes that in order for the "free competition for a free vote" to exist, some conditions external to the electoral process itself must be met.

13. Research regarding civil society assistance includes Allison and Beschel 1992; Azpuru et al. 2008; Bernard et al. 1998; Blair 1998; Grugel 1999; Hearn and Robinson 2000; Ottaway and Carothers 2000; Sundstrom 2006; and Thijn and Bernard 1998.

14. From 1989 to 1994, the international community made commitments to Central and Eastern Europe, namely to Poland, Czechoslovakia (after 1993 the Czech Republic and Slovakia), and Hungary, of approximately $44.3 billion (Quigley 1997, 1).

15. Scholars have vigorously discussed the development of Central and Eastern

European civil society for a long time (Mendelson 2001; Mendelson and Glenn 2002; Petrescu 2000; Quigley 1997, 2000; Richter 2002), but researchers have also focused attention on other regions, such as Latin America (Allmand 1998; Schifter 2000), the Middle East (Brouwer 2000), Africa (Bratton and van de Walle 1997; Hearn and Robinson 2000; Landsberg 2000; Sedogo 1998), and Asia (Adamson 2002; Golub 2000; Racelis 2000; Weinthal and Luong 2002; Win 1998).

16. NED's Discretionary Proposal Guidelines and Procedures may be found at www.ned.org/grantseekers.

17. The term "Roundtable Talks" here refers to negotiations that took place in Poland in 1989 between the representatives of the communist regime and the opposition, as a result of which the transformation in Poland began (Ćwiek-Karpowicz and Kaczyński 2006; Osiatynski 1996). See also Elster 1996 and Huntington 1991 for the typology of political transitions.

18. Carl Gershman, the president of NED during Solidarity and the Future of Democratization, a conference held at Georgetown University in May 2009 to commemorate the twentieth anniversary of Poland's Roundtable Talks, said that the idea of assisting civil society groups through cross-border work originated from the Solidarity movement and spread to other countries around the world.

19. For comparative transition literature that highlights Poland as a special case, see, for example, Crawford and Lijphart 1995 or King 2000.

20. According Polity IV or Freedom House rankings and economic data, Poland is a consolidated democracy with a prospering free-market economy. Poland's accomplishments in the political and economic spheres have been internationally recognized by its inclusion in international organizations. Poland became member of the International Monetary Fund (IMF) and the World Bank in 1996 (it was a founding member of both in 1946 but withdrew in 1954); the Council of Europe in 1991; the Organization for Economic Co-operation and Development (OECD) in 1996; the World Trade Organization (WTO) in 1995; and NATO in 1999. However, the main indicator of Poland's successful transformation was the achievement of the Copenhagen criteria regarding accomplishments in democratization and creation of a market economy and accession to the European Union (EU), which Poland joined on May 1, 2004.

21. For more information about funding for Polish civil society, see CSCE 1994; Friszke 2006; Juros et al. 2004; and Zimmer and Priller 2004.

22. In December 2004, Poland provided the impetus that led to the EU intervention in Ukraine. In the event, Javier Solana, EU high representative for common foreign and security policy, joined Polish president Aleksander Kwaśniewski and Lithuania's Valdas Adamkus and traveled to Ukraine to resolve the ongoing standoff over the disputed presidential vote. As a result, the agreement between Prime Minister Viktor Yanukovych and his challenger, Viktor Yushchenko, was reached, and the conflicting sides agreed to work toward eliminating the use of force in resolving the election crisis (RFE/RL Newsline 2004).

23. From the fourteenth to the twentieth centuries, Belarus and Ukraine, together with Poland and Lithuania, shared similar historical circumstances (Burant 1993). Poles, Belarusians, Ukrainians, and Lithuanians were united under a common sovereign as a result of the marriage of Lithuania's Grand Duke Jagiełło to Poland's Queen Jadwiga in the fourteenth century. Later, these countries, together with the Polish crown, jointly formed the Polish-Lithuanian Commonwealth, or Rzeczpospolita Obojga Narodow (literally, Republic of Two Nations) for more than 400 years (Snyder 2003). In 1918, after 123 years of partitions by Austria-Hungary, Germany, and Russia, Poland regained its independence. The Second Polish Republic and Bolshevik Russia disputed their borders and control over lands, which led to the Polish-Soviet War (1919–21). After World War I, in December 1919, the Allied Supreme Council declared a demarcation line, called the Curzon Line, between these countries, but the line did not play any role in establishing the Polish-Soviet border in 1921. Instead, the Riga Peace Treaty (1921), which ended the Polish-Soviet War, divided Ukraine's and Belarus's western and eastern lands between Poland and Soviet Russia (Leslie 1983, 137–38). The areas that belonged to Poland were called Kresy (the eastern territories) and polonized. The Molotov-Ribbentrop Pact of August 1939 united most of the Ukrainian and Belarusian areas; however, the Soviet influence from 1945 to 1991 had a critical influence on the countries' political, economic, social, and cultural developments and determined their later transformations (Ekiert and Hanson 2003; Lieven 1999, 32; Magdziak-Mieszewska 2002).

24. Social scientists acknowledge the role of international networks in civil society building, but there are not many studies that address this topic empirically (Keck and Sikkink 1998; Smith et al. 1997; Tarrow 1998, 2005) and there is almost no research on civil society assistance networks composed of domestic civil society groups and neighbor-based democracy assistance providers.

25. On the one hand, there were countries like Belarus, which backslid to authoritarianism despite some prospects for democratization at the beginning of the 1990s (Dawisha and Parrott 1997; Diamond and Plattner 2001; Fish 2001, 2005; Ishiyama and Kennedy 2001; Mihalisko 1997). On the other side, there are the CEE countries, including the Baltic states, that successfully democratized and underwent transition to a market economy; their accomplishments were internationally recognized by inclusion into the Western mainstream (Baldwin 1995; Haerpfer 2002; Pridham 2005; Pridham et al. 1997; Rose and Haerpfer 1995; Schimmelfennig and Sedelmeir 2005). Other countries, like Ukraine or Georgia, although having some brief experience with democratization before, underwent democratic breakthroughs marked by electoral revolutions, but their democracies are not yet consolidated (Åslund and McFaul 2006; D'Anieri 2007b; Flikke 2008; Tudoroiu 2007; Wilson 2006; Zhurzhenko 2005).

26. While revising the manuscript for the publication, I learned that many Belarusian organizations were harassed when Belarusian television identified their links with Polish NGOs. For more information, see http://wiadomosci.ngo.pl/wiadomosci/793519.html.

Chapter 1. Belarus's and Ukraine's Quests for Democracy

1. It should be mentioned that Belarus had a brief independence period in 1918, when, while under German occupation, it first declared independence and formed the Belarusian People's Republic. However, this period did not last long because during the Polish-Soviet War, the territory of Belarus was split between Poland and Soviet Russia.

2. To read more about Belarusian political developments from the beginning of independence, see the works by Hill (2005), Silitski (2003), Specter (1994), and White and Korosteleva (2005).

3. Rudling (2008) divides Belarus's political evolution into three phases: (1) independence, liberalization, and establishment of democratic national institutions (1991–94); (2) conflict between president and parliament, strengthening of the presidential powers, and weakening of democratic institutions and independence (1994–96); and (3) one-man authoritarian rule (since 1997).

4. Hill (2005) reports that in a referendum on the amended version of the constitution, 78 percent of voters supported the idea of a strong president.

5. For more about Lukashenko's rise to power and the sociopolitical roots of authoritarianism in Belarus, see Eke and Kuzio 2000.

6. Applebaum (2010), Englund (2010), and OSCE/ODIHR Election Observation Mission reports (OSCE/ODIHR 2001, 2006) describe events surrounding the elections.

7. Nearly seventeen hundred local governments exist, and there is a three-level hierarchy: regional (*voblasc*), district (*raion*), and village or (in urban areas) township (Silitski 2008).

8. For more information, see reports by the Belarusian Helsinki Committee at http://belhelcom.org/en/node/10181.

9. For more about the repressive Lukashenko regime, see works by Korosteleva (2003), Marples and Padhol (2002), and Lindner (2007).

10. Corruption is widespread in Belarus. Transparency International publishes an annual Corruption Perceptions Index (CPI) and classifies countries according to "the degree to which corruption is perceived to exist among public officials and politicians." Transparency International, http://www.transparency.hu/Corruption_Perceptions_Index. Scores range from 1 to 10, and a higher score means less corruption. Belarus was ranked 123 out of 176 countries surveyed in the Transparency International 2012 Corruption Perceptions Index.

11. The winter of 2006–7 brought the Russia-Belarus energy crisis, with a short-term embargo of oil sales to Belarus in January 2007. The Russian government made a decision to raise energy prices and develop market-based relations with Belarus. The dispute ended with a deal allowing Gazprom, the Russian gas monopoly, to purchase a 50 percent stake in Beltransgaz—the key Belarusian gas distribution and transportation network—in exchange for a five-year-long transition to European-level energy prices for Belarus (Silitski 2008). Lindner (2007) is of the opinion that the days when transactions with Russia were bringing the Belarusian economy huge profits are

gone. Realizing this, in May 2007, the government began to look for some savings by abolishing the wide-scale system of social privileges and subsidies, such as free public transport for students and medical subsidies for pensioners.

12. Paweł Kazanecki, president of the board, East European Democratic Centre (EEDC), interview by author, Warsaw, July 14, 2008.

13. See Freedom House 2008a and Taras 2007.

14. One Polish NGO, the East European Democratic Center, in 2007 issued a report about the status of Belarusian society that contains analysis conducted by Polish and Belarusian scholars and practitioners. In this chapter I relied on works by Dynko (2007), Usau (2007b), Pankaviec (2007), and Šałajeva (2007).

15. Valer Bulhakau, an editor of the journal *Arche* who fled Belarus after politically motivated allegations against him, informed me that there is some Western cultural influence in Belarus. He cited as an example the occasional concerts given by popular music bands.

16. The text of the interview is available at the official website of the president of Belarus, http://president.gov.by/en/.

17. Belarusians show a high degree of russification, and Russian is a preferred tongue for everyday communication (Eke and Kuzio 2000). On the Russian influence in the development of Belarusian culture, see Yekadumaw 2003.

18. For more on Russia's influence in Belarusian politics, see works by Maksymiuk (2003), Rontoyanni (2005), and Wallander (2004).

19. For more about Belarusian identity and Lukashenko's russification attempts, see works by Hill (2005), Ioffe (2003), Jocelyn (1998), Eke and Kuzio (2000), Stent (2007), and Zaprudnik (2003).

20. According to the Central Election and National Referendum Commission of Belarus (1995), referendum results show that 83 percent of people voted to recognize Russian as a second state language; 83 percent supported the idea of modified versions of the Soviet-era flag. However, it is questionable whether this referendum was free and fair.

21. Eke and Kuzio (2000) draw on the definition of Smith (1991, 9), which involves some sense of a political community, some common institutions, a single code of rights and duties, an economic and a social space with clearly demarcated boundaries with which the citizens identify, and on Parekh's (1975, 225) definition, which adds that national identity refers to a "territorially organized community" or "polity." Also, Linz and Stepan (1978, 62–65) refer to national identity as an important factor contributing to democratization, but, at the same time, the authors point out that cultural and linguistic nationalism in multinational states makes the stability of democracy less likely.

22. US president George W. Bush included Belarus in "his "axis of evil," while Secretary of State Condoleezza Rice, in her Senate hearings prior to her confirmation as secretary of state in January 2005, included Belarus as the sole European country among countries such as Cuba, Myanmar, and Zimbabwe in a list of "outposts of tyranny." In her Senate confirmation hearings, Rice said, "To be sure, in our world

there remain outposts of tyranny—and America stands with oppressed people on every continent—in Cuba, and Burma, and North Korea, and Iran, and Belarus, and Zimbabwe" (US Senate Committee 2005). With regard to the "outposts of tyranny," the main concerns are about their potential possession of weapons of mass destruction and support for terrorist organizations. However, with Belarus, the United States seems primarily concerned about the authoritarian rule and lack of human rights. Although relations with Belarus are frosty, it remains one of only two "outposts of tyranny" (along with Zimbabwe) to still maintain official diplomatic relations with the United States.

23. Freedom House rates countries on political rights and civil liberties. The FH rating process is based on a checklist of questions. Freedom House then assigns a numerical rating to each country and territory—on a scale of 1 to 7—for political rights and analogous ratings for civil liberties. A rating of 1 indicates the highest degree of freedom and 7, the lowest level of freedom. Those countries whose ratings average 1.0 to 2.5 are considered free, from 3.0 to 5.0 means partly free, and from 5.5 to 7.0 indicates not free (Freedom House 2009a).

24. Data and reports evaluating countries are available in Freedom in the World, by Freedom House, http://www.freedomhouse.org/report-types/freedom-world.

25. In order to present a well-rounded picture of civil society in Belarus, in this section I relied on both academic analyses as well as practitioners' views, specifically by Buchvostau (2007), Čavusau (2007), Chernov (2008), Conkievich (2002), Ekiert (1996), Gershman and Allen (2006), Gromadzki and Veselý (2006), Howard (2003), Lipskaya (2000), Lindner (2007), Poczobut (2007), Raik (2006), Sannikov and Kuley (2006), Taras (2007), Uładamirski (2007), Usau (2007), Vidanava (2007), Wilde (2002), Zhuchkov (2004), and Żejmis (2003).

26. Information from the Ministry of Justice is available at http://www.minjust.by/struct/ua.htm and http://en.ngo.by/.

27. Grzegorz Gromadzki, director of International Cooperation Program, and Agnieszka Komorowska, coordinator of the Civil Initiatives in Eastern Europe Program, Stefan Batory Foundation, interviews by author, Warsaw, June 12, 2008.

28. Čavusau (2007, 12) reports that KGB chief Ściapan Sucharenka accused the United States of using funds from international and foreign NGOs to form and train special groups for staging street protests in Belarus, and the nonregistered opposition groups Malady Front and Zubr were expected to play leading roles in protests.

29. According to Taras (2007, 59), in 2005, the Ministry of Information closed down newspapers, such as *Navinki* and *Molodyozhny Prospekt.* In 2006, the Belarusian Supreme Economic Court ordered the closure of *Zhoda,* the weekly newspaper of the Belarusian Social Democratic Party. Financial constraints forced other newspapers, such as *Delovaya Gazeta* and *Salidarnaść,* to stop publishing.

30. For a report by the Committee to Protect Journalists, see http://cpj.org/2009/02/attacks-on-the-press-in-2008-belarus.php.

31. On the Belarusian crackdown on the Polish minority that resulted in sanctioning the arrest of ethnic Polish activists and evicting prominent Polish groups,

as well as the reaction of the Polish government and the EU to those events, see Lobjakas 2010.

32. See Komorowska and Kuzawińska 2004; and Gromadzki and Veselỳ 2006.

33. Chernov (2008) reports that sixty-eight and twenty-six organizations were closed down in the wake of court decisions in 2005 and 2007, respectively. (There are no data for 2006.)

34. The "For Freedom" campaign, established by Aleksandr Milinkevich in 2006, united the Belarusian democratic forces and the people of Belarus to work for civil, social, cultural, and other rights. The strategic objectives of the For Freedom movement are free elections, preservation of Belarus as an independent nation, raising the quality of life in Belarus to European standards, and, ultimately, integration of Belarus into the European Union. For more information, see the For Freedom website, http://www.pyx.by/.

35. Sean McCormack, spokesman, US State Department, press statement, Washington, DC, August 16, 2008, http://minsk.usembassy.gov.

36. In December 2007, Lukashenko lifted a requirement for citizens to obtain a travel permit before going abroad, effective from the beginning of 2008. At the same time, the government created a database that was expected to include nearly one hundred thousand people who cannot leave the country (Freedom House 2008a).

37. Marples (2006) poses the question of why the opposition was not united and why another opposition candidate, Kazulin, decided to oppose Milinkevich. Was his decision made because of party loyalty, personal ambitions, or rivalries with other opposition candidates? It also remains debatable whether Kazulin's campaign helped or hindered that of Milinkevich. Marples (2006) argues that because the election was held much earlier than anticipated, opposition forces lacked sufficient time to prepare to campaign, visit all areas of the country, and unite. He also gives credit to Kazulin for his bravery and to Milinkevich for his growing confidence and the way in which he managed to attract large crowds despite working in exceedingly difficult conditions.

38. Recent developments in the Belarusian opposition, as reported by the ForBelarus.eu (2009) Internet portal, demonstrate that divisions in opposition went even further.

39. Observing different outcomes of transition from communist rule, scholars find that some countries were influenced by communist legacies more than others (Bunce 1999; Crawford and Lijphart 1995, 179; Crawford and Lijphart 1997; D'Anieri 2007b; Geddes 1995; Hanson 1995; Jowitt 1992; Kubicek 2000; Linz and Stepan 1996; McDaniel 1996; van Zon 2005a). Hanson (1995) calls the legacy of communism the "Leninist legacy," and the term refers to a common ideology hostile to capitalism and democracy; the Communist Party as an economic, political, and social monopoly; the political culture; social structure; and institutions created under communism that have influenced the choices made by postcommunist leaders.

40. Scholars who have analyzed Kuchma's rise to power and his presidency include D'Anieri (2007b), Fritz (2007), Harasymiw (2002), Kuzio (1997), Markov (1993), Protsyk (2004), Wilson (2002), Wolczuk (2002), and Zimmer (2006).

41. According to the Constitution (Constitution of Ukraine 1996, art. CVI), the president is the head of state, with the cabinet of ministers subordinated under him as the highest executive body. An essential reinforcement of the president's position was the establishment of "vertical power" reaching down to the oblast and local levels. Other significant features of the constitution included the following provisions: the president appoints a prime minister following his approval by the parliament; the president appoints members of the cabinet of ministers and chairs of local state administrations; the president dissolves the legislature; the parliament can override a presidential veto by a two-thirds majority, and it can hold a vote of no confidence in the cabinet of ministers by a simple majority. Whereas legislative authority was meant to remain with the unicameral parliament, according to the Constitution, the president had the right to issue economic decrees approved by the prime minister for a three-year period (Constitution of Ukraine 1996, chap. XV).

42. Similar statements about Kuchma's "linkages" have been made by Åslund (2006), Bondarenko (2002), Fritz (2007), Way (2005a), Whitmore (2005), and Wilson (2006). Zimmer (2006) and van Zon (2001) argue that Ukraine under Kuchma developed into a neo-patrimonial state, with the ruler using public administration for his own interests and political and economic elites subordinated to him. In such a system, elites were in constant competition and conflict with one another, and their recruitment for public offices that offered access to resources and opportunities for rent-seeking depended on personal loyalty based on fear and rewards (Zimmer 2006, 282–87). Relations based on authority, domination, material incentives, and rewards resembled the Soviet style of politics and confirmed that the "communist legacy" in Ukraine had been preserved (Kitschelt 2003).

43. For example, in 2002, Kuchma appointed Viktor Medvedchuk, chair of the Socialist Democratic Party of Ukraine (SDPU) and business oligarch, as head of the presidential administration in order to increase government control over media. Evidence demonstrating Kuchma's ability to manipulate the oligarchic group was apparent when transcripts of secret tapes recorded by a security guard in the presidential office were published (Zimmer 2006, 286). This incident revealed Kuchma's role behind fraud in the 1999 presidential elections (Fritz 2007, 147; Wilson 2006, 51–56). See also the book by Kubicek (2000), who examines emerging business confederations in post-Soviet Ukraine and their ties to the state.

44. See Levitsky and Way 2002; Way 2005a, 131.

45. D'Anieri (2007b), Fritz (2007), Kuzio (2000a), Nahaylo (1999), Wilson (2006), and Zimmer (2006) called Ukraine a "hybrid regime." "Hybrid regimes" have some attributes of democratic political life (e.g., regular elections and democratic constitutions) but suffer from serious democratic deficits, including poor representation of citizens' interests, low levels of political participation beyond voting, frequent abuse of the law by government officials, elections of uncertain legitimacy, very low levels of public confidence in state institutions, and so forth. There are different expressions for such regimes, including "semi-democracies," "formal democracies," "electoral democracies," "pseudodemocracies," "weak democracies," and

"partial democracies," but the most popular is "semi-authoritarian countries." For more on such regimes, see Carothers 2002; Diamond 2002; Epstein et al. 2006; O'Donnell and Schmitter 1986; and Ottaway 2003.

46. For three months in 2001 street demonstrations occurred in Kiev under the banner "Ukraine without Kuchma." These were the first mass democratic demonstrations in Ukraine since independence. These scandals also divided the presidential "coalition," and Kuchma's position was seriously weakened (Fritz 2007, 147; Karatnycky 2006).

47. Åslund and McFaul (2006), Kuzio (2006), and Wilson (2006) have also expressed this view.

48. Yushchenko's pre-election campaign was hindered first by controlled media, which nearly excluded him from coverage, and then by dioxin poisoning, which severely weakened the candidate's health and disfigured his face (Way 2005a, 131–32; Wilson 2006, 96). Emerson (2007, 220) argues that Yushchenko's position was even enhanced when it became clear that he had been poisoned during a dinner with the director of the Ukrainian Security Service.

49. In the first round of the election, with a very close vote, Yanukovych was declared the winner. However, since neither candidate received 50 percent of the returns, the second round was scheduled for three weeks later. In the run-off election, held on November 21, exit polls predicted a Yushchenko victory, but the Central Election Commission declared Yanukovych the victor with 49.5 percent of the vote, compared with Yushchenko's 46.6 percent (Central Election Commission 2004a). Given that the third-place candidate from the first round (Moroz) had explicitly endorsed Yushchenko, these results were hard to believe. Observers (Ukrainian and international, including the OSCE) reported fraud in the second round of the election.

50. See Tudoroiu 2007 and Fritz 2007 for descriptions of the events surrounding the Orange Revolution.

51. For more about the situation of civil society and its role during the Orange Revolution, see the works by Åslund and McFaul (2006), Demes and Forbrig (2006), Diuk (2006), Kuzio (2006), Way (2005a), Wilson (2006), and van Zon (2005b).

52. The Pora campaign officially closed at the end of January 2005 but has its successors. One of them is the Pora political party, officially registered on June 1, 2005 (Demes and Forbrig 2006, 99).

53. Jan Fedirko, program coordinator, Foundation for Young Democracy, interview by author, Lublin, June 6, 2008.

54. For more about the role of the international community and its support for civil society in Ukraine, see the works by Åslund and McFaul (2006), McFaul (2007), Ledsky (2005), Kuzio (2005b), and Sushko and Prystayko (2006).

55. For example, under Ukrainian law, a newly formed parliamentary coalition must decide on a candidate for prime minister and submit the nomination to the president for consideration. However, the parliamentary majority ignored this provision knowing that, even if Yushchenko decided to ask the government to resign, he would not have enough votes in parliament.

56. The vote, which international observers described as an "impressive display of democratic election," gave Yanukovych a 3.48 percent lead over his rival, Prime Minister Yulia Tymoshenko (Central Election Commission of Ukraine 2010; Galpin 2010; Marson 2010).

57. Feifer (2010) reports on the election of Yanukovych.

58. The analysis of the collapse of the "Orange" forces in Ukraine by D'Anieri (2011) mentions this erosion of competition as one of the factors undermining consolidation of power in Ukraine and other post-Soviet societies.

59. Local governance in Ukraine has a four-level administrative structure. Ukraine is divided into twenty-four regions known as oblasts, the Autonomous Republic of Crimea, and cities with oblast status (Kiev and Sevastopol). Each region is divided into between eleven and twenty-seven districts (known as raions) and cities with raion status. The districts are divided into towns and villages (Zimmer 2006, 293–94).

60. Emerson (2007) and *Economist* articles (2005, 2008) provide some discussion about the economic situation in Ukraine.

61. See Transparency International's assessment, "Fighting Corruption in Ukraine: A Serious Challenge," http://www.transparency.org/news/feature/fighting_corruption_in_ukraine_a_serious_challenge.

62. Sindelar (2012) reports some of the cases on Radio Free Europe/Radio Liberty.

63. See detailed discussion in Harmash 2005 and Maksymiuk 2005b.

64. Jan Piekło, director, PAUCI, interview by author, Warsaw, June 30, 2008. At a NATO summit in Bucharest in 2008, Russian president Vladimir Putin told US president George W. Bush, "You understand, George, that Ukraine is not even a state!" (*Economist* 2009).

65. In 2005–6 the Russian energy monopoly Gazprom decreased gas deliveries to Ukraine after negotiators failed to resolve a price dispute. The move caused drastic shortfalls in Europe, which gets about one-fifth of its supplies from Russia via Ukraine (RFE/RL Newsline 2006).

66. See articles by D'Anieri (2011) and Colton (2011).

67. Fedirko interview.

68. Piekło interview.

69. Paweł Kazanecki, president of the board, East European Democratic Centre (EEDC), interview by author, Warsaw, July 14, 2008; Fedirko interview.

70. Piekło interview; also Wilson 2006.

71. Fedirko interview.

72. Artur Radziwiłł, vice president of the board, Center for Social and Economic Research (CASE), interview by author, Warsaw, July 1, 2008. Anders Åslund, of the Institute of International Economics in Washington and a member of the advisory council of the Center for Social and Economic Research (CASE), Warsaw, also argues that the emergence of oligarchs can be a positive element in economic development, because oligarchs have conflicting interests and are stimulators of democracy. See, for example, Åslund 2005.

73. See, for example, Whitmore 2005.

74. Scholars exploring the concept of "quality of democracy" include Diamond and Morlino (2005), for example.

75. Several scholars argue that regional division has the greatest salience in Ukrainian politics; see works by Colton (2011), D'Anieri (2011), Laverty (2008), Osipian and Osipian (2012), and Way (2012).

76. Paweł Bobołowicz, president of the board, Foundation for Young Democracy, interview by author, Lublin, June 6, 2008.

77. Some electoral studies suggest that Ukraine has more than two geographic and cultural subdivisions. Birch (2000) distinguishes five distinct regions in Ukraine.

78. For earlier discussions about regionalism in Ukraine, see D'Anieri 2007a; Barrington 2002; Barrington and Herron 2004; Hesli et al. 1998; Kuzio 2006; Osipian and Osipian 2006; Shulman 2005; Wilson 2006; and van Zon 2005b.

79. Several thousand people protested in Kiev against President Viktor Yushchenko's threat to dissolve the parliament, which was controlled by a pro-Russian coalition (Agence France Presse 2007). The gatherings on the Maidan in 2007 were not the work of spontaneous, self-organized civil society, as had been the case in 2004. Rather, they were the product of a civil society funded and managed by Prime Minister Viktor Yanukovych's Party of Regions through the use of so-called "political tourism" (Kuzio 2007a). The website maidan.org.ua reprinted information distributed in eastern Ukraine, offering the opportunity to undertake paid political tourism in Kiev (Kuzio 2007a). Residents of Kharkiv were offered a full day's "pay" of 150 hryvni (thirty dollars). Students in Poltava were offered 80 hryvni (without food) or 50 (with food) to go to Kiev (Kuzio 2007a). Senior political tourists obtained between 100 and 150 hryvni per day, while students in general were offered 90. Political tourists were not necessarily committed Party of Regions supporters. The Parliamentary Assembly of the Council of Europe's experts on Ukraine have pointed out that the "blue Maidan" demonstrations in downtown Kiev were incompatible with democracy (Kuzio 2007a). However, at the same time, pro-Yushchenko supporters rallied in favor of early elections, and this action seemed to be artificially managed as well (Agence France Presse 2007; Kuzio 2007a).

80. Osipian and Osipian (2012, 636) summarize this situation well: "People of the West and the Center see the South-east as an agent of Russia or the empire that intends to swallow Ukraine and convert Ukrainians into Russians. People of the South-east believe that the Center, and especially the West, of Ukraine want to enter NATO and, in doing this, break the old ties with Russia and forcefully ukrainize the people of the South-east. That is why all national elections—presidential and parliamentary— turn into an apocalyptic confrontation of 'us' versus 'them,' an absolute good against an absolute evil." See also Colton's (2011) analysis of regional voting patterns in 2010 and raw data on the website of Central Election Commission of Ukraine, http://www .cvk.gov.ua.

Chapter 2. Polish Governmental Aid Programs

1. ODA is the sum of donations and loans given to developing countries by official government institutions of donor countries or by international organizations. The

aid is intended to support economic and political progress in recipient countries. Postcommunist countries are categorized as non-Development Assistance Committee (DAC) OECD countries. OECD data are available at http://www.oecd-ilibrary.org/ statistics.

2. OECD Statistics, ODA by donor, data extracted from http://stats.oecd.org/, October 4, 2012.

3. Author's calculations based on the OECD Statistics and World Development Indicators (WDI) compiled by the World Bank. According to the WDI, Polish GDP (in current US$) was nearly $470 billion in 2009 (data extracted on October 4, 2012).

4. The official documents regarding Polish foreign assistance include "The Strategy for Poland's Development Cooperation," adopted by the Polish Council of Ministers in 2003, as well as documents produced annually by the Polish Ministry of Foreign Affairs (MFA).

5. For more information on the Millennium Development Goals, see the UN Millennium Declaration, http://www.un.org/millennium/declaration/ ares552e.pdf. For the full text of the Paris Declaration, see http://www.oecd.org/ dataoecd/11/41/34428351.pdf.

6. For more information on the European Consensus, see http://europa.eu/ scadplus/leg/en/lvb/r12544.htm.

7. In 2005, the Council of the European Union set the level of assistance to the GDP ratio for the old and new EU members. For the old EU members, this ratio is 0.51 percent by 2010 and 0.7 percent by 2015 (Polish Ministry of Foreign Affairs 2006, 20).

8. Mirosław Sycz, vice-director, and Agata Czaplinska, head of the Implementation of Development Assistance Program, Development Cooperation Department, Polish Ministry of Foreign Affairs (MFA), interview by author, Warsaw, June 27, 2008.

9. Ibid.

10. Other governmental bodies that have dealt with aid provision are primarily the Ministry of Science and Higher Education and the Ministry of Finance. The Ministry of Finance grants reduction and conversion of debts, preferential loans, and the like, as well as making transfer payments to international financial institutions in which Poland has membership. Poland provides preferential loans, which, according to the norms of the OECD Development Assistance Committee, are loans that contain a donation amounting to at least 25 percent of the total loan, debt relief to developing countries and those democratizing, and contributions to international financial institutions. Polish loans are provided mainly for environmental, educational, and health projects, as well as for modernization of infrastructure, agriculture, and public transportation. In 2007, Polish financial aid recipients were China, Montenegro, Uzbekistan, Nicaragua, and the International Development Association (IDA) within the World Bank (Polish Ministry of Foreign Affairs 2007a).The Ministry of Science and Higher Education, however, focuses on educational aid in the form of scholarships and internships. Of all types of Polish assistance, scholarships offered to international students have the longest tradition. Citizens of recipient countries receive funds from the Polish government to complete undergraduate, graduate, and postdoctoral

programs at Polish universities. The biggest group of recipients comprises citizens from Belarus, Ukraine, Albania, Moldova, Afghanistan, and Macedonia. Also, other government agencies involved, to lesser extent, in aid provision include the Ministry of National Education (MNE), the Office of the Committee for European Integration, the Ministry of Economy, the Ministry of Culture and National Heritage, the Ministry of Interior and Administration, the Ministry of Agriculture and Rural Development, the Ministry of National Defense, the Ministry of Construction, the Ministry of the Environment, the Ministry of Health, and the Ministry of Labor and Social Policy. However, it should be noted that since 2011, when the Solidarity Fund PL was reconstructed, many of these governmental bodies have delegated their tasks to this fund.

11. For more about the Solidarity Fund PL's programs, see its website, http://solidarityfund.pl/en/fundacja1/o-fundacji.

12. The financial resources that the MFA receives come from a special portion of the Polish budget, called the Implementation of the Polish Program for Global Development and Support for International Cooperation for Democracy and Civil Society. According to the Polish Constitution (1997), chapter 10, article CCXXIV, the Cabinet (the Council of Ministers) prepares a draft state budget, supervises its implementation, passes a resolution on the closing of the state's accounts, and prepares a report on the implementation of the budget. The parliament's lower chamber (the Sejm) adopts the state budget for the fiscal year by means of a budget act (the budget law is also subject to consideration by the senate). Announcement of the budget act requires the signature of the president, who may refuse to sign the bill and instead send it for examination by the Constitutional Court.

13. Sycz and Czaplinska interview.

14. Ibid.

15. The aim of Visegrad 4 Eastern Partnership Program (V4EaP) was to enhance cooperation between the Visegrad region and the countries of the Eastern Partnership—Armenia, Azerbaijan, Belarus, Georgia, Moldova, and Ukraine. The idea was to share experience with social and economic transformation and democratization through the development of civil society and cooperation among local governments, academia, and individual citizens. For more information about this program, see the Visegrad Fund's website at http://visegradfund.org/v4eap/.

16. President Lech Kaczynski, speech to the UN General Assembly 2006, "May Our Efforts Be Inspired by Solidarity," http://www.president.pl/x.node?id=6042877.

17. A similar statement may be found on the Polish MFA's website, http://www.polskapomoc.gov.pl/Why,We,Provide,Assistance,204.html.

18. The article (Hanrahan 2009) further reports that the Poles are proud of two things: that they started the 1989 revolutions and that, instead of receiving international aid, they are now strong enough to donate it.

19. The year 2006 was established by the Polish parliament as the year of Jerzy Giedroyc. Thus, there were many exhibitions and publications devoted to his person in 2006. One of the sources that discusses Giedroyc's view on eastern foreign policy is

available at the official website of Poland's former president, Aleksander Kwaśniewski, http://www.kwasniewskialeksander.pl/int.php?mode=view&id=2207.

20. Geremek was the social historian and politician who in August 1980 joined the Gdańsk workers' protest movement and became one of the advisers of Solidarity, working closely with Lech Wałęsa. Later, Geremek prepared proposals for peaceful democratic transformation in Poland, and, in 1989, he played a crucial role during the debates between Solidarity and the authorities. Geremek referred to Giedroyc's impact on the shape of Polish foreign policy in his speech at the Polish Institute of International Affairs on November 28, 2000. The text (in Polish) is available at http://www.pism.pl/files/cykl/cykl%20I_Geremek.pdf.

21. For example, the Lomé IV Agreement of 1989 between the EU and the ACP countries can serve as an example.

22. Joanna Rohozińska, National Endowment for Democracy, interview by author, Washington, DC, November 20, 2008.

23. At the 1993 Copenhagen summit, the European Union put into words "the model of European democracy," which comprised the only points of reference for postcommunist Europe. In order to be considered for membership, states must have achieved "stability of institutions guaranteeing democracy, the rule of law, human rights and the respect for and protection of minorities." Moreover, since the regimes that were being dismantled in Central and Eastern Europe were very different in structure from the authoritarian regimes in southern Europe, candidate countries, in addition to fulfilling the political criteria, must have achieved "the existence of a functioning market economy." Thus, the transition to a market economy was viewed as an integral component of democratization (European Commission: Enlargement 2009). This definition of democracy is now incorporated in the Treaty of Nice that entered into force on February 1, 2003 (European Commission: Treaty of Nice 2002).

24. The European Neighborhood Policy applies to the EU's immediate neighbors by land or sea, namely Algeria, Armenia, Azerbaijan, Belarus, Egypt, Georgia, Israel, Jordan, Lebanon, Libya, Moldova, Morocco, the Occupied Palestinian Territory, Syria, Tunisia, and Ukraine. Although Russia is also a neighbor of the EU, relations are instead developed through a strategic partnership covering four "common spaces" (European Commission: ENP 2009).

25. Earlier, EU assistance was provided through TACIS to focus on humanitarian aid and activities related to the effects of the Chernobyl nuclear disaster. Aid strategies included humanitarian aid in the form of baby food and medicines or vacations abroad for thousands of children living in the Chernobyl radiation zones. Almost 70 percent of the radioactive fallout emitted in the Chernobyl explosion on April 26, 1986, fell on the territory of Belarus (Hill 2005).

26. On November 21, 2006, Benita Ferrero-Waldner, the European commissioner for external relations and ENP, launched a document entitled "What the European Union Could Bring to Belarus," which offers a strategy for what the people of Belarus might gain from joining the ENP process, if the Belarusian government engages in democratization and respect for human rights and rule of law (European Commission: External Relations 2006).

27. The EU finds it difficult to address the erosion of democracy under Lukashenko, and the scale, scope, and impact of EU support have been very limited. The fact is that the EU deals only with the Belarusian government. Since Lukashenko consolidated his authoritarian regime, actions taken by the EU toward Belarus have been exclusively in response to the actions taken by Lukashenko. This type of policy can be described as reactive. The EU has condemned Belarusian authorities for the authoritarian methods used toward the political opposition, media, and civil society and has demonstrated its disapproval using different restrictive measures. The EU rejected recognition of Lukashenko's unconstitutional actions. In 1997, along with the decision of the Council of Europe to suspend the guest status of Belarus, the European Union suspended high-level political contacts and the continuation of the ratification of the Partnership for Cooperation Agreement (PCA) with Belarus, signed in 1995 (Wieck 2002, 372). With a few exceptions, the EU did not renew technical assistance programs in the humanitarian, social, and democratization fields. Moreover, the EU, as a whole, introduced sanctions against the Belarusian authorities—among others, the visa ban against the highest political officials. Also, the EU froze all funds and economic resources of persons who were responsible for violations of international electoral standards and the crackdown on civil society during and after the 2006 presidential elections (Council of the European Union 2006a).

In December 2006, in response to violations of civil and trade union rights, the EU authorized the exclusion of Belarus from its Generalized System of Preferences (GSP) (Lindner 2007). Taking some liberalizing measures in the first half of 2007 to regain trade preference status, Lukashenko emphasized that the government acted in the interest of the economy first and that the Belarusian government did not intend to make any real political changes. Once the EU made it clear that, without a complete cessation of political repression, no compromise on GSP was possible, the Belarusian government fully resumed its previous practices (Belarusian Institute for Strategic Studies 2007). To date, the policy of restricted relations over the years in protest against the lack of democratization and economic reform in Belarus has not produced the serious moves toward reform and cooperation desired by the EU (Dumasy 2003).

In addition to restrictive measures aimed at the Belarusian government, the EU has taken some other actions that harm Belarusians and hamper EU democracy assistance efforts in Belarus. Charging sixty euros for a single entry visa certainly sends the wrong signal to Belarusian citizens (Lindner 2007, 71). The cost of the visa makes it is harder for Belarusians to enter the European Union, to travel to meet people, to participate in conferences. If it is harder to get in touch with the EU and its people, it is less likely that the legitimacy of the Belarusian regime will be weakened in the eyes of Belarusians; at the same time, the EU efforts to encourage democratization are questioned (Lindner 2007).

28. More information on the European Partnership for Democracy is available at its website, http://www.eupd.eu.

29. The US Congress passed the bill unanimously on October 4, 2004, and President George W. Bush signed it into law on October 20.

30. The USAID has been the principal independent US federal government

agency to provide assistance to countries recovering from disaster, trying to improve their economic situations, and engaging in democratic reforms. The organization spends less than one-half of 1 percent of the federal budget for assistance to five regions of the world—sub-Saharan Africa, Asia, Latin America and the Caribbean, Europe and Eurasia, and the Middle East. USAID works in such areas as agriculture, democracy and governance, economic growth, the environment, education, health, global partnerships, and humanitarian assistance. According to the agency financial report for 2007, the USAID spent $1.3 billion on programs aimed at strengthening democratic institutions, such as parliaments, judiciaries, and political parties (USAID 2007, 13). The objectives of investing in people (education) and economic growth represent the largest investments, at 32.6 percent and 32.3 percent of the net cost of operations, respectively. The agency invested 14 percent of its net cost of operations in the democracy and governance objective, compared to 14.9 percent on humanitarian assistance. Thus, the USAID technical assistance aimed at democracy promotion is a small fraction of the total amount of aid provided.

31. Rodger Potocki, director, Europe and Eurasia Region, National Endowment for Democracy, interview by author, Washington, DC, November 20, 2008.

32. Ibid.

33. See, for example, McFaul 2005.

34. Narozhna's (2004) findings refer to the USAID, the Canadian International Development Agency (CIDA), and the EU/EC program in Ukraine.

35. These partners receive MFA funds through a procedure that begins with a call for proposals, organized since 2004 for NGOs, since 2005 for central administration entities, and since 2006 for local institutions. Assistance initiatives are also undertaken by Polish embassies through the Small Grants Fund.

36. The administrative division of Poland since 1999 has been based on three levels of subordination. The territory of Poland is divided into voivodeships (provinces); these are further divided into *powiat*s (counties), and these in turn are divided into *gmina*s (communes or municipalities). In 2012, Poland had 16 voivodeships, 379 powiats (including 65 cities with powiat status), and 2,478 gminas.

37. Some examples of Polish applicants include the Oil and Gas Institute, Department of Geology and Geological Concessions in the Ministry of the Environment, Polish National Police, Agricultural Market Agency, and the Polish Agency for Enterprise Development.

38. Sycz and Czaplinska interview.

39. A list of Polish organizations, funding amounts, and descriptions of projects that were granted with the governmental support in 2010 is available at the website of Polish Aid, http://www.polskapomoc.gov.pl.

40. Sycz and Czaplinska interview.

41. Paweł Bobołowicz, president of the board, Foundation for Young Democracy, interview by author, Lublin, June 6, 2008.

42. Sycz and Czaplinska interview.

43. Such an argument corresponds with scholars' analyses of Belarusian national

identity (Eke and Kuzio 2000; Ioffe 2003; Jocelyn 1998). Eke and Kuzio (2000), in their analysis of failures of democratization in Belarus, point to lack of national identity as a factor that prevents Belarus from having democracy. Jocelyn (1998, 73, 81) argues that in Belarus "national consciousness is a highly problematic concept" and adds that "Belarusian national identity is fragmented, and its roots lead in different directions." Throughout the history of Belarus, there were many efforts to destroy Belarusian society, its sense of statehood, and cultures; as a result, no single Belarusian identity has ever had a chance to develop (Ioffe 2003). During the Soviet period, while there was a strong Ukrainian identity, the Byelorussian Soviet Socialist Republic had a much weaker nationalist identity and thus was less prepared for independence than Ukraine (Stent 2007).

44. There is unlimited access to accurate information about Belarusian history, literature, and the social and political situation in Belarus. All publications are provided in the Belarusian language. In the second half of 2007, the Kamunikat.org website was viewed an average of seventeen thousand times a month—a fact that speaks to its popularity (Polish Ministry of Foreign Affairs 2007a).

45. Konstanty Kalinowski was the leader of the January Uprising of 1863 in the lands of the former Grand Duchy of Lithuania. He also promoted the good traditions of democracy, tolerance, and freedom of the Polish-Lithuanian Commonwealth and opposed national oppression of cultures dominated by imperial Russia. For more information, see Kordowicz 1955 or http://www.belarusguide.com/culture1/people/Kastus.html.

46. In July 2006, I had the opportunity to meet some of the Belarusian students accepted for the first year of the program during the Warsaw East European Conference organized by the Center for East European Studies at Warsaw University.

47. *Gazeta Wyborcza* has anticommunist roots and was an outcome of the Polish Roundtable Agreement. Its founders were political opponents affiliated with the Solidarity movement. The newspaper began publication on May 8, 1989, under the motto, "Nie ma wolności bez Solidarności" (There's no freedom without Solidarity). The newspaper was to serve as the voice of Solidarity during the run-up to semi-free elections to be held June 4, 1989 (hence its title). The newspaper's editor-in-chief since its founding has been Adam Michnik—a leading organizer of the illegal democratic opposition in Poland (http://wyborcza.pl/0,80370.html).

48. For information about the project, see the Polish Robert Schuman Foundation's website, http://www.schuman.org.pl/modules.php?name=Content&pa=showpage&pid=667.

49. For information about the project, see the Center for Social and Economic Research website, http://www.case.com.pl/strona—ID-ukraina,nlang-710.html.

50. Ibid.

51. Paweł Kucharczyk, president of the executive board, Institute of Public Affairs (IPA), interview by author, Warsaw, June 30, 2008.

52. The expression "democratic deficit" is used in the EU literature to refer to the legitimacy problems of international institutions, like the EU, which by design are

not directly accountable to the voters or their elective representatives (Majone 1998; Moravcsik 2004). Here, the usage *democratic deficit* encompasses Carothers's (2002) conceptualization of democratic deficit and other weaknesses of Ukraine's political system, such as the Ukrainian democratic government's lack of capacity to work with effectiveness, frequent abuse of the law by government officials, rent-seeking, low levels of public confidence in state institutions, and so forth.

53. There are many arguments in the literature demonstrating the merits of local government. John Stuart Mill denoted the limits of central government and suggested that accountability can be improved by increasing the autonomy of local elected governments. Beetham (1996) demonstrates that local governments score more highly than central government on accountability, responsiveness, and representativeness. Andrew and Goldsmith (1998, 110) point out that questions of freedom of speech, democratic governance, and nondiscrimination are all areas of political rights in which local governments have important opportunities for action. Other scholars provide connections between local government and effectiveness of governing and exercise of local choices (Sharpe 1988; Stewart 1983). Some scholars perceive decentralization as a way of checking the centralized state, which had discredited itself in the eyes of citizens through rent-seeking, corruption, and other abuses of power (Ostrom et al. 1993).

54. See also Linz and Stepan 1996.

55. The generic form of this thesis is associated with Lipset's (1959) work, and it has been shared and developed by others, such as Rueschemeyer et al. (1992), Huber et al. (1993), Boix and Stokes (2003), and Epstein et al. (2006), who have maintained that economic development facilitates democratization. However, the effect is far from linear, and the argument runs as follows: in societies with higher levels of economic wealth, people become more educated (the middle class increases) and tend to generate trust, tolerance, and participation, thus pushing for civil liberties and democratic governance.

56. Whereas recent empirical research shows mixed results, many studies on democratization find it important to control for economic development. Political scientists' findings vary as to whether economic growth leads to democracy or vice versa and how to operationalize economic development.

57. The visa issue was also mentioned in the Fedirko interview.

58. In the EPD's board of directors are many prominent activists and scholars associated with Central and Eastern Europe who played an important role in establishing this initiative; they include Jacques Rupnik, Jacek Kucharczyk, and Martin Bútora. For more information about EPD, see http://www.eupd.eu/.

59. For scholarly work on the Eastern Partnership, see, for example, Korosteleva 2011.

60. The summit was attended by European Commission president Manuel Barroso, EU foreign policy chief Catherine Ashton, European Parliament president Jerzy Buzek, European Council president Herman Van Rompuy, German chancellor Angela Merkel, French prime minister François Fillon, and Ukrainian president Viktor Yanukovych.

61. Jan Andrzej Dąbrowski, president of the board, College of Eastern Europe, interview by author, Wrocław, June 18, 2008.

62. Magda Dębkowska, director, East European Democratic Centre (EEDC), interview by author, Warsaw, June 5, 2008.

63. The Parliamentary Assembly of the Council of Europe investigates, recommends, and advises many European institutions on a wide range of issues significant in the European political context. It meets in Strasbourg. See the PACE website, http://assembly.coe.int/Main.asp?link=/Sessions/PreviousSessions_e.htm.

64. Andrzej Bobiński, program coordinator, Center for International Relations (CIR), interview by author, Warsaw, July 15, 2008.

65. Grzegorz Gromadzki, director of the International Cooperation Program, and Agnieszka Komorowska, coordinator of the Civil Initiatives in Eastern Europe Program, Stefan Batory Foundation, interview by author, Warsaw, June 12, 2008.

Chapter 3. The Solidarity Movement's Lasting Legacy

1. Although the majority of the Polish UN Associations' activities were financed by the state, the local branches could have their own fund-raising activities, which, later in the 1980s, allowed for their independence from the central budget. The associations gave priority to issues such as security and cooperation in Europe, human rights, UN peacekeeping operations and their Polish contingent, and the growing problem of environmental protection in the heavily polluted areas of the Silesia region (Fryzowska 1995).

2. Other civil society groups included social, scientific, and cultural organizations, such as the Center for Documentation and Analysis (CDiA) and the Social Committee for Science (SKN); farmers' organizations, such as Solidarność Wiejska and the All-Poland Farmers' Resistance Committee (OKOR); and political groups and other organizations concerned with national self-determination, such as the Confederation for an Independent Poland (KPN) and the Committee for National Self-Determination (KPSN).

3. For more on the emergence and the fate of the Solidarity movement in subsequent years, see Ash 2002.

4. On the Soviet interventions in Hungary and Czechoslovakia, see, for example, Volkogonov 1998. The issue of the possible military intervention of the Soviet Union is disputed among some researchers and political elites in Poland. For example, according to Kamiński's (2007) research, General Jaruzelski had asked Moscow to intervene, but his request was rejected by the Political Bureau of the Central Committee of the Communist Party of the Soviet Union at the beginning of December 1981.

5. The Independent Students' Association was formed in October 1980, in the aftermath of the antigovernment strike actions. During the life of Solidarity, the NZS was its student suborganization.

6. Some of these improvements could be attributed to the fact that Poland was a signatory of the Helsinki Final Act 1975. The Commission on Security and Cooperation in Europe is also known as the US Helsinki Commission.

7. Moreover, the Act on Foundations of 1984 was implemented, permitting some Polish foundations to work independently, but the majority were still controlled by the government. It should be stressed, however, that this step was the first attempt in the region since World War II to allow the legal existence of nonprofit institutions. This act was in some ways quite liberal because a foundation could be created only by two people. In other ways, however, the legislation was still strict, because the establishment of the foundation required approval and the supervision of an appropriate government ministry. In 1991, the Polish law on foundations was amended to remove the requirement of prior ministry approval. The same law is in force today, with only few changes (Rymsza 2007).

8. Poland's transformation process resulted from the combined actions (e.g., negotiations and agreements) of the government and opposition groups; hence, the change is called a "pacted transition" (Huntington 1991, 615; Ekiert 2003, 90; Osiatynski 1996). The negotiations were conducted in three groups: economy and social policy, political reforms, and trade unions' pluralism.

9. All seats in the newly created Senate were to be elected democratically, as were 161 seats (35 percent of the total) in the Sejm. The remaining 65 percent of seats in the Sejm were guaranteed for the ruling Polish Communist Party (PZPR) (Ćwiek-Karpowicz and Kaczyński 2006, 27; Osiatynski 1996, 44–47). In the election of June 4, 1989, Solidarity won 99 percent of all the seats in the Senate and all of the 35 percent electorally determined seats in the Sejm. Although the elections were not entirely democratic, they paved the way for creation of Tadeusz Mazowiecki's cabinet and a peaceful transition to democracy, which was confirmed after the first truly free parliamentary election, in 1991. The 65/35 percent division was officially abolished.

10. After the Roundtable Talks and the June 1989 election, the Communist Party fell like a "house of cards," and a new party, Social-Democracy of the Republic of Poland, was formed in January 1990. Most of the old leaders did not join the new party, and new leaders were mostly people politically shaped in the 1980s and directly engaged in the Roundtable negotiations. Since 1989, Solidarity has become a more traditional trade union. Solidarity also played an important pro-transformational role: the organization performed an important political function in serving as a base of social support for right-center political parties.

11. Klon/Jawor Association is a nongovernmental organization that supports the Polish third sector by collecting and disseminating information. It also offers a communication platform for organizations. For more data, see the Klon/Jawor database, http://klon.org.pl. This website is a good source of information about the third sector in Poland. The Klon/Jawor Association also is an operator of the databank on nongovernmental organizations in Poland.

12. In 1983 and 1984, the AFL-CIO channeled about US$200,000 each year to Solidarity, and $300,000 in both 1985 and 1986 (Friszke 2006, 110).

13. The great majority of Polish third-sector organizations were established on the basis of the Associations Law of 1989, passed under the Solidarity government.

14. Most of the large multinational institutions in the West, such as the

International Monetary Fund, the World Bank, and the European Bank for Reconstruction and Development, focused the majority of their resources on macroeconomic stabilization policies in the region (Siegel and Yancey 1992). These resources consisted of credits, loans, and technical support to facilitate macroeconomic changes, and only a very small percentage of this aid went for democracy assistance in CEE countries.

15. For more information about the PHARE program, see http://europa.eu/ legislation_summaries/enlargement/2004_and_2007_enlargement/e50004_en.htm.

16. For more information about the Department for International Development's program, see http://www.dfid.gov.uk/funding/khf.asp.

17. The 1989 Support for East European Democracy (SEED) act reads, "The President should ensure that the assistance provided to Eastern European countries pursuant to this Act is designed: (1) to contribute to the development of democratic institutions and pluralism characterized by: (a) the establishment of fully democratic and representative political systems based on free and fair elections, (b) effective recognition of fundamental liberties and individual freedoms, including freedom of speech, religion, and association, (c) termination of all laws and regulations which impede the operation of a free press and the formation of political parties, (d) creation of an independent judiciary, and (e) establishment of non-partisan military, security, and polices forces" (SEED 1989).

18. Renata Koźlicka-Glińska, of the Polish-American Freedom Foundation (PAFF) and one of the interviewees for this study, used to work in the delegation's office in Brussels before taking a position with PAFF.

19. The first reform took place in 1990 and resulted in the creation of *gminy* (municipalities). The final stage of reform came into force on January 1, 1999, and introduced the three-level hierarchy of territorial divisions. The reform was designed to build local government, increase authorities' activities in the region, and bring them closer to the citizens.

20. Katarzyna Morawska, project specialist in the management office, Foundation in Support of Local Democracy (FSLD), interview by author, Warsaw, June 5, 2008. The foundation was established by oppositionists and former members of the Lech Wałęsa Civic Committee who were deeply engaged with foreign foundations from the first phase of their efforts to assist Poland.

21. Morawska interview.

22. In accordance with the Polish Constitution (article CX), parliamentary committees are appointed to examine and prepare the work of the Sejm (http://www .sejm.gov.pl/komisje/komisje.html). There are two types of Sejm committees: standing committees and special committees. The Sejm has more than twenty standing legislative committees in which Polish NGOs can be engaged.

23. For more information about this association's current work, see its official website, http://www.ofop.engo.pl/x/297532.

24. Renata Koźlicka-Glińska, program officer, Polish-American Freedom Foundation (PAFF), interview by author, Warsaw, June 12, 2008.

25. Zbigniew Pisarski, president of the board, Casimir Pulaski Foundation, interview by author, Warsaw, July 14, 2008.

26. Andrzej Bobiński, program coordinator, Center for International Relations (CIR), interview by author, Warsaw, July 15, 2008.

27. Jan Andrzej Dąbrowski, president of the board, College of Eastern Europe, interview by author, Wrocław, June 18, 2008. Bogumiła Berdychowska is a Polish journalist who specializes in the history of Ukraine in the twentieth century and relations between Poland and Ukraine. She is the author of many publications in these areas (see for example Stefan Batory Foundation 2005). She is director of the stipends department in the National Cultural Center in Warsaw, which allocates grants to people doing cultural and scientific work in the former Soviet Union, and coordinates the Polish-Ukrainian youth exchange (Narodowe Centrum Kultury, http://www.nck .pl/). Zdzisław Najder is a Polish historian of literature internationally renowned for his work on Joseph Conrad, a former opponent of the communist government in Poland, and former director of the Polish section of Radio Free Europe (Hoover Institution, Stanford University, http://hoorferl.stanford.edu/bios/8.php). Agnieszka Magdziak-Miszewska is a teacher, journalist, and diplomat. She was director of the Center for International Relations (CIR) in Warsaw (specializing in Eastern matters). She worked at the Polish embassy in Moscow as a counselor-minister, and in 2006 she was appointed to be ambassador to Israel (Polish Embassy, Israel, http://www.telavivpl .org/index.php?m=268&ln=en). Henryk Wujec was a Solidarity activist, a participant in the Roundtable Talks, a member of parliament, and a former deputy minister of agriculture (Encyclopedia of Solidarity, http://www.encyklopedia-solidarnosci.pl/ wiki/index.php?title=Henryk_Wujec). In 2010, he became social affairs adviser to the president of Poland, Bronisław Komorowski.

28. For example, the Institute of Public Affairs was an organization established to support social and political reforms and to provide a forum for debate on social, political, and economic issues in Poland. Later, however, the IPA also began to prepare reform proposals, conduct research and societal analysis, and present policy recommendations not only in Poland but also in other countries in the postcommunist region. The IPA publishes the results of its activities in the form of books and policy papers, which are distributed to members of parliament, government officials, the media, and nongovernmental organizations in Poland and in the postcommunist countries.

29. During the 1990s, many Polish NGOs were also specializing in humanitarian aid to victims of natural disasters and armed conflicts, followed by material development aid, monitoring, and counseling. The Polish Red Cross, Caritas Poland, and, since 1994, the Polish Humanitarian Organization (PHO) provide aid for all conflict victims who are in need. PHO has, for example, provided support for the reconstruction of schools and water and sanitary systems as well as for sewage treatment plants for hospitals in Iraq, Afghanistan, Chechnya, the Palestinian Territories, and many African countries. Caritas Poland also offers material aid to educational, social, and health-promoting projects, as well as to prisoners; it also

conducts rehabilitation projects. Smaller organizations provide training programs for doctors from abroad, provide food and medical help, and run projects for children with AIDS and other illnesses (Zagranica Group 2003).

30. Grzegorz Gromadzki, Stefan Batory Foundation, interview by author, Warsaw, June 12, 2008. See also official Solidarity's website, http://www.solidarnosc.gov .pl/?document=89.

31. Katarzyna Bielawska, Democratic Society East Foundation (DSE), interview by author, Warsaw, July 15, 2008.

32. Przemysław Fenrych, Foundation in Support of Local Democracy (FSLD), interview by author, Szczecin, July 22, 2008.

33. Smolar was co-organizer of the twenty-fifth anniversary celebrations of the Solidarity Trade Union (August 2005) and program director of an international conference: From Solidarność to Freedom (Center for International Relations, http:// www.csm.org.pl/).

34. Konopka was an assistant and spokesman for Lech Wałęsa and served as the Solidarity spokesman at the 1989 Roundtable Agreement negotiations (Ludzie Wprost: Sylwetki, Cytaty, Fakty [People direct: profiles, quotes, facts], http://ludzie .wprost.pl/sylwetka/Piotr-Nowina-Konopka/).

35. For more about the activities of Polish-Czechoslovak Solidarity and Charter 77, see Kenney 2002, 122–56.

36. Fenrych interview.

37. Rodger Potocki, National Endowment for Democracy, interview by author, Washington, DC, November 20, 2008. Carl Gershman, president of NED, made a similar statement during the Solidarity and the Future of Democratization conference commemorating the twentieth anniversary of Poland's Roundtable Talks, held in May 2009 at Georgetown University.

38. Jan Nowak-Jeziorański became a prominent figure both in Poland and the United States. He was a famous "Kurier from Warsaw" who informed the Western governments of the situation in Poland under German and Soviet occupation. In World War II, he was the first to report the Warsaw ghetto uprising. After the war, he worked as the head of the Polish section of Radio Free Europe, and, during his residence in the United States, he was a member of the Polish American Congress, an organization he headed between 1979 and 1996. He also worked as an adviser to the US National Security Agency and Presidents Ronald Reagan and Jimmy Carter (Radio Free Europe/Radio Liberty 2005a).

39. Dąbrowski interview.

40. Funded by the Polish-American Enterprise Fund, PAFF first operated only in the United States; in 2000, it opened a representative office in Poland. The Polish-American Enterprise Fund was founded in 1991 to deal with the economic and business spheres in Poland, such as entrepreneurship development, development of companies, placing them on the stock market, and so forth. The fund had been successfully managed, earning $100 million, so there was a decision to establish PAFF with this money. Since then, the fund has been active in the financial market, and

PAFF receives annual interest income of $10 million to $11 million, which is used for operational and administrative activities (Koźlicka-Glińska interview). For more information, see the PAFF website, www.pafw.pl.

41. Koźlicka-Glińska interview.

42. PAFF does not itself implement operating activities but only transfers funds to organizations to carry out programs. However, these programs are often written by the foundation or together with the cooperating partner organizations (Koźlicka-Glińska interview). An example of such a program is the large grant to RITA. It is administered by the Education for Democracy Foundation (known as FED) and aims to support free and democratic transition in other postcommunist countries, notably through the sharing of the Polish experience. RITA has existed from the beginning of the presence of PAFF in Poland and will run as long as the funds of the foundation last. RITA provides funding from 5 to 30,000 PLN (about fifteen hundred to ten thousand dollars) for a recipient organization that can implement its own projects or do regranting (Koźlicka-Glińska interview). For more information about RITA, see http://rita.edudemo.org.pl/.

43. Lane Kirkland was a longtime head of the AFL-CIO; he stepped down in the mid-1990s.

44. Gromadzki and Komorowska interview.

45. Grzegorz Gromadzki, director of International Cooperation Program, Stefan Batory Foundation, interview by author, Warsaw, June 12, 2008.

46. Gromadzki and Komorowska interview.

47. This information comes from the Batory Foundation website, http://www .batory.org.pl/english/east/index.htm.

48. Artur Radziwiłł, vice president of the board, Center for Social and Economic Research (CASE), interview by author, Warsaw, July 1, 2008.

49. Potocki interview.

50. Ibid.

51. Magda Dębkowska, director, East European Democratic Center (EEDC), interview by author, Warsaw, June 5, 2008.

52. Paweł Kazanecki, president of the board, East European Democratic Center (EEDC), interview by author, Warsaw, July 14, 2008.

53. Aleksandra Kujawska, program coordinator, Education for Democracy Foundation (FED), interview by author, Warsaw, July 15, 2008.

54. Quigley (1997, 50) reports that, in 1994, the FSLD was funded by some six American foundations, two German foundations, and the Fondation de France.

55. Katarzyna Morawska, project specialist in the management office, Foundation in Support of Local Democracy (FSLD), interview by author, Warsaw, June 5, 2008.

56. Ibid.; Kazanecki interview. Also, Quigley (1997, 49–51) highlights the role of Regulski and Regulska in obtaining funding from diverse public and private sources.

57. Paweł Bobołowicz, president of the board, Foundation for Young Democracy, interview by author, Lublin, June 6, 2008.

58. Fenrych interview.

59. Morawska interview.

60. Gromadzki and Komorowska interview.

61. Katarzyna Bielawska, board member, Democratic Society East Foundation, interview by author, Warsaw, June 27, 2008.

62. Ibid.

63. Gromadzki interview.

64. Bielawska interview.

65. Paweł Kucharczyk, president of the executive board, Institute of Public Affairs (IPA), Warsaw, June 30, 2008.

66. Kujawska interview.

67. Rafał Dymek, Robert Schuman Foundation, interview by author, Warsaw, June 12, 2008.

68. Morawska interview.

69. Ibid.

70. Ibid.

71. Bobołowicz interview.

72. Fenrych interview.

73. Ibid.

74. For example, Polish NGOs avoid using the term *Kresy* in relation to its eastern neighbors, because the term, which means the outskirts or borderlands of Poland, is viewed negatively in those countries.

75. Rafał Dymek, general director, Polish Robert Schuman Foundation, interview by author, Warsaw, July 14, 2008.

76. Fenrych interview.

77. Concord is a confederation representing NGOs from EU member states. It is a tool for political and institutional coordination, as well as a forum of exchange for its members. Concord members have been deepening their relations with the NGOs from new member states through the Trialog project. For more information, see http://www.concordeurope.org/Public/Page.php?ID=4.

78. For more information, see the EU Presidency Fund website, http://www.presidencyfund.org/wcm/index.php.

79. This information comes from the Robert Bosch Stiftung website, http://www.bosch-stiftung.de/content/language2/html/index.asp.

80. Bobołowicz interview.

81. Morawska interview.

82. Bobołowicz interview.

83. Euroregion represents a specific type of cross-border cooperation between two (or more) territories located in different European countries.

84. Potocki interview.

85. Data from NED provided at the author's request. The data for cross-border work are summarized in table A4.1 (app. 4).

86. This statement is based on the data received from NED. See table A4.1 (app. 4).

87. Potocki interview.

88. Ibid.

89. Between 2003 and 2008, Western donors disbursed a total of more than $500

million to Polish and Ukrainian organizations (Jan Piekło, director, PAUCI, interview by author, Warsaw, June 30, 2008).

90. Gromadzki and Komorowska interview.

91. This information comes from Zagranica Group materials obtained from Marta Pejda, executive secretary, Zagranica Group, in interview by author, Warsaw, June 27, 2008, and from the Zagranica Group website, http://www.zagranica.org.pl/index .php?option=com_content&task=blogcategory&id=48&Itemid=132.

92. Piekło interview.

93. Kazanecki interview.

94. Jakub Boratyński's expressed this opinion during a meeting the Zagranica Group organized during the fourth Polish Forum for Non-Governmental Initiatives, in 2005.

95. During interviews, many representatives of Polish NGOs frequently referred to the role of the EU in beginning to offer aid to other countries because it was the Polish government's decision to engage in democracy assistance.

96. Koźlicka-Glińska interview.

97. Bobiński interview.

Chapter 4. Demystifying Cross-Border Networks

1. Rafał Dymek, Polish Robert Schuman Foundation, interview by author, Warsaw, July 14, 2008.

2. Katarzyna Bielawska, member of the board, Democratic Society East Foundation (DSE), interview by author, Warsaw, June 27, 2008.

3. For security reasons, the names of the organization and its representative who provided this information are not disclosed. This procedure will be followed, where necessary, throughout this chapter.

4. The concept of "activation" corresponds with Putnam's (1994) argument that the civic community is marked not only by trust and cooperation but also by an active and public-spirited citizenry. He finds that active engagement in community affairs is one of the factors contributing to stable democracy in the regions he studied.

5. Arkadiusz Goliński, vice-director, St. Maximilian Kolbe House for Meetings and Reconciliation (DMK), interview by author, Gdańsk, July 2, 2008.

6. Przemysław Fenrych, program coordinator, Foundation in Support of Local Democracy (FSLD), interview by author, Szczecin, July 22, 2008.

7. This statement is based on the FSLD list of projects obtained from Katarzyna Morawska, project specialist in the management office, Foundation in Support of Local Democracy (FSLD), in interview by author, Warsaw, June 5, 2008.

8. Marta Pejda, executive secretary, Zagranica Group (ZG), interview by author, Warsaw, June 27, 2008.

9. Jan Andrzej Dąbrowski, president of the board, Jan Jezierański College of Eastern Europe, interview by author, Wrocław, June 18, 2008.

10. Ibid.

11. Bielawska interview.

12. Working for Radio Racyja offers Belarusians the chance to be part of a Belarusian-speaking team and to fight for an independent and democratic Belarus. As the station's brochure indicates, Radio Racyja seems to perform the function that Radio Free Europe had in Poland under communism, but the president of Radio Racyja claims that the founders never intended to replicate the success of Radio Free Europe (Belarusian Information Center 2008). The station also has its own online service at www.racyja.com, where one can find current news from Belarus.

13. The list of Polish organizations that arranged internships and workshops in Poland for young journalists and students from Belarus or for representatives of Belarusian nongovernmental organizations and independent media is long. In order to protect the participants, I have chosen not to include it here.

14. Fenrych interview.

15. There are also instances when Polish volunteers for Polish NGOs who are not permanent employees go to live in local communities in Belarus for some time, in order to organize and activate the local community as well as to facilitate cooperation there.

16. Goliński interview.

17. See, for example, Siegel and Yancey 1992.

18. Fenrych interview.

19. This observation was also made by Wróbel (2003, 16).

20. For more on data regarding the Polish third sector, see http://www.bazy.ngo.pl, which is the largest and most popular Polish database of foundations, organizations, and other entities whose activity is connected with the nongovernmental sector.

21. Paweł Kazanecki, president of the board, East European Democratic Center (EEDC), interview by author, Warsaw, July 14, 2008.

22. The term "resurrection of Ukrainian civil society" is borrowed from O'Donnell and Schmitter (1986).

23. Jan Fedirko, program coordinator, Foundation for Young Democracy, interview by author, Lublin, June 6, 2008.

24. Kazanecki interview.

25. Dymek interview.

26. Fedirko interview.

27. Fedirko's notes translated from Polish by the author.

28. Fedirko interview.

29. Fedirko's notes translated from Polish by the author.

30. Some interviewees expressed the view that Poles' involvement in the Orange Revolution was also a perfect moment to improve Polish-Ukrainian relations. Fedirko noted that, although political relations were good, there is still an awareness of the massacres of Poles in Volhynia that took place during and after World War II. Fedirko interview.

31. Aleksandra Kujawska, program coordinator, Education for Democracy Foundation (FED), interview by author, Warsaw, July 15, 2008.

32. Fedirko interview.

33. Information from the database obtained during the Morawska interview.

34. Ibid.

35. Paweł Bobołowicz, president of the board, Foundation for Young Democracy, interview by author, Lublin, June 6, 2008.

36. Information from the database obtained during the Morawska interview.

37. Magda Dębkowska, director, East European Democratic Center (EEDC), interview by author, Warsaw, June 5, 2008.

38. Information from the Democratic Society East Foundation, http://www.tdw.org.pl/index.php?option=content&task=view&id=81.

39. Paweł Kucharczyk, president of the executive board, Institute of Public Affairs (IPA), interview by author, Warsaw, June 30, 2008.

40. Jan Piekło, director, Poland-Ukrainian Cooperation Foundation (PAUCI), interview by author, Warsaw, June 30, 2008.

41. Kazanecki interview.

42. Fedirko interview.

43. The FSLD has cooperated with the Agency for the Development of Local Self-Government in Donetsk since 2005 and with the Regional Development Agency in Luhansk oblast in a project aimed at supporting these units in their functioning in a democratic state and cooperation with civil society, through training meetings with NGO representatives and visits to Poland. This is information is based on the FSLD project database acquired in the Morawska interview.

44. For example, the project "European Standards in Public Sector Initiatives: Local Governments and NGOs" was implemented by the European Center for Sustainable Development in Wrocław with a Stefan Batory Foundation grant and focused on exchanges for representatives of local government and nongovernmental organizations in Poland and Ukraine (Stefan Batory Foundation 2007). Another example of joint Polish-Ukrainian projects bringing together NGOs and local authorities is the Polish-Ukrainian School of Social Activists, financed by PAFF. One of the main objectives of the project was training a group of activists in the local communities. Included in the initiative were organized study visits in Poland for the Ukrainian employees of cultural centers of three regions in central Ukraine. Information about this project was obtained from the Local Activity Support Center's annual report for 2005, http://www.cal.org.pl/lib/spaw2/uploads/files/raport_StowarzyszenieCAL_2005.pdf.

45. Easton (1975) writes that the demands of society may be articulated directly, by society members themselves, or by others on their behalf, such as organizations or other organized constituencies.

46. Bobołowicz interview. As Sundstrom (2006) finds, the better the cooperation between local authorities and civil society groups, the more local political factors are favorable to the development of civil society and the better the position of civil society vis-à-vis a government (thus, the greater chances for the development of the civil society sector as well).

47. Bobołowicz interview.

48. Fenrych interview.

49. Grzegorz Gromadzki, director of the International Cooperation Program,

and Agnieszka Komorowska, coordinator of the Civil Initiatives in Eastern Europe Program, Stefan Batory Foundation, interview by author, Warsaw, June 12, 2008.

50. Piekło interview.

51. International organizations have been noted for their ability to constrain the actions of member states. Specifically, it is argued that joining intergovernmental organizations is a credible way to lock in policies or reforms to guard against future policy reversals (Goldstein 1998, 143–44). Membership can be perceived as "a tactic used by governments to 'lock-in' and consolidate democratic institutions, thereby enhancing their credibility and stability vis-à-vis nondemocratic political threats" (Moravcsik 2000, 220). Membership in some organizations is sometimes conditional upon domestic liberalization. For example, the European Union requires all members to be liberal, free-market democracies, as does the Council of Europe (European Commission: Treaty of Nice 2002). Pevehouse (2002) finds regional organizations to be "an external sustainer of democracy" for at least two main reasons. First, the high costs imposed by these organizations (e.g., sanctions or expulsion) create a clear incentive to work within the rules of the system (Pevehouse 2002, 614). Second, Pevehouse argues that the higher the average level of democracy of each member state in regional organizations, like the EU, the more likely the organization will be to serve this role of external guarantor (Pevehouse 2002, 616).

52. Fedirko interview.

53. Piekło interview.

54. For example, Ukrainians were invited to come to Poland to observe an accession referendum on the EU. Sociologists and politicians from Ukraine watched the referendum campaign and the voting, and they worked closely with Polish experts on future recommendations for Ukraine (Fedirko interview). Ukrainians who traveled to Poland to observe the referendum also participated in roundtable debates on the possible accession of Ukraine, as well as other prospective countries, to the EU. These events were organized by Polish NGOs in close cooperation with Latvian and Slovakian partners (Kucharczyk interview).

55. Piekło interview. Moreover, in cooperation with the Center for US-Ukrainian Relations in New York and the German Konrad-Adenauer Foundation, PAUCI holds annually a conference on the Euro-Atlantic integration of Ukraine that attracts renowned experts from the United States, Poland, Ukraine, and Germany. For more information about the Center for US-Ukrainian Relations, see http:// usukrainianrelations.org/index.php?option=com_content&task=blogcategory&id=14 &Itemid=78.

56. Gromadzki and Komorowska interview.

57. Piekło interview.

58. Bobołowicz interview.

59. Dymek interview. Some Polish NGOs, like the Foundation for Young Democracy, also share their experience at information centers established in public places and dedicated to providing details about integration into the European Union (Bobołowicz interview). As a result, European Union information centers were established in Lutsk, Ukraine. Currently, it is the Soros Foundation in Ukraine, called

the International Renaissance Foundation (IRF), that is actively working on the creation of these European Union information centers (Fedirko interview).

60. Zbigniew Pisarski, president of the board, Casimir Pulaski Foundation, interview by author, Warsaw, July 14, 2008.

61. Piekło interview.

62. Bobołowicz interview. The Schengen Zone comprises twenty-six European countries that have abolished passport and immigration controls at their common borders. Countries in this zone also adopted a common visa policy. For more information, see the European Commission's webpage on this initiative, http://ec.europa.eu/dgs/home-affairs/what-we-do/policies/borders-and-visas/schengen/.

63. Fedirko interview.

64. Andrzej Bobiński, program coordinator, Center for International Relations (CIR), interview by author, Warsaw, July 15, 2008.

65. Gromadzki and Komorowska interview.

66. Artur Radziwiłł, vice president of the board, Center for Social and Economic Research (CASE), interview by author, Warsaw, July 1, 2008. It should be said that although all EU countries have to begin requiring visas for nonmember states' citizens according to EU visa policies that are imposed on all members, many countries interpret the common regulations in different ways and thus apply them differently. Therefore, Polish NGOs found it important to engage in some projects in cooperation with partners from the new EU member states—Czech Republic, Slovakia, and the Baltic states—in order to exchange opinions and develop recommendations on how the visa system might be improved. Poland had a different rule for issuing visas to Ukrainians than did the Czech Republic, and the Czech Republic later adopted some of the more liberal Polish solutions (Kucharczyk interview).

67. Pisarski interview.

68. Given the capacity of the project, it is coordinated by three organizations—the Jan Nowak-Jeziorański College of Eastern Europe, the Angelus Silesius Meeting House in Wrocław, and the Borusia Foundation in Olsztyn. See the Study Tours to Poland website, http://www.studytours.pl/.

69. Study Tours to Poland website, http://www.studytours.pl/.

70. Dąbrowski interview.

71. This program is named after Lane Kirkland of the AFL-CIO, the organization that strongly supported the Solidarity movement in the 1980s. At the beginning, the operator of the Kirkland program was the Center for East European Studies at Warsaw University, which ran the program for one year. Since the center planned to be in charge of the Kalinowski Scholarship Program from the Polish government (discussed in chap. 2), the Fulbright Commission took over administration of the Kirkland program.

72. From the beginning, the program included candidates from Ukraine, Belarus, Lithuania, Slovakia, and Kaliningrad oblast in Russia. Later, the program was extended to include participants from Georgia, Moldova, Armenia, and Azerbaijan.

In the years 2000–2007, a total of 275 scholars completed the program (Urszula Sobiecka, coordinator of the Lane Kirkland Scholarship Program, Polish-American Fulbright Commission, interview by author, Warsaw, July 1, 2008).

73. This information is from a fact sheet about the program obtained during the Sobiecka interview.

74. Renata Koźlicka-Glińska, program officer, Polish-American Freedom Foundation (PAFF), interview by author, Warsaw, June 12, 2008.

75. Piekło interview.

76. Ibid.

77. Bielawska interview. One night in 1944, on Stalin's orders, the Crimean Tatars were suddenly evicted from their homes and exiled to Uzbekistan—and forced to leave everything behind. At the end of the 1990s, after fifty years, the survivors and their families returned to Crimea.

78. The Tatars' activism dates to late Soviet times, and General Petro Grigorenko (a high-ranking Soviet army commander of Ukrainian descent and later a prominent Soviet human rights activist) used to work on their behalf. Thus, in discussing the activism of the Crimean Tatars, it important to take into account a long history of activism that goes back to the Brezhnev era. See Vardys 1971 for scholarship on this area. See also, for example, the speech of Petro Grigorenko to the Crimean Tatars in 1968, at the website of the International Committee for Crimea, http://www.iccrimea .org/surgun/grigorenko.html.

79. Kujawska interview. Polish NGOs have also conducted training seminars on independent media, civic education, youth activism, and NGO development for thousands of representatives from independent groups in Crimea. They have also provided advice and infrastructure for democracy-building NGOs and organized internships and networking visits for Crimean activists to Kiev, L'viv, and Warsaw. Another Polish organization, the Association of Educators, has trained teachers, school inspectors, and student activists in order to improve the quality of Crimean schools, promote self-government and democracy within these schools, foster civic education, and address local problems by designing and implementing projects that involve local communities (Rodger Potocki, National Endowment for Democracy, interview by author, Washington, DC, November 20, 2008).

80. Kujawska interview.

Chapter 5. Why Polish Democracy Assistance Matters

1. Paweł Kazanecki, president of the board, East European Democratic Center (EEDC), interview by author, Warsaw, July 14, 2008.

2. This is the author's general observation, but the quotation containing the questions is from Aleksandra Kujawska, program coordinator, Education for Democracy Foundation (FED), interview by author, Warsaw, July 15, 2008. FED was one of the first organizations in Poland that received international aid for their activities during the transformation process in Poland.

3. Carothers (1999, 209) points out that the inclination toward civil society assistance also was facilitated by pragmatic factors; many officials in the administration of US president Bill Clinton had come from the NGO community, and because federal budgets were being cut, NGO aid officials had to do more with less because the government was granting them fewer funds.

4. Przemysław Fenrych, program coordinator, Foundation in Support of Local Democracy (FSLD), interview by author, Szczecin, July 22, 2008. There were some efforts of the St. Maximilian Kolbe House for Meetings and Reconciliation to implement a project in cooperation with the local authorities, but the project had to be shut down because of Lukashenko's official attack on it and his threat to regional authorities (Arkadiusz Goliński, vice-director, St. Maximilian Kolbe House for Meetings and Reconciliation [DMK], interview by author, Gdańsk, July 2, 2008).

5. Katarzyna Morawska, Project Specialist in the Management Office, Foundation in Support of Local Democracy (FSLD), interview by author, Warsaw, June 5, 2008.

6. Grzegorz Gromadzki, director of international cooperation program, and Agnieszka Komorowska, coordinator of the Civil Initiatives in Eastern Europe Program, Stefan Batory Foundation, Warsaw, June 12, 2008.

7. Ibid.

8. This information is from the Stefan Batory Foundation website, http://www .batory.org.pl/english/prog.htm.

9. Gromadzki and Komorowska interview.

10. Kazanecki interview.

11. Ibid.

12. Paweł Bobołowicz, president of the board, Foundation for Young Democracy, interview by author, Lublin, June 6, 2008.

13. Ibid.

14. Mirosław Sycz, vice-director, Development Co-operation Department, and Agata Czaplinska, head of implementation, Development Assistance Program, Polish Ministry of Foreign Affairs (MFA), interview by author, Warsaw, June 27, 2008. The Polish Ministry of Foreign Affairs does not provide funds for projects that do not incorporate the recipient country's local partners. In order to receive funds from the Ministry of Foreign Affairs, Polish NGOs, while applying for financial support, have to demonstrate that they will involve partners from the aid recipient country by attaching letters, agreements, and other documents. Sources of information about these procedures are available on the Polish Aid website, http://www.polskapomoc.gov.pl.

15. Morawska interview.

16. Rodger Potocki, director for Europe and Eurasia, and Joanna Rohozińska, program officer for Europe and Eurasia, National Endowment for Democracy, interview by author, Washington, DC, November 20, 2008.

17. Kujawska interview.

18. Rafał Dymek, general director, Polish Robert Schuman Foundation, interview by author, Warsaw, July 14, 2008.

19. Kazanecki interview.

20. Kujawska interview. Similar observations were shared by Jan Fedirko, program

coordinator, Foundation for Young Democracy, in an interview by the author, Lublin, June 6, 2008.

21. For security reasons, the author has omitted the source of this information here and subsequently—when necessary—throughout the chapter.

22. Zbigniew Pisarski, president of the board, Casimir Pulaski Foundation, interview by author, Warsaw, July 14, 2008.

23. Morawska interview.

24. Pisarski interview.

25. Dymek interview.

26. Kazanecki interview.

27. Fenrych interview.

28. Bielawska interview.

29. Jan Piekło, director, Poland-Ukrainian Cooperation Foundation (PAUCI), interview by author, Warsaw, June 30, 2008.

30. Bobołowicz interview.

31. Gromadzki and Komorowska interview.

32. Bobołowicz interview.

33. Kashubians were able to preserve their unique language and culture in Poland. Today, in some towns and villages in northern Poland, Kashubian is the second language spoken after Polish, and it enjoys legal protection in Poland as an official regional language. It is the only language in Poland with this status, granted by an act of the Polish parliament. This language is taught in regional schools, and many geographical names of Kashubia (in north-central Poland) are written in this language. For more about Kashubians, see http://kaszubia.com/.

34. Bielawska interview.

35. Kujawska interview.

36. Pisarski interview.

37. Fedirko interview.

38. Marta Pejda, of the Zagranica Group, interview by author, Warsaw, June 27, 2008.

39. Bielawska interview.

40. Kujawska interview.

41. Bobołowicz interview; Jan Andrzej Dąbrowski, president of the board, College of Eastern Europe, interview by author, Wrocław, June 18, 2008.

42. Piekło interview.

43. Urszula Sobiecka, coordinator of the Lane Kirkland Scholarship Program, Polish-American Fulbright Commission, interview by author, Warsaw, July 1, 2008.

44. Ibid.

45. Ibid.

46. Dąbrowski interview.

47. Sobiecka interview.

48. Ibid.

49. Ibid.

50. Kujawska interview.

51. Kazanecki interview.

52. Ibid.

53. Dymek interview.

54. Ibid.

55. Carothers (1999, 267) makes a similar point when he briefly acknowledges that some American democracy groups were also making use of third-country trainers and experts by sending Polish experts to Ukraine, Chileans to Bolivia, and South Africans to Malawi.

56. Andrzej Bobiński, program coordinator, Center for International Relations (CIR), interview by author, Warsaw, July 15, 2008.

57. Gromadzki and Komorowska interview.

58. Fenrych interview.

59. Artur Radziwiłł, vice president of the board, Center for Social and Economic Research (CASE), interview by author, Warsaw, July 1, 2008.

60. Morawska interview.

61. See Stemplowski 2001.

62. Goliński interview.

63. Bobiński interview.

64. Kazanecki interview.

65. Historian Jan Malicki, director of the Center for East European Studies, was a participant in and organizer of several underground initiatives between 1981 and 1985. In 1985, he was tried and sentenced for political crimes. For more about the center and its educational activities, see the center's website, http://www.studium .uw.edu.pl.

66. Kazanecki interview. The situation of Eastern European studies also is described in a report from the Slavic Research Center in Japan, http://src-h.slav .hokudai.ac.jp/coe21/publish/no7/05bremer.pdf.

67. Dymek interview.

68. Bobołowicz interview.

69. Bielawska interview.

70. Goliński interview.

71. Pisarski interview.

72. Magdalena Dębkowska, East European Democratic Center, interview by author, Warsaw, June 5, 2008.

73. Jan Nowak-Jeziorański's statement is from the *New Eastern Europe* website, http://www.new.org.pl/o_nas.html . The quotation, like others from Polish-language sources, was translated by the author.

74. Fenrych interview.

75. Morawska interview.

76. Ibid.

77. Potocki and Rohozińska interview.

78. Ibid.

79. Ibid.

80. Ibid.

81. Ibid.

82. Ibid. Prime Minister Vladimir Meciar belonged to the old elites who continued to rule after the collapse of communism. He was prime minister of Slovakia in 1990–91, 1992–94, and 1994–98. His leadership was later associated with autocratic policies, corruption, and failing economic conditions. His rule also influenced the development of the civil society sector.

83. Data on NED cross-border projects in Belarus implemented by Polish NGOs goes back to 1993; however, the author obtained detailed descriptions only of those projects funded between 2000 and 2007. The information refers only to projects specifically targeted to Belarus and those directed toward the whole postcommunist region, in which Belarus is one of the targeted countries.

84. Cross-border projects directed toward Ukraine dominate NED assistance to Polish NGOs in terms of monies spent—55 percent of total grants for Polish NGOs between 1993 and 2007.

85. Based on data from NED cross-border projects with Belarus and Ukraine obtained during the Potocki and Rohozińska interview.

86. Potocki and Rohozińska interview.

References

ACAP (American Committee for Aid to Poland, Inc). 1995. *American Private Voluntary Organizations Active in Poland: Including Some in East Central Europe and the Newly Independent States.* Washington, DC: NED Democracy Resource Center.

Adamson, Fiona B. 2002. "International Democracy Assistance in Uzbekistan and Kyrgyzstan: Building Civil Society from the Outside?" In *The Power and Limits of NGOs: A Critical Look at Building Democracy in Eastern Europe and Eurasia,* edited by Sarah E. Mendelson and John K. Glenn, 177–206. New York: Columbia University Press.

Agence France Presse (AFP). 2007. "Thousands Rally in Kiev against President." April 2. Ebscohost, http://ehis.ebscohost.com.

———. 2008. "Ukraine President Postpones Elections Due to Financial Crisis." October 20. http://afp.google.com/article/ALeqM5iosNEc3C40SuNSi_e1COuQQcwobA.

Aksartova, Sada. 2005. "Civil Society from Abroad: U.S. Donors in the Former Soviet Union." PhD dissertation, Princeton University.

Alesina, Alberto, and David Dollar. 2000. "Who Gives Foreign Aid to Whom and Why?" *Journal of Economic Growth* 5 (1): 33–63.

Allison, Graham T., and R. Beschel. 1992. "Can the United States Promote Democracy?" *Political Science Quarterly* 107 (1): 89–98.

Allmand, Mónica. 1998. "Networking Civil Society in Latin America." In *Civil Society and International Development,* edited by Amanda Bernard, Henny Helmich, and Percy B. Lehning, 121–26. Paris: North-South Centre of the Council of Europe and Development Centre Studies of the Organization for Economic Co-operation and Development.

Almond, Gabriel A., and Sidney Verba. 1963. *The Civic Culture: Political Attitudes and Democracy in Five Nations.* Princeton: Princeton University Press.

Andrew, Caroline, and Michael Goldsmith. 1998. "From Local Government to Local Governance: And Beyond?" *International Political Science Review* 19 (2): 101–17.

Applebaum, Anne. 2010. "In Belarus, a Slide toward Eastern Aggression." *Washington Post,* December 21. http://www.washingtonpost.com/wp-dyn/content/article/2010/12/20/AR2010122003971.html.

Armijo, Elliott, Thomas J. Biersteker, and Abraham F. Lowenthal. 1994. "The Problems of Simultaneous Transitions." *Journal of Democracy* 5 (4): 161–75.

Ash, Timothy Garton. 2002. *The Polish Revolution: Solidarity.* New Haven: Yale University Press.

Åslund, Anders. 2005. "Comparative Oligarchy: Russia, Ukraine and the United States." Studies and Analyses, Center for Social and Economic Research, Warsaw. http://www.case-research.eu/upload/publikacja_plik/4931074_SA%20296last.pdf.

———. 2006. "The Ancien Régime: Kuchma and the Oligarchs." In *Revolution in Orange: The Origins of Ukraine's Democratic Breakthrough,* edited by Anders Åslund and Michael McFaul, 9–28. Washington, DC: Carnegie Endowment for International Peace.

———, and Michael McFaul, eds. 2006. *Revolution in Orange: The Origins of Ukraine's Democratic Breakthrough.* Washington, DC: Carnegie Endowment for International Peace.

Azpuru, Dinorah, Steven E. Finkel, Aníbal Pérez-Liñán, and Mitchell A. Seligson. 2008. "Trends in Democracy Assistance: What Has the United States Been Doing?" *Journal of Democracy* 19 (2): 150–59.

Balcerowicz, Leszek, Barbara Blaszczyk, and Marek Dabrowski. 1997. "The Polish Way to the Market Economy, 1989–1995." In *Economies in Transition: Comparing Asia and Eastern Europe,* edited by Wing Thye Woo, Stephen Parker, and Jeffrey D. Sachs, 131–60. Cambridge, MA: MIT Press.

Baldwin, Richard E. 1995. "The Eastern Enlargement of the European Union." *European Union Review* 39:474–81.

Ballentine, Karen. 2002. "International Assistance and the Development of Independent Mass Media in the Czech and Slovak Republics." In *The Power and Limits of NGOs: A Critical Look at Building Democracy in Eastern Europe and Eurasia,* edited by Sarah E. Mendelson and John K. Glenn, 91–125. New York: Columbia University Press.

Barrington, Lowell W. 2002. "Examining Rival Theories of Demographic Influence on Political Support: The Power of Regional, Ethnic, and Linguistic Divisions in Ukraine." *European Journal of Political Research* 41 (4): 455–91.

———, and Erik S. Herron. 2004. "One Ukraine or Many? Regionalism in Ukraine and Its Political Consequences." *Nationalities Papers* 32 (1): 53–86.

BBC News. 2006. "Dozens Arrested in Belarus Demos." February 16. http://news.bbc .co.uk/2/hi/europe/4722362.stm.

———. 2008. "Snap Election Called in Ukraine." October 8. http://news.bbc.co.uk/2/hi/ europe/7660058.stm.

———. 2009. "EU Launches 'Eastern Partnership.'" May 8. http://news.bbc.co.uk/2/hi/ europe/8040037.stm.

———. 2012. "Belarus Election: Opposition Shut Out of Parliament." September 24. http://www.bbc.co.uk/news/world-europe-19690249.

Beetham, D. 1996. "Theorizing Democracy and Local Government." In *Rethinking Local Democracy,* edited by D. King and G. Stoker. London: Macmillan.

Belarusian Information Center. 2008. *Belarusian Radio Racyja 2008.* Brochure.

Belarusian Institute for Strategic Studies. 2007. "Belarus Exclusion from GSP: Possible Repercussions." http://www.belinstitute.eu/images/stories/documents/biss_gsp_ eng.pdf.

Berman, Sheri. 1997. "Civil Society and the Collapse of the Weimar Republic." *World Politics* 49 (3): 401–29.

Bermeo, Nancy. 2003. *Ordinary People in Extraordinary Times: The Citizenry and the Breakdown of Democracy.* Princeton: Princeton University Press.

Bernard, Amanda, Henny Helmich, and Percy B. Lehning, eds. 1998. *Civil Society and International Development.* Paris: North-South Centre of the Council of Europe and Development Centre Studies of the Organization for Economic Co-operation and Development.

Bernhard, Michael. 1993. "Civil Society and Democratic Transition in East Central Europe." *Political Science Quarterly* 108 (2): 307–26.

Biekart, Kees. 1999. *The Politics of Civil Society Building: European Private Aid Agencies and Democratic Transitions in Central America.* Utrecht: International Books; Amsterdam: Transnational Institute.

Birch, Sarah. 2000. "Interpreting the Regional Effect in Ukrainian Politics." *Europe-Asia Studies* 52 (6): 1017–41.

Blair, Harry. 1998. "Civil Society and Building Democracy: Lessons from International Donor Experience." In *Civil Society and International Development,* edited by Amanda Bernard, Henny Helmich, and Percy B. Lehning, 65–80. Paris: North-South Centre of the Council of Europe and Development Centre of the Organization for Economic Co-operation and Development.

Boix, Carles. 2003. *Democracy and Redistribution.* Cambridge: Cambridge University Press.

———, and Susan Carol Stokes. 2003. "Endogenous Democratization." *World Politics* 55 (4): 517–49.

Bondarenko, Kost. 2002. "Ukraine's Oligarchs Emerge from Soviet System." *Kyiv Post,* April 4.

Boone, Peter. 1996. "Politics and the Effectiveness of Foreign Aid." *European Economic Review* 40 (2): 289–329.

Boratyński, Jakub. 2005. "The Zagranica Group's Meeting on the Role of Polish NGOs in Shaping Polish Foreign Policy toward the East." September 24. Wiadomosci NGO [NGO news], http://wiadomosci.ngo.pl/wiadomosci/128473.html.

Bratton, Michael, and Nicholas van de Walle. 1997. *Democratic Experiments in Africa: Regime Transitions in Comparative Perspective.* Cambridge: Cambridge University Press.

Brinks, Daniel, and Michael Coppedge. 2006. "Diffusion Is No Illusion: Neighbor Emulation in the Third Wave of Democracy." *Comparative Political Studies* 39 (7): 1–23.

Brouwer, Imco. 2000. "Weak Democracy and Civil Society Promotion: The Cases of Egypt and Palestine." In *Funding Virtue: Civil Society and Democracy Promotion,* edited by Marina Ottaway and Thomas Carothers, 21–48. Washington, DC: Carnegie Endowment for International Peace.

Buchvostau, Aleksandr. 2007. "Trade Unions in Belarus." In *Hopes, Illusions, Perspectives: Belarusian Society 2007.* Warsaw and Minsk: East European Democratic Center.

Bunce, Valerie J. 1995. "Should Transitologists Be Grounded?" *Slavic Review* 54 (1): 111–27.

———. 1999. "The Political Economy of Postsocialism." *Slavic Review* 58 (4): 756–93.

———. 2000. "Comparative Democratization: Big and Bounded Generalizations." *Comparative Political Studies* 33 (6–7): 703–34.

Bunce, Valerie J., and Sharon L. Wolchik. 2006. "International Diffusion and Postcommunist Electoral Revolutions." *Communist and Post-Communist Studies* 39 (3): 283–304.

———. 2011. *Defeating Authoritarian Leaders in Postcommunist Countries.* Cambridge: Cambridge University Press.

Burant, Stephen R. 1993. "International Relations in a Regional Context: Poland and Its Eastern Neighbors; Lithuania, Belarus, Ukraine." *Europe-Asia Studies* 45 (3): 395–418.

Burnell, Peter. 2000. *Democracy Assistance: International Co-operation for Democratization.* London: Frank Cass.

———. 2008. "International Democracy Promotion: A Role for Public Goods Theory?" *Comparative Politics* 14 (1): 37–52.

Carothers, Thomas. 1997. "The Observers Observed." *Journal of Democracy* 8 (3): 17–31.

———. 1999. *Aiding Democracy Abroad: The Learning Curve.* Washington, DC: Carnegie Endowment for International Peace.

———. 2002. "The End of the Transition Paradigm." *Journal of Democracy* 13 (1): 5–21.

———. 2004. *Critical Mission: Essays on Democracy Promotion.* Washington, DC: Carnegie Endowment for International Peace.

———. 2009. "Democracy Assistance: Political vs. Developmental?" *Journal of Democracy* 20 (1): 5–19.

Čavusau, Jury. 2007. "Belarus' Civic Sector." In *Hopes, Illusions, Perspectives: Belarusian Society 2007.* Warsaw and Minsk: East European Democratic Center.

Central Election and National Referendum Commission of Belarus. 2006. "Message: Election of the President of the Republic of Belarus." March 19. http://rec.gov.by/.

Central Election Commission of Ukraine. 2000. Referendum. April 16. http://www.cvk.gov.ua/.

———. 2004a. Presidential Election 2004: Results of Elections for the President of Ukraine. November 21. http://www.cvk.gov.ua/pls/vp2004/wp0011e.

———. 2004b. Presidential Election 2004: Results of Elections for the President of Ukraine [repeated balloting]. December 26. http://www.cvk.gov.ua/pls/vp2004/wp0011e.

———. 2006. Parliamentary Election 2006. Results of Voting on Parties (blocs of parties) in Ukraine. March 26. http://www.cvk.gov.ua/pls/vp2004/wp0011e.

———. 2007. Parliamentary Election 2007. Results of Voting on Parties (blocs of parties) in Ukraine. September 30. http://www.cvk.gov.ua/pls/vnd2007/w6p001e.

———. 2010. Presidential Election 2010. Results of Voting: The Elections of the President of Ukraine. January 17. http://www.cvk.gov.ua/pls/vp2010/WP0011.

Charter 97. 2007. "Youth Protests the Compulsory BRSM Membership." September 21. http://www.charter97.org/bel/news/2007/09/21/protiv.

Cheibub, Jose Antonio, Adam Przeworski, Fernando Papaterra Limongi Neto, and Michael M. Alvarez. 1996. "What Makes Democracies Endure?" *Journal of Democracy* 7 (1): 39–55.

Chernov, Viktor. 2008. "Third Sector in Belarus." *Nashe Mneniye*, February 18. http://nmnby.eu/news/analytics/1315.html.

Chimiak G. 2004. "Motywacje spolecznikow dzialajacych w organizacjach pozarzadowych w Polsce: Proba typologii" [Motivations of civil society activists working in nongovernmental organizations in Poland: An attempt to provide typology]. In *Samoorganizacja spoleczenstwa polskiego: III sector i wspolnoty lokalne w jednoczacej sie Europie* [Polish self-organization of society: The third sector and local communities in the uniting Europe], edited by P. Glinski, B. Lewenstein, and A. Sicinski. Warsaw: Wydawnictwo IfiS PAN.

Cieszkowski, Andrzej. 2007. "The Foreign Policy of the Republic of Poland and the European Neighborhood Policy." Address presented at Between East and West—the Role of Poland in the European Union's Eastern Policy—Political, Cultural and Spiritual Consequences of Poland's Location at the Eastern Borders of the EU, conference organized by the Cardinal Stefan Wyszynski University and the Forum of Young Diplomats in cooperation with the Konrad Adenauer Foundation in Poland under the auspices of the German Presidency of the Council of the European Union, April 17, Warsaw.

Cohen, Jean L., and Andrew Arato. 1997. *Civil Society and Political Theory.* Cambridge, MA: MIT Press.

Cohen, Joshua, and Joel Rogers. 1992. "Secondary Associations and Democratic Governance." *Politics and Society,* special issue, 20 (4): 393–472.

Colton, Timothy J. 2011. "An Aligning Election and the Ukrainian Political Community." *East European Politics and Societies* 25 (1): 4–27.

Conkievich, Elaine M. 2002. "The NGOs Approach: Possibilities for Positive Engagement in Belarus." In *Independent Belarus: Domestic Determinants, Regional Dynamics, and Implications for the West,* edited by Margarita M. Balmaceda, James I. Clem, and Lisbeth L. Tarlow. Cambridge, MA: Ukrainian Research Institute of Harvard University and the Davis Center for Russian and Eurasian Studies.

Constitution of the Republic of Belarus. 1994. http://president.gov.by/en/press10669 .html.

Constitution of the Republic of Poland. 1997. http://www.sejm.gov.pl/prawo/konst/ angielski/kon1.htm.

Constitution of the Ukrainian Soviet Socialist Republic. 1978. http://gska2.rada.gov .ua/site/const/istoriya/1978.html (Ukrainian version).

Constitution of Ukraine. 1996. http://www.rada.gov.ua/const/conengl.htm (English version).

———. Amendments to the Constitution of Ukraine. 2004. European Commission for

Democracy through Law CDL(2005)036. http://www.venice.coe.int/docs/2005/CDL(2005)036-e.pdf

Council of Europe. 2008. "Resolution of the Conference on Democratization of the Mass Media in Belarus." Warsaw, June 6–7.

Council of the European Union. 2006a. "Belarus—Council Adopts Financial Restrictive Measures." Brussels, May 18, 9531/06 (Presse 146). http://www.consilium.europa.eu/ueDocs/cms_Data/docs/pressdata/en/misc/89641.pdf.

———. 2006b. "Belarus—Council Adopts Financial Restrictive Measures. Constitution of Ukraine. 1996" (with 2004 amendments). http://www.president.gov.ua/en/content/constitution.html.

Counterpart Creative Center. 2006. "Civil Society Organizations in Ukraine: The State and Dynamics 2002–2006." http://ccc-tck.org.ua/en-default/file/biblioteka/cso_e.pdf.

Crawford, Beverly, and Arend Lijphart. 1995. "Explaining Political and Economic Change in Post-Communist Eastern Europe: Old Legacies, New Institutions, Hegemonic Norms, and International Pressures." *Comparative Political Studies* 28 (2): 171–99.

———, eds. 1997. *Liberalization and Leninist Legacies: Comparative Perspectives on Democratic Transitions.* Berkeley, CA: International and Area Studies.

Crawford, Gordon. 2000. "European Union Development Co-operation and the Promotion of Democracy." In *Democracy Assistance: International Co-operation for Democratization,* edited by Peter Burnell, 90–127. London: Frank Cass.

Cremona, Marise. 2004. "The European Neighborhood Policy: Legal and Institutional Issues." Working Paper. Center on Democracy, Development, and the Rule of Law (CDDRL), Stanford Institute for International Studies No. 25.

Crescenzi, Mark J. C., and Andrew J. Enterline. 1999. "Ripples from the Waves? A Systemic, Time-Series Analysis of Democracy, Democratization, and Interstate War." *Journal of Peace Research* 36:75–94.

CSCE (Commission on Security and Cooperation in Europe). 1994. "Human Rights and Democratization in Poland." Washington, DC. January.

Ćwiek-Karpowicz, Jarosław, and Piotr Maciej Kaczyński. 2006. *Assisting Negotiated Transition to Democracy: Lessons from Poland 1980–1999.* Warsaw: Institute of Public Affairs.

Czubek, Grażyna. 2002. *Social Diplomacy: The Case of Poland; International Activity of Polish NGOs and Their Dialogue with Government.* Warsaw: Stefan Batory Foundation.

Dahl, Robert A. 1971. *Polyarchy: Participation and Opposition.* New Haven: Yale University Press.

———. 1989. *Democracy and Its Critics.* New Haven: Yale University Press.

———. 1997. "Development and Democratic Culture." In *Consolidating the Third Wave Democracies: Themes and Perspectives,* edited by Larry Diamond, 34–39. Baltimore: Johns Hopkins University Press.

D'Anieri, Paul. 2007a. "Ethnic Tensions and State Strategies: Understanding the

Survival of the Ukrainian State." *Journal of Communist Studies and Transition Politics* 23 (1): 33–58.

———. 2007b. *Understanding Ukrainian Politics: Power, Politics, and Institutional Design.* Armonk, NY: M. E. Sharpe.

———. 2011. "Structural Constraints in Ukrainian Politics." *East European Politics and Societies* 25 (1): 28–46.

Darden, Keith A. 2001. "Blackmail as a Tool of State Domination: Ukraine under Kuchma." *East European Constitutional Review* 10 (2–3).

Dawisha, Karen, and Bruce Parrott. 1997. *Democratic Changes and Authoritarian Reactions in Russia, Ukraine, Belarus, and Moldova.* Cambridge: Cambridge University Press.

della Porta, Donatella, and Sidney G. Tarrow, eds. 2005. *Transnational Protest and Global Activism.* Lanham, MD: Rowman and Littlefield.

Demes, Pavol, and Joerg Forbrig. 2006. "Pora—'It's Time' for Democracy in Ukraine." In *Revolution in Orange: The Origins of Ukraine's Democratic Breakthrough,* edited by Anders Åslund and Michael McFaul, 85–102. Washington, DC: Carnegie Endowment for International Peace.

De Quetteville, Harry. 2008. "Poland Takes on Russia with 'Eastern Partnership' Proposal." *Daily Telegraph,* May 25. http://www.telegraph.co.uk/news/2027636/ Poland-takes-on-Russia-with-Eastern-Partnership-proposal.html.

Deutsch, Karl W. 1961. "Social Mobilization and Political Development." *American Political Science Review* 55 (September): 634–47.

Diamond, Larry. 1992. "Promoting Democracy." *Foreign Policy* 87 (1): 25–46.

———. 1994. "Rethinking Civil Society: Toward Democratic Consolidation." *Journal of Democracy* 5 (3): 4–17.

———. 1996. "Toward Democratic Consolidation." In *The Global Resurgence of Democracy,* edited by Larry Diamond and Marc F. Plattner, 227–40. 2nd ed. Baltimore: Johns Hopkins University Press.

———. 1997. "Introduction: In Search of Consolidation." In *Consolidating the Third Wave Democracies: Regional Challenges,* edited by Larry Diamond, Marc F. Plattner, Yun-han Chu, and Hung-mao Tien, xiii–xlvii. Baltimore: Johns Hopkins University Press.

———. 1999. *Developing Democracy: Toward Consolidation.* Baltimore: Johns Hopkins University Press.

Diamond, Larry, Juan José Linz, and Seymour Martin Lipset. 1989. *Democracy in Developing Countries: Latin America.* London: Adamantine Press.

———. 2002. "Thinking about Hybrid Regimes." *Journal of Democracy* 13 (2): 21–35.

Diamond, Larry, and Leonardo Morlino. 2005. *Assessing the Quality of Democracy.* Baltimore: Johns Hopkins University Press.

Diamond, Larry, and Marc F. Plattner, eds. 2001. *The Global Divergence of Democracies.* Baltimore: Johns Hopkins University Press.

Diani, Mario, and Doug McAdam. 2003. *Social Movements and Networks: Relational Approaches to Collective Action.* Oxford: Oxford University Press.

Diuk, Nadia. 2006. "Triumph of Civil Society." In *Revolution in Orange: The Origins of Ukraine's Democratic Breakthrough,* edited by Anders Åslund and Michael McFaul, 69–84. Washington, DC: Carnegie Endowment for International Peace.

Dumasy, Teresa. 2003. "Belarus's Relations with the European Union: A Western Perspective." In *Contemporary Belarus: Between Democracy and Dictatorship,* edited by Elena A. Korosteleva, Colin W. Lawson, and Rosalind J. Marsh, 179–92. London and New York: RoutledgeCurzon.

Dynko, Andrej. 2007. "Language of Streets and Language of the Ploshcha: Evolution and Status of the Belarusian Language after 2000." In *Hopes, Illusions, Perspectives: Belarusian Society 2007.* Warsaw and Minsk: East European Democratic Center.

Easton, David. 1975. "A Re-Assessment of the Concept of Political Support." *British Journal of Political Science* 5 (4): 435–57.

East View Information Services Inc. 2005. *Current Digest of the Post-Soviet Press* 16 (57): May 18.

———. 2009. "President, PM Spar Over Ukraine Economic Collapse." *Current Digest of the Post-Soviet Press* 60 (51–52): January 13.

Economist. 2005. "The Viktor and Yulia Show." June 18, 45–46.

———. 2008. "A Political Soap-Opera, Continued." May 31, 53–54.

———. 2009. "Dear Viktor, You're Dead, Love Dmitry." August 22, 47–48.

EEDC (East European Democratic Center). 2007. "Annual Activity Report." Warsaw.

Eke, Steven M., and Taras Kuzio. 2000. "Sultanism in Eastern Europe: The Socio-Political Roots of Authoritarian Populism in Belarus." *Europe-Asia Studies* 52 (3): 523–47.

Ekiert, Grzegorz. 1996. *The State against Society: Political Crises and Their Aftermath in East Central Europe.* Princeton: Princeton University Press.

———. 2003. "Patterns of Post-Communist Transformation in Central and Eastern Europe." In *Capitalism and Democracy in Central and Eastern Europe: Assessing the Legacy of Communist Rule,* edited by Grzegorz Ekiert and Stephen E. Hanson, 89–119. Cambridge: Cambridge University Press.

———, and Stephen E. Hanson, eds. 2003. *Capitalism and Democracy in Central and Eastern Europe: Assessing the Legacy of Communist Rule.* Cambridge: Cambridge University Press.

Elster, Jon, ed. 1996. *The Roundtable Talks and the Breakdown of Communism.* Chicago: University of Chicago Press.

Emerson, Michael. 2005. *Democratization in the European Neighborhood.* Brussels: Centre for European Policy Studies (CEPS).

———. 2007. "Ukraine and the European Union." In *The New Eastern Europe: Ukraine, Belarus, and Moldova,* edited by Daniel Hamilton and Gerhard Mangott, 215–38. Washington, DC: Center for Transatlantic Relations; Vienna: Austrian Institute for International Affairs.

———, and Gergana Noutcheva. 2004. "Europeanization as a Gravity Model of Democratization." CEPS Working Documents, No. 214.

Englund, Will. 2010. "Belarus Looks East, West as Vote Nears." *Washington*

Post, December 18. http://www.washingtonpost.com/wp-dyn/content/ article/2010/12/17/AR2010121706576.html.

Enterline, Andrew J., and J. Michael Greig. 2005. "Beacons of Hope? The Impact of Imposed Democracy on Regional Peace, Democracy, and Prosperity." *Journal of Politics* 67 (4): 1075–98.

Epstein, David L., Robert Bates, Jack Goldstone, Ida Kristensen, and Sharyn O'Halloran. 2006. "Democratic Transitions." *American Journal of Political Science* 50 (3): 551–69.

Ethier, Diane. 2003. "Is Democracy Promotion Effective? Comparing Conditionality and Incentives." *Democratization* 10 (1): 99–120.

European Commission: Enlargement. 2009. "Accession Process." http://ec.europa.eu/ enlargement/index_en.htm.

European Commission: ENP. 2009. "The Policy: What Is the European Neighborhood Policy?" http://ec.europa.eu/world/enp/policy_en.htm.

European Commission: External Cooperation Programs. 2009. "European Neighborhood and Partnership Instrument." http://ec.europa.eu/europeaid/ where/neighbourhood/overview/index_en.htm.

European Commission: External Relations. 2006. "Non Paper: What Can the European Union Bring to Belarus?" November 23. http://eeas.europa.eu/delegations/ belarus/documents/eu_belarus/non_paper_1106.pdf.

———. 2009. "Eastern Partnership." http://eeas.europa.eu/eastern/index_en.htm.

European Commission: Treaty of Nice. 2002. "Official Journal C 325." December 24. http://ec.europa.eu/dgs/secretariat_general/nice_treaty/index_en.htm.

European Parliament. 1998. "Democracy and Respect for Human Rights in the Enlargement Process of the European Union." April 1. Briefing No. 20, http:// www.europarl.europa.eu/enlargement/briefings/pdf/20a1_en.pdf.

Fairbanks, Charles H., Jr. 2004. "Georgia's Rose Revolution." *Journal of Democracy* 15 (2): 110–24.

———. 2007. "Revolution Reconsidered." *Journal of Democracy* 18 (1): 42–57.

FED (Education for Democracy Foundation). 2005. "Program RITA: 5 lat współpracy" [RITA program: 5 years of cooperation]. http://rita.edudemo.org.pl/blans- programu.html.

Feifer, Gregory. 2010. "Yanukovych Sworn in as Ukraine President." RFE/RL, February 25. http://www.rferl.org/content/Yanukovych_To_Be_Sworn_In_As_President_ Of_Ukraine/1967742.html.

Finkel, Steven E., Aníbal Pérez-Liñán, and Mitchell A. Seligson. 2006. "Effects of US Foreign Assistance on Democracy Building: Results of a Cross-National Quantitative Study." Final Report, USAID. http://pdf.usaid.gov/pdf_docs/ Pnade694.pdf.

Fish, M. Steven. 2001. "The Dynamics of Democratic Erosion." In *Postcommunism and the Theory of Democracy*, edited by Richard D. Anderson, M. Steven Fish, Stephen E. Hanson, and Philip G. Roeder, 54–95. Princeton: Princeton University Press.

———. 2005. *Democracy Derailed in Russia: The Failure of Open Politics*. New York: Cambridge University Press.

Flikke, Geir. 2008. "Pacts, Parties and Elite Struggle: Ukraine's Troubled Post-Orange Transition." *Europe-Asia Studies* 60 (3): 375–96.

ForBelarus.eu. 2009. "Split within Belarusian Opposition." April 5. http://forbelarus .eu/article_info.php?articles_id=167&osCsid=0a36ccbeccda4d97be6a83c799 aa3456.

Forbrig, Joerg, David R. Marples, and Pavol Demeš, eds. 2006. *Prospects for Democracy in Belarus.* 2nd ed. Washington, DC: German Marshall Fund of the United States and Heinrich Böll Stiftung.

Freedom House. 2005. "How Freedom Is Won: From Civic Resistance to Durable Democracy." http://www.icnl.org/research/journal/vol7iss3/special_3.htm.

———. 2008a. "Freedom in the World—Belarus." www.freedomhouse.org.

———. 2008b. "Freedom in the World—Ukraine." www.freedomhouse.org.

———. 2009a. "Freedom in the World Methodology." www.freedomhouse.org.

———. 2009b. "Nations in Transit (NIT) Ratings." www.freedomhouse.org.

Freres, Christian L. 1999. "European Actors in Global Change: The Role of European Civil Societies in Democratization." In *Democracy without Borders: Transnationalization and Conditionality in New Democracies,* edited by Jean Grugel, 42–56. London: Routledge.

Friszke, Andrzej. 2006. *Solidarność Podziemna 1981–1989* [Solidarity Underground 1981–1989]. Warsaw: Instytut Studiów Politycznych Polskiej Akademii Nauk, Stowarzyszenie "Archiwum Solidarności."

Fritz, Verena. 2007. *State-Building: A Comparative Study of Ukraine, Lithuania, Belarus, and Russia.* Budapest: Central European University Press.

Fryzowska, Ewa. 1995. "The United Nations Association of Poland." In *The Role of Non-Governmental Organizations in the New European Order,* edited by Jürgen Schramm. Baden-Baden: Nomos Verlagsgesellschaft.

FSLD (Foundation in Support of Local Democracy). 2007. "Annual Report 2007." http://www.frdl.org.pl/downloads/raport2007.pdf.

Fukuyama, Francis. 1992. *The End of History and the Last Man.* London: Penguin.

Galpin, Richard. 2010. "Waiting on Word from Ukraine's Tymoshenko." *BBC News,* February 9. http://news.bbc.co.uk/2/hi/8505309.stm.

Garnett, Sherman W., and Robert Legvold. 1999. *Belarus at the Crossroads.* Washington, DC: Carnegie Endowment for International Peace.

Gazeta Wyborcza. 2004. "Polscy politycy o sytuacji na Ukrainie" [Polish politicians on the situation in Ukraine]. November 23. http://wyborcza.pl/1,75248,2407894.html.

Geddes, Barbara. 1995. "A Comparative Perspective on the Leninist Legacy in Eastern Europe." *Comparative Political Studies* 28 (2): 239–74.

George, Alexander L., and Andrew Bennett. 2005. *Case Studies and Theory Development in the Social Sciences.* Cambridge, MA: MIT Press.

Geremek, Bronislaw. 1996. "Civil Society Then and Now." In *The Global Resurgence of Democracy,* edited by Larry Diamond and Marc F. Plattner, 241–50. Baltimore: Johns Hopkins University Press.

Gershman, Carl, and Michael Allen. 2006. "The Assault on Democracy Assistance." *Journal of Democracy* 17 (2): 36–51.

Gillespie Richard, and Richard Youngs. 2002. "Themes in European Democracy Promotion." *Democratization* 9 (1): 1–16.

Gleditsch, Kristian, and Michael D. Ward. 2006. "Diffusion and the International Context of Democratization." *International Organization* 60 (4): 911–33.

Gliński, Piotr. 2006. *Style działań organizacji pozarzadowych w Polsce* [Different forms of NGOs' activities in Poland]. Warsaw: IFiS PAN.

Goldstein, Judith. 1998. "International Institutions and Domestic Politics: GATT, WTO, and the Liberalization of International Trade." In *The WTO as an International Organization,* edited by Anne O. Kruger, 133–60. Chicago: University of Chicago Press.

Golub, Stephen J. 2000. "Democracy as Development: A Case for Civil Society Assistance in Asia." In *Funding Virtue: Civil Society Aid and Democracy Promotion,* edited by Marina Ottaway and Thomas Carothers, 135–58. Washington, DC: Carnegie Endowment for International Peace.

Gromadzki, Grzegorz, and Luboš Veselý. 2006. *Aktywnie i wspólnie: UE wobec Białorusi* [Actively and collectively: The EU toward Belarus]. Warsaw: Fundacja Batorego.

Grugel, Jean. 1999. *Democracy without Borders: Transnationalization and Conditionality in New Democracies.* London: Routledge.

Gunther, Richard P., Nikiforos Diamandouros, and Hans-Jürgen Puhle. 1995. *The Politics of Democratic Consolidation: Southern Europe in Comparative Perspective.* Baltimore: Johns Hopkins University Press.

Hadenius, Axel, and Fredrik Uggla. 1998. "Shaping Civil Society." In *Civil Society and International Development,* edited by Amanda Bernard, Henny Helmich, and Percy B. Lehning, 43–56. Paris: North-South Centre of the Council of Europe and Development Centre Studies of the Organization for Economic Co-operation and Development.

Haerpfer, Christian W. 2002. *Democracy and Enlargement in Post-Communist Europe: The Democratization of the General Public in Fifteen Central and Eastern European Countries, 1991–1998.* London: Routledge.

Hanrahan, Brian. 2009. "How Poland Became an Aid Donor." *BBC News,* April 16. http://news.bbc.co.uk/2/hi/europe/8002550.stm.

Hanson, Stephen E. 1995. "The Leninist Legacy and Institutional Change." *Comparative Political Studies* 28 (2): 306–14.

Harasymiw, Bohdan. 2002. *Post-Communist Ukraine.* Edmonton: Canadian Institute of Ukrainian Studies.

Harmash, Serhii. 2005. "'Rehiony' zminyuyut' oblychchya, abo Akhmetov y roli prem'yera" [The Party of Regions is changing its face, or Akhmetov in the role of prime minister]. *Ukraïns'ka Pravda,* December 1. http://www.pravda.com.ua/articles/2005/12/1/3025607/.

Haukkala, Hiski, and Arkady Moshes. 2004. *Beyond "Big Bang": The Challenges of the EU's Neighborhood Policy in the East.* Report 9. Helsinki: Finnish Institute of International Affairs (FIIA).

Hearn, Julie, and Mark Robinson. 2000. "Civil Society and Democracy Assistance in

Africa." In *Democracy Assistance: International Co-operation for Democratization*, edited by Peter Burnell, 241–62. London: Frank Cass.

Henderson, Karen, ed. 1999. *Back to Europe: Central and Eastern Europe and the European Union*. London: Routledge.

Henderson, Sarah. 2000. "Importing Civil Society: Foreign Aid and the Women's Movement in Russia." *Demokratizatsiya* 8 (1): 65–82.

———. 2002. "Selling Civil Society: Western Aid and the Nongovernmental Organization Sector in Russia." *Comparative Political Studies* 35 (March): 139–67.

———. 2003. *Building Democracy in Contemporary Russia: Western Support for Grassroots Organizations*. Ithaca, NY: Cornell University Press.

Herron, Erik S. 2007. "State Institutions, Political Context, and Parliamentary Election Legislation in Ukraine, 2000–2006." *Journal of Communist and Transition Studies* 23 (1): 57–76.

Hesli, Vicki L., William M. Reisinger, and Arthur H. Miller. 1998. "Political Party Development in Divided Societies: The Case of Ukraine." *Electoral Studies* 17:244.

Hill, Ronald J. 2005. "Post-Soviet Belarus: In Search of Direction." In *Postcommunist Belarus*, edited by Stephen White, Elena Korosteleva, and John Löwenhardt, 1–15. Lanham, MD: Rowan and Littlefield.

Howard, Marc Morjé. 2003. *The Weakness of Civil Society in Post-Communist Europe*. Cambridge: Cambridge University Press.

Huber, Evelyne, Dietrich Rueschemeyer, and John D. Stephens. 1993. "The Impact of Economic Development on Democracy." *Journal of Economic Perspectives* 7 (3): 71–85.

Human Rights House Network. 2009. "Abolition of Article 193.1 of the Criminal Code." July 2. http://humanrightshouse.org/Articles/11225.html.

Huntington, Samuel P. 1968. *Political Order in Changing Societies*. New Haven: Yale University Press.

———. 1991. *The Third Wave: Democratization in the Late Twentieth Century*. Norman: University of Oklahoma Press.

Inglehart, Ronald, 1988. "The Renaissance of Political Culture." *American Political Science Research* 82 (4): 1203–30.

International Center for Not-for-Profit Law (ICNL). 2006. "Belarus: Presidential Decree No. 8 on Certain Measures of Regulation of Procedure of Receipt and Use of Foreign Gratuitous Aid." http://www.icnl.org/research/library/index.php.

Ioffe, Grigory. 2003. "Understanding Belarus: Belarusian Identity." *Europe-Asia Studies* 55 (8): 1241–72.

Ishiyama, John T., and Ryan Kennedy. 2001. "Superpresidentialism and Political Party Development in Russia, Ukraine, Armenia, and Kyrgyzstan." *Europe-Asia Studies* 53 (8): 1177–91.

Iwański, Tadeusz. 2012. "The Press and Freedom of Speech in Ukraine Ahead of Parliamentary Elections." OSW Commentary, September 20. http://www.osw.waw.pl/en/publikacje/osw-commentary/2012-09-24/press-and-freedom-speech-ukraine-ahead-parliamentary-elections.

Jacoby, Wade. 2006. "Inspiration, Coalition, and Substitution: External Influences on Postcommunist Transformations." *World Politics* 58 (4): 623–51.

Jarábik, Balázs. 2006. "International Democracy Assistance to Belarus: An Effective Tool?" In *Prospects for Democracy in Belarus,* edited by Joerg Forbrig, David R. Marples, and Pavol Demeš, 85–94. 2nd ed. Washington, DC: German Marshall Fund of the United States and Heinrich Böll Stiftung.

Jocelyn, Ed. 1998. "Nationalism, Identity and the Belarusian States." In *National Identities and Ethnic Minorities in Eastern Europe,* edited by Ray Taras, 73–93. Basingstoke, England: Macmillan.

Jowitt, Kenneth. 1992. *New World Disorder: The Leninist Extinction.* Berkeley: University of California Press.

Juros, Andrzej, E. Les, S. Nalecz, I. Rybka, and M. Rymsza. 2004. "From Solidarity to Subsidarity: The Nonprofit Sector in Poland." In *Future of Civil Society: Making Central European Nonprofit-Organizations Work,* edited by Annette Zimmer and Eckhard Priller, 557–601. Wiesbaden: VS Verlag für Socialwissenschaften/GWV Fachverlage GmbH.

Kamiński, Łukasz. 2007. *Przed i po 13 grudnia: Państwa bloku wschodniego wobec kryzysu w PRL 1980–1982, t. 1* [Before and after the 13th of December: Behind the Iron Curtain countries' attitude toward the crisis in PRL 1980–1982, vol. 1]. Warsaw: Institute of National Remembrance.

Kantorosinski, Zbigniew, comp. 1991. *The Independent Press in Poland, 1976–1990: Holdings in the European and Prints and Photographs Divisions, Library of Congress.* Washington, DC: Library of Congress. http://www.loc.gov/rr/european/ polpress/indepres1.html#fore.

Karatnycky, Adrian. 2005. "Ukraine's Orange Revolution." *Foreign Affairs* 84 (2): 32–52.

———. 2006. "The Fall and Rise of Ukraine's Political Opposition: From Kuchmagate to the Orange Revolution." In *Revolution in Orange: The Origins of Ukraine's Democratic Breakthrough,* edited by Anders Åslund and Michael McFaul, 29–44. Washington, DC: Carnegie Endowment for International Peace.

Karniajenka, Viktar. 2007. "Analysis of the 2006 Political Campaign." In *Hopes, Illusions, Perspectives: Belarusian Society 2007.* Warsaw and Minsk: East European Democratic Center.

Kausch, Kristina, David Mathieson, Irene Menendez, and Richard Youngs. 2006. "Survey of European Democracy Promotion Policies 2000–2006." Fundación para las Relaciones Internacionales y el Diálogo Exterior (FRIDE). http://www.fride.org/ publication/132/survey-of-european-democracy-promotion-policies-2000-2006.

Keane, John. 1998. *Civil Society: Old Images, New Visions.* Stanford: Stanford University Press.

Keck, Margaret E., and Kathryn Sikkink. 1998. *Activists beyond Borders: Advocacy Networks in International Politics.* Ithaca, NY: Cornell University Press.

Kelley, Judith. 2006. "New Wine in Old Wineskins: Promoting Political Reforms through the New European Neighborhood Policy." *Journal of Common Market Studies* 44 (1): 29–55.

Kelly, Matt. 2004. "US Money Has Helped Opposition in Ukraine." *San Diego Union Tribune*, December 11. http://www.signonsandiego.com/uniontrib/20041211/ news_1n11usaid.html.

Kenney, Padraic. 2002. *A Carnival of Revolution: Central Europe 1989*. Princeton: Princeton University Press.

King, Charles. 2000. "Post-Postcommunism: Transition, Comparison, and the End of Eastern Europe." *World Politics* 53 (1): 143–72.

King, Gary, Robert O. Keohane, and Sidney Verba. 1994. *Designing Social Inquiry: Scientific Inference in Qualitative Research*. Princeton: Princeton University Press.

Kitschelt, Herbert. 2003. "Accounting for Postcommunist Regime Diversity: What Counts as a Good Cause." In *Capitalism and Democracy in Central and Eastern Europe: Assessing the Legacy of Communist Rule*, edited by Grzegorz Ekiert and Stephen E. Hanson, 49–88. Cambridge: Cambridge University Press.

Komorowska, Agnieszka, and Bożena Kuzawińska. 2004. *Belarus: Catching Up with Europe*. Warsaw: Stefan Batory Foundation. http://www.batory.org.pl/doc/pogon_ ang.pdf.

Konieczna, Joanna. 2002. "Wartosci polityczne w okresie transformacji w Polsce, na Ukrainie i w innych krajach Europy Wschodniej" [The political values in the period of transition in Poland, Ukraine, and other countries of Eastern Europe]. In *Polacy wsrod Europejczykow* [Poles among Europeans], edited by A. Jasinska-Kania and M. Marody. Warsaw: Scholar.

Kopstein, Jeffrey S. 2006. "The Transatlantic Divide over Democracy Promotion." *Washington Quarterly* 29 (spring): 85–98.

———, and David A. Reilly. 2000. "Geographic Diffusion and the Transformation of the Postcommunist World." *World Politics* 53 (1): 1–37.

Kordowicz, Wiktor. 1955. *Konstanty Kalinowski: Rewolucyjna demokracja polska w powstaniu styczniowym na Litwie i Białorusi* [Konstanty Kalinowski: Polish democracy in a January uprising in Lithuania and Belarus]. Warsaw: Ludowa Spółdzielnia Wydawnicza.

Korosteleva, Elena A. 2003. "Party System Development in Post-Communist Belarus." In *Contemporary Belarus: Between Democracy and Dictatorship*, edited by Elena A. Korosteleva, Colin W. Lawson, and Rosalind J. Marsh, 68–84. London and New York: RoutledgeCurzon.

———. 2011. *Eastern Partnership: A New Opportunity for the Neighbours?* London: Routledge.

Kovalova, Elena. 2007. "Ukraine's Role in Changing Europe." In *The New Eastern Europe: Ukraine, Belarus, and Moldova*, edited by Daniel Hamilton and Gerhard Mangott, 171–94. Washington, DC: Center for Transatlantic Relations; Vienna: Austrian Institute for International Affairs.

Koźlicka, R. 2002. *Trzeci sektor w Unii Europejskiej* [The third sector in the European Union]. Warsaw: Stowarzyszenie Klon/Jawor.

Kubicek, Paul James. 1994. "Delegative Democracy in Russia and Ukraine." *Communist and Post-Communist Studies* 27 (4): 423–42.

———. 2000. *Unbroken Ties: The State, Interest Associations, and Corporatism in Post-Soviet Ukraine.* Ann Arbor: University of Michigan Press.

———. 2005. "The European Union and Democratization in Ukraine." *Communist and Post-Communist Studies* 38 (2): 269–92.

Kupryashkina, Svetlana. 2000. "Civil Society without Political Influence." *Give and Take: A Journal on Civil Society in Eurasia* 3 (3): 15–16.

Kuts, Svitlana, Alex Vinnikov, Leo Abramov, Vasyl Polyiko, Maxym Filiak, Lyuba Palyvoda, and Julia Tyhomyrova. 2001. "Deepening the Roots of Civil Society in Ukraine: Findings from an Innovative and Participatory Assessment Project on the Health of Ukrainian Civil Society." Civicus Index on Civil Society. http://info .worldbank.org/etools/docs/library/7410/Deepening_Roots_Ukraine.pdf.

Kuzio, Taras. 1997. *Ukraine under Kuchma: Political Reform, Economic Transformation, and Security Policy in Independent Ukraine.* New York: St. Martin's Press.

———. 2000a. "The National Factor in Ukraine's Quadruple Transition." *Contemporary Politics* 6 (2): 143–64.

———. 2000b. *Ukraine: Perestroika to Independence.* London: Macmillan.

———. 2005a. "The Opposition's Road to Success." *Journal of Democracy* 16 (2): 117–30.

———. 2005b. "From Kuchma to Yushchenko: Ukraine's 2004 Presidential Elections and the Orange Revolution." *Problems of Post-Communism* 52 (2): 29–44.

———. 2006. "Everyday Ukrainians and the Orange Revolution." In *Revolution in Orange: The Origins of Ukraine's Democratic Breakthrough,* edited by Anders Åslund and Michael McFaul, 45–68. Washington, DC: Carnegie Endowment for International Peace.

———. 2007a. "Political Tourism and Managed Civil Society in Ukraine." *Eurasia Daily Monitor,* May 22. http://www.jamestown.org/single/?no_cache=1&tx_ ttnews%5Btt_news%5D=32759.

———. 2007b. "Prospects for the Political and Economic Development of Ukraine." In *The New Eastern Europe: Ukraine, Belarus, and Moldova,* edited by Daniel Hamilton and Gerhard Mangott, 25–54. Washington, DC: Center for Transatlantic Relations; Vienna: Austrian Institute for International Affairs.

Lahusen, Christian. 1999. "International Campaigns in Context: Collective Action between the Local and the Global." In *Social Movements in a Globalizing World,* edited by Donatella della Porta, Hanspeter Kriesi, and Dieter Rucht, 189–205. New York: St. Martin's Press.

Lalpychak, Chrystyna. 1991. "Independence." *Ukrainian Weekly* 49 (December 8). http://www.ukrweekly.com/archive/pdf3/1991/The_Ukrainian_Weekly_1991–49 .pdf.

Lancaster, Carol. 2007. *Foreign Aid: Diplomacy, Development, Domestic Politics.* Chicago: University of Chicago Press.

Landsberg, Christopher. 2000. "Voicing the Voiceless: Foreign Political Aid to Civil Society in South Africa." In *Funding Virtue: Civil Society and Democracy*

Promotion, edited by Marina Ottaway and Thomas Carothers, 105–34. Washington, DC: Carnegie Endowment for International Peace.

Laverty, Nicklaus. 2008. "The Problem of Lasting Change: Civil Society and the Colored Revolutions in Georgia and Ukraine." *Demokratizatsiya: The Journal of Post-Soviet Democratization* 16 (2): 143–62.

Ledsky, Nelson C. 2005. Prepared statement in *Ukraine—Developments in the Aftermath of the Orange Revolution: Hearing before the Subcommittee on Europe and Emerging Threats of the Committee on International Relations, House of Representatives.* 109th Congress, 1st session, July 27. http://democrats .foreignaffairs.house.gov/archives/109/22653.pdf.

Legvold, Robert, and Celeste A. Wallander. 2004. *Swords and Sustenance: The Economics of Security in Belarus and Ukraine.* Cambridge, MA: American Academy of Arts and Sciences and MIT Press.

Lehning, Percy B. 1998. "Towards a Multi-Cultural Civil Society: The Role of Social Capital and Democratic Citizenship." In *Civil Society and International Development,* edited by Amanda Bernard, Henny Helmich, and Percy B. Lehning, 27–42. Paris: North-South Centre of the Council of Europe and Development Centre Studies of the Organization for Economic Co-operation and Development.

Lenzi, Mark. 2002. "Lost Civilization: The Thorough Repression of Civil Society in Belarus." *Demokratizatsiya* 10 (3): 401–24.

Leś, Ewa, Slawomir Nalecz, and Stefan Toepler. 1999. "Poland." In *Global Civil Society: Dimensions of the Nonprofit Sector, Volume 1,* edited by Lester M. Salamon and S. Wojciech Sokolowski. Bloomfield, CT: Kumarian Press.

———. 2004. "Poland." In *Global Civil Society: Dimensions of the Nonprofit Sector, Volume 2,* edited by Lester Salamon and S. Wojciech Sokolowski. Bloomfield, CT: Kumarian Press.

Leslie R. F. 1983. *The History of Poland since 1863.* Cambridge: Cambridge University Press.

Levitsky, Steven, and Lucan A. Way. 2002. "Competitive Authoritarianism: Elections without Democracy." *Journal of Democracy* 13 (2): 51–64.

Lieven, Anatol. 1999. *Ukraine and Russia: A Fraternal Rivalry.* Washington, DC: United States Institute of Peace.

Lijphart, Arend. 2004. "Constitutional Design for Divided Societies." *Journal of Democracy* 15 (2): 96–109.

Linden, Ronald H. 2002. *Norms and Nannies: The Impact of International Organizations on the Central and East European States.* Lanham, MD: Rowman and Littlefield.

Lindner, Rainer. 2007. "Neighborhood in Flux: EU-Belarus-Russia Prospects for the European Union's Belarus Policy." In *The New Eastern Europe: Ukraine, Belarus, and Moldova,* edited by Daniel Hamilton and Gerhard Mangott, 55–76. Washington, DC: Center for Transatlantic Relations; Vienna: Austrian Institute for International Affairs.

Linz, Juan J. 2000. *Totalitarian and Authoritarian Regimes.* Boulder, CO: Lynne Rienner Publishers.

Linz, Juan J., and Alfred Stepan. 1978. *The Breakdown of Democratic Regimes.* Baltimore: Johns Hopkins University Press.

———. 1996. *Problems of Democratic Transition and Consolidation: Southern Europe, South America, and Post-Communist Europe.* Baltimore: Johns Hopkins University Press.

Lipset, Seymour M. 1959. "Some Social Requisites for Democracy: Economic Development and Political Legitimacy." *American Political Science Review* 53 (1): 69–105.

Lipskaya, Elena. 2000. "Re-registration of NGOs in Belarus." Report for the European Foundation Centre, Brussels.

Lobjakas, Ahto. 2010. "Poland Takes Belarus Offensive to Brussels." Radio Free Europe/Radio Liberty, February 24. http://www.rferl.org/content/Poland_Takes_Belarus_Offensive_To_Brussels/1967523.html.

Löwenhardt, John. 2005. "Belarus and the West." In *Postcommunist Belarus,* edited by Stephen White, Elena Korosoteleva, and John Löwenhardt. Lanham, MD: Rowman and Littlefield.

Lozowy, Ivan. 2004. "Ukraine: A Tide Colored Orange." Transitions Online, December 21. http://www.ceeol.com/aspx/issuedetails.aspx?issueid=1dab3350–8ff0–440d-a933-c4ed75421d42&articleId=c58596c5–9542–48c3–8647-e878570aeb33.

Lynch, Dov. 2006. "A European Strategy towards Belarus: Becoming 'Real.'" In *Prospects for Democracy in Belarus,* edited by Joerg Forbrig, David R. Marples, and Pavol Demeš, 156–63. 2nd ed. Washington, DC: German Marshall Fund of the United States and Heinrich Böll Stiftung.

MacMahon, Margery. 1997. "Aleksandr Lukashenko, President, Republic of Belarus." *Journal of Communist Studies and Transition Politics* 13 (4): 129–37.

Maddox, Bronwen. 2004. "Poland's Solidarity Brings Ukraine Closer to Europe." *Times Online,* November 30. http://209.157.64.201/focus/f-news/1292023/posts.

Magdziak-Miszewska, Agnieszka. 2002. "Belarus: Poland's Strange Neighbor." In *Independent Belarus: Domestic Determinants, Regional Dynamics, and Implications for the West,* edited by Margarita M. Balmaceda, James I. Clem, and Lisbeth L. Tarlow. Cambridge, MA: Ukrainian Research Institute of Harvard University and the Davis Center for Russian and Eurasian Studies.

Majone, Giandomenico. 1998. "Europe's Democratic Deficit." *European Law Journal* 4 (1): 5–28.

Maksymiuk, Jan. 2003. "Belarus: Freedom to Submit." *Foreign Policy* 139 (36): 35–37.

———. 2005a. "Lukashenka Plans 'No Democratic Change' for Belarus." *RFE/RL Belarus and Ukraine Report,* April.

———. 2005b. "Ukraine: Parties Get Down to Crucial Election Campaign." *RFE/RL Belarus, Ukraine, and Moldova Report,* December 16. http://www.rferl.org/content/article/1063683.html.

Mansfeldová, Zdenka, S. Nalecz, E. Priller, and A. Zimmer. 2004. "Civil Society in Transition: Civic Engagement and Nonprofit Organizations in Central and Eastern Europe after 1989." In *Future of Civil Society: Making Central European Nonprofit-*

Organizations Work, edited by Annette Zimmer and Eckhard Priller. Wiesbaden: VS Verlag für Sozialwissenschaften / GWV Fachverlage GmbH.

Markov, Ihor. 1993. "The Role of the President in the Ukrainian Political System." *RFE/ RL Research Report* 2 (48): 32.

Marples, David R. 2005. "Europe's Last Dictatorship: The Roots and Perspectives of Authoritarianism in 'White Russia.'" *Europe-Asia Studies* 57 (6): 895–908.

———. 2006. "Color Revolutions: The Belarus Case." *Communist and Post-Communist Studies* 39 (3): 351–64.

———, and Uladzimir Padhol. 2002. "The Opposition in Belarus: History, Potential and Perspectives." In *Independent Belarus: Domestic Determinants Regional Dynamics, and Implications for the West,* edited by Margarita M. Balmaceda, James I. Clem, and Lisbeth L. Tarlow. Cambridge, MA: Ukrainian Research Institute of Harvard University and the Davis Center for Russian and Eurasian Studies.

Marson, James. 2010. "Ukraine's New President: Is the Orange Revolution Over?" *Time,* February 11. http://www.time.com/time/world/article/0,8599,1963613,00. html.

McDaniel, Tim. 1996. *The Agony of the Russian Idea.* Princeton: Princeton University Press.

McFaul, Michael. 2005. "Democracy Promotion as a World Value." *Washington Quarterly* 28 (1): 147–63.

———. 2007. "Ukraine Imports Democracy: External Influences on the Orange Revolution." *International Security* 32 (2): 45–83.

McMahon, Patrice. 2000. "Building Civil Societies in East Central Europe: The Effect of American Non-Governmental Organizations on Women's Groups." In *Civil Society in Democratization,* edited by Peter Burnell. London: Frank Cass.

———. 2002. "International Actors and Women's NGOs in Poland and Hungary." In *The Power and Limits of NGOs: A Critical Look at Building Democracy in Eastern Europe and Eurasia,* edited by Sarah E. Mendelson and John K. Glenn, 29–53. New York: Columbia University Press.

———. 2004. "Building Civil Societies in East Central Europe: The Effect of American Non-governmental Organizations on Women's Groups." In *Civil Society in Democratization,* edited by Peter Burnell and Peter Calvert. New York: Routledge.

Meckel, Markus. 2006. "A European Foundation for Democracy." In *Prospects for Democracy in Belarus,* edited by Joerg Forbrig, David R. Marples, and Pavol Demeš, 164–69. 2nd ed. Washington: German Marshall Fund of the United States.

Mendelson, Sarah E. 2001. "Democracy Assistance and Political Transition in Russia." *International Security* 25 (4): 68–106.

Mendelson, Sarah E., and John K. Glenn. 2000. "Democracy Assistance and NGO Strategies in Post-Communist Societies." Carnegie Endowment for International Peace Working Paper No. 8. February. http://carnegieendowment.org/files/final .pdf.

Mendelson, Sarah E., and John K. Glenn. 2002. *The Power and Limits of NGOs: A Critical Look at Building Democracy in Eastern Europe and Eurasia.* New York:

Columbia University Press.

Michałowski, Jacek. 2005. Comment in Program RITA: 5 lat współpracy [RITA program: 5 years of cooperation]. http://powiatkolobrzeg.home.pl/ngo/ DOKUMENTY/RITA_5_LAT.PDF.

Michnik, Adam. 1993. *The Church and the Left.* Edited, translated, and with an introduction by David Ost. Chicago: University of Chicago Press.

Mihalisko, Kathleen. 1997. "Belarus: Retreat to Authoritarianism." In *Democratic Changes and Authoritarian Reaction in Russia, Ukraine, Belarus, and Moldova,* edited by Karen Dawisha and Bruce Parrott, 223–81. Cambridge: Cambridge University Press.

Milcher, Susanne, Ben Slay, and Mark Collins. 2007. "The Economic Rationale of the European Neighborhood Policy." In *Europe after Enlargement,* edited by Anders Åslund and Marek Dąbrowski, 165–88. Cambridge: Cambridge University Press.

Milinkevich, Aleksandr. 2006. Foreword to *Prospects for Democracy in Belarus,* edited by Joerg Forbrig, David R. Marples and Pavol Demeš, 9–10. 2nd ed. Washington, DC: German Marshall Fund of the United States and Heinrich Böll Stiftung.

Mingarelli, Hugues. 2006. "ENP as a Mechanism and Tool of Transformation and Deepening Integration with the EU: The European Commission." In *The Eastern Dimension of the European Neighborhood Policy,* 19–22. Warsaw: Center for International Relations.

Mitlin, Diana. 1998. "The NGO Sector and Its Role in Strengthening Civil Society and Securing Good Governance." In *Civil Society and International Development,* edited by Amanda Bernard, Henny Helmich, and Percy B. Lehning, 81–98. Paris: North-South Centre of the Council of Europe and Development Centre Studies of the Organization for Economic Co-operation and Development.

Moravcsik, Andrew. 2000. "The Origins of Human Rights Regimes: Democratic Delegation in Postwar Europe." *International Organization* 54 (2): 217–52.

———. 2004. "Is There a 'Democratic Deficit' in World Politics? A Framework for Analysis." *Government and Opposition* 39 (2): 336–63.

Motyl, Alexander J. 1993. *Dilemmas of Independence: Ukraine after Totalitarianism.* New York: Council on Foreign Relations Press.

Muller, Edward N., and Mitchell A. Seligson. 1994. "Civic Culture and Democracy: The Question of Causal Relationship." *American Political Science Review* 88 (3): 635–52.

Mulvey, Stephen. 2004. "Behind the Scenes at Kiev's Rally." *BBC News,* November 28. http://news.bbc.co.uk/2/hi/europe/4050187.stm.

Nahaylo, Bohdan. 1999. *The Ukrainian Resurgence.* Toronto: University of Toronto Press.

Nanivska, Vira. 2001. "NGO Development in Ukraine." International Centre for Policy Studies, Kiev, Ukraine. http://www.icps.com.ua/files/articles/36/71/ngo_development_eng.pdf.

Narozhna, Tanya. 2004. "Foreign Aid for a Post-Euphoric Eastern Europe: The Limitations of Western Assistance in Developing Civil Society." *Journal of*

International Relations and Development 7:243–66.

NED (National Endowment for Democracy). 2006. "Annual Report: Eurasia Grantee Spotlight; Polish-Czech-Slovak Solidarity Foundation." http://www.ned.org/publications/annual-reports/2009-annual-report/eurasia/crossborder.

O'Brennan, John, and Pat Cox. 2006. *The Eastern Enlargement of the European Union.* London: Routledge.

O'Donnell, Guillermo. 1988. "Challenges to Democratization in Brazil." *World Policy Journal* 5 (2): 281–300.

———. 2001. "Democracy, Law, and Comparative Politics." *Journal Studies in Comparative International Development* 36 (1): 7–36.

O'Donnell, Guillermo, Jorge Vargas Cullell, and Osvaldo M. Iazzetta. 2004. *The Quality of Democracy: Theory and Applications.* Notre Dame, IN: University of Notre Dame Press.

O'Donnell, Guillermo, and Philippe C. Schmitter. 1986. *Transitions from Authoritarian Rule: Tentative Conclusions about Uncertain Democracies.* Baltimore: Johns Hopkins University Press.

OECD. Aid Statistics. 2009. Creditor Reporting System (CRS) Dataset. http://www.oecd.org/dac/stats/directivesforreportingtotheaidactivitydatabasecreditorreportingsystem.htm.

Offe, Claus. 2004. "Capitalism by Democratic Design? Democratic Theory Facing the Triple Transition in East Central Europe." *Social Research: An International Quarterly of Social Sciences* 71 (3): 501–28.

O'Loughlin, John, Michael D. Ward, Corey L. Lofdahl, Jordin S. Cohen, David S. Brown, David Reilly, Kristian S. Gleditsch, and Michael Shin. 1998. "The Diffusion of Democracy, 1946–1994." *Annals, Association of American Geographers* 88 (4): 545–74.

Olsen, Gorm Rye. 2000. "Promotion of Democracy as a Foreign Policy Instrument of 'Europe': Limits to International Idealism." *Democratization* 7 (2): 142–67.

OSCE/ODIHR. 2005. "A Final Report on the 2004 Presidential Election in Ukraine." http://www.osce.org/odihr/elections/ukraine/14674.

OSCE/ODIHR Election Observation Mission. 2006. "Republic of Belarus Presidential Election." March 9. http://www.osce.org/odihr/elections/belarus/19395.

———. 2007. "Ukraine: Pre-Term Parliamentary Elections, 30 September 2007." December 20. http://www.osce.org/odihr/elections/ukraine/29970.

OSCE/ODIHR Limited Observation Mission. 2001. "Republic of Belarus Presidential Election." September 9. http://www.osce.org/odihr/elections/belarus/14459.

Osiatynski, Wiktor. 1996. "The Roundtable Talks in Poland." In *The Roundtable Talks and the Breakdown of Communism,* edited by Jon Elster, 21–68. Chicago: University of Chicago Press.

Osipian, Ararat L., and Alexandr L. Osipian. 2006. "Why Donbass Votes for Yanukovych: Confronting the Ukrainian Orange Revolution." *Demokratizatsiya* 14 (4): 495–517.

———. 2012. "Regional Diversity and Divided Memories in Ukraine: Contested Past as

Electoral Resource, 2004–2010." *East European Politics and Societies* 26 (3): 616–42.

Ostrom, Elinor, Larry Schroeder, and Susan Wynne. 1993. *Institutional Incentives and Sustainable Development: Infrastructure Policies in Perspective.* Oxford: Westview Press.

Ottaway, Marina. 2003. *Democracy Challenged: The Rise of Semi-Authoritarianism.* Washington, DC: Carnegie Endowment for International Peace.

Ottaway, Marina, and Thomas Carothers, eds. 2000. *Funding Virtue: Civil Society Aid and Democracy Promotion.* Washington, DC: Carnegie Endowment for International Peace.

Ottaway, Marina, and Theresa Chung. 1999. "Debating Democracy Assistance: Toward a New Paradigm." *Journal of Democracy* 10 (4): 9–113.

Padhol, Uladzimir, and David R.Marples. 2005. "The Dynamics of the 2001 Presidential Election." In *Postcommunist Belarus,* edited by Stephen White, Elena Korosteleva, and John Löwenhardt. Lanham, MD: Rowan and Littlefield.

Pankaviec, Żmicier. 2007. "Sport as an Ideological Weapon." In *Hopes, Illusions, Perspectives: Belarusian Society 2007.* Warsaw and Minsk: East European Democratic Center.

Parekh, Bhikhu. 1975. "The Concept of National Identity." *New Community* 21 (2): 255–68.

Pateman, Carole. 1970. *Participation and Democratic Theory.* Cambridge: Cambridge University Press.

PAUCI. 2005. "Creating Lasting Partnerships." Brochure.

———. 2007a. "Annual Report."

———. 2007b. "Młodzież Razem: Odległość nie jest przeszkodą" [Young people together: Distance is not an obstacle]. Brochure.

Pavliuk, Oleksandr. 2001. *Unfulfilling Partnership: Ukraine and the West, 1991–2001.* Kiev: East-West Institute.

Payne, Leigh A. 2000. *Uncivil Movements: The Armed Right Wing and Democracy in Latin America.* Baltimore: Johns Hopkins University Press.

Pérez-Díaz, Víctor. 1993. *The Return of Civil Society: The Emergence of Democratic Spain.* Cambridge, MA: Harvard University Press.

Petrescu, Dan. 2000. "Civil Society in Romania: From Donor Supply to Citizen Demand." In *Funding Virtue: Civil Society and Democracy Promotion,* edited by Marina Ottaway and Thomas Carothers, 217–42. Washington, DC: Carnegie Endowment for International Peace.

Pevehouse, Jon C. 2002. "Democracy from the Outside-In? International Organizations and Democratization." *International Organization* 56 (3): 515–49.

———. 2005. *Democracy from Above: Regional Organizations and Democratization.* Cambridge: Cambridge University Press.

Pinder, John. 1991. "The European Community and Democracy in Central and Eastern Europe." In *Building Democracy? The International Dimension of Democratization in Eastern Europe,* edited by G. Pridham, E. Herring, and G. Sanford, 119–43. New York: St. Martin's Press.

Pinto-Duschinsky, Michael. 1997. "The Rise of 'Political Aid.'" In *Consolidating the Third Wave Democracies: Regional Challenges,* edited by Larry Diamond, Marc F. Plattner, Yun-han Chu, and Hung-mao Tien, 295–324. Baltimore: Johns Hopkins University Press.

Poczobut, Andrzej. 2007. "Situation of Organizations Uniting the Polish Minority in Belarus: The Past, the Present, and the Outlook." In *Hopes, Illusions, Perspectives: Belarusian Society 2007.* Warsaw and Minsk: East European Democratic Center.

Polish Ministry of Foreign Affairs. 2006. "Annual Report." Development Co-operation Department. Warsaw.

———. 2007a. "Annual Report." Warsaw.

———. 2007b. "Polish Aid Program Administered by the Ministry of Foreign Affairs of the Republic of Poland." Warsaw.

———. 2008a. "Polish Aid Program Administered by the Ministry of Foreign Affairs of the Republic of Poland." Warsaw.

———. 2008b. "Polish Aid: Co-operation with Eastern Europe, South Caucasus and Central Asia." Brochure.

———. 2010. "Polish Aid Program Administered by the Ministry of Foreign Affairs of the Republic of Poland." Warsaw.

Pridham, Geoffrey. 1994. "The International Dimension of Democratization: Theory, Practice, and Inter-regional Comparisons." In *Building Democracy? The International Dimension of Democratization in Eastern Europe,* edited by G. Pridham, E. Herring, and G. Sanford. New York: St. Martin's Press.

———. 1999. "The European Union, Democratic Conditionality, and Transnational Party Linkages: The Case of Eastern Europe." In *Democracy without Borders: Transnationalization and Conditionality in New Democracies,* edited by Jean Grugel, 59–75. London: Routledge.

———. 2005. *Designing Democracy: EU Enlargements and Regime Change in Post-Communist Europe.* New York: Palgrave Macmillan.

Pridham, Geoffrey, Eric Herring, and George Sanford, eds. 1997. *Building Democracy? The International Dimension of Democratisation in Eastern Europe.* Rev. ed. Leicester: Leicester University Press.

Prizel, Ilya. 1997. "Ukraine between Proto-democracy and 'Soft' Authoritarianism." In *Democratic Changes and Authoritarian Reactions in Russia, Ukraine, Belarus, and Moldova,* edited by Karen Dawisha and Bruce Parrott. Cambridge: Cambridge University Press.

———. 2002. "Ukraine's Hollow Decade." *East European Politics and Societies* 16 (2): 363–85.

Protsyk, Oleh. 2004. "Ruling with Decrees: Presidential Decree Making in Russia and Ukraine." *Europe-Asia Studies* 56 (5): 637–60.

Prytula, Olena. 2006. "The Ukrainian Media Rebellion." In *Revolution in Orange: The Origins of Ukraine's Democratic Breakthrough,* edited by Anders Åslund and Michael McFaul, 103–24. Washington, DC: Carnegie Endowment for International Peace.

Przeworski, Adam. 1991. *Democracy and the Market: Political and Economic Reforms in Eastern Europe and Latin America.* Cambridge: Cambridge University Press.

Przeworski, Adam, Michael E. Alvarez, Jose Antonio Cheibub, and Fernando Limongi. 2000. *Democracy and Development: Political Institutions and Well-Being in the World, 1950–1990.* Cambridge: Cambridge University Press.

Przeworski. Adam, and Fernando Limongi. 1997. "Modernization: Theories and Facts." *World Politics* 49 (2): 155–83.

Puglisi, Rosaria. 2003. "The Rise of the Ukrainian Oligarchs." *Democratization* 10 (3): 99–123.

Putnam, Robert D. 1994. *Making Democracy Work: Civic Traditions in Modern Italy.* Princeton: Princeton University Press.

———, Robert Leonardi, Raffaella Y. Nanetti, and Franco Pavoncello. 1983. "Explaining Institutional Success: The Case of Italian Regional Government." *American Political Science Review* 77 (1): 55–74.

Quigley, Kevin F. F. 1997. *For Democracy's Sake: Foundations and Democracy Assistance in Central Europe.* Washington, DC: Woodrow Wilson Center Special Studies.

———. 2000. "Lofty Goals, Modest Results: Assisting Civil Society." In *Funding Virtue: Civil Society and Democracy Promotion,* edited by Marina Ottaway and Thomas Carothers, 191–216. Washington, DC: Carnegie Endowment for International Peace.

Racelis, Mary. 2000. "New Visions and Strong Actions: Civil Society in the Philippines." In *Funding Virtue: Civil Society and Democracy Promotion,* edited by Marina Ottaway and Thomas Carothers, 159–90. Washington, DC: Carnegie Endowment for International Peace.

Radio Free Europe/Radio Liberty. 2005a. "Legendary RFE Polish Service Director Jan Nowak Dead at 91." January 21. http://www.rferl.org/content/pressrelease/1105757.html.

———. 2005b. "Transcript: What Do Melnychenko's Tapes Say about Gongadze Case?" March 3. http://www.rferl.org/content/article/1057789.html.

———. 2006. "Russia/ Ukraine: Does Gas Deal Signal 'Victory for Common Sense?'" January 4. http://www.rferl.org/content/article/1064402.html.

———. 2009a. "Ukrainian Media Union Demands Public List of Slain Journalists." September 10. http://www.rferl.org/content/Ukrainian_Media_Union_Demands_Public_List_Of_Slain_Journalists/1819371.html.

———. 2009b. "Ukrainian Journalists Mark Anniversary of Gongadze's Murder." September 17. http://www.rferl.org/content/Ukrainian_Journalists_Mark_Anniversary_Of_Gongadzes_Murder/1824929.html.

———. 2010. "Lukashenka Claims Victory amid Mounting Criticism." December 12. http://www.rferl.org/content/belarus_lukashenka_election_vote_crackdown_fraud/2253668.html.

———. 2012a. "Ukraine: OSCE Criticizes Ukraine Elections." October 29. http://www.rferl.org/content/yanukovych-claims-ukraine-win/24753842.html.

———. 2012b. "Russia: Clinton Calls Eurasian Integration an Effort to 'Re-Sovietize.'" December 7. http://www.rferl.org/content/clinton-calls-eurasian-integration-effort-to-resovietize/24791921.html.

Radio Free Europe/Radio Liberty News. 2009. "Ethnic Polish Organization in Belarus Holds Congress." March 16. http://www.rferl.org/content/Ethnic_Polish_ Organization_In_Belarus_Holds_Congress/1511107.html.

Raik, Kristi. 2006. "Making Civil Society Support Central to EU Democracy Assistance." In *Prospects for Democracy in Belarus,* edited by Joerg Forbrig, David R. Marples, and Pavol Demeš, 170–77. 2nd ed. Washington, DC: German Marshall Fund of the United States and Heinrich Böll Stiftung.

Rasler, Karen, and William R. Thompson. 2004. "The Democratic Peace and a Sequential, Reciprocal, Causal Arrow Hypothesis." *Comparative Political Studies* 37 (8): 879–908.

Regulska, Joanna. 1998. "The Rise and Fall of Public Administration Reform in Poland: Why Bureaucracy Does Not Want to Be Reformed." In *Local Development and Public Administration in Transition,* edited by Max Barlow, Imre Lengyel, and Richard Welch. Szeged, Hungary: József Attila University.

Rettman, Andrew. 2011. "Poland: West Should Use Cold War Tactics to Free Belarus." *EU Observer,* January 11. http://euobserver.com/24/31621.

RFE/RL (Radio Free Europe/Radio Liberty) Newsline. 2004a. "Ukraine's Yushchenko, Yanukovych Move toward Political Compromise." December 4. http://www.hri .org/news/balkans/rferl/2004/04-12-02.rferl.html#32.

———. 2004b. "Poland Urges Ukraine to Hold Fair Presidential Vote." November 15. http://www.rferl.org/content/Article/1143282.html.

———. 2006. "Belarus: Russia/Ukraine: Does Gas Deal Signal 'Victory For Common Sense'?" January 4. http://www.rferl.org/content/article/1064402.html.

Richter, James. 2002. "Promoting Civil Society? Democracy Assistance and Russian Women's Organizations." *Problems of Post-Communism* 48 (1): 30–41.

Roeder, Philip G. 1994. "Varieties of Post-Soviet Authoritarian Regimes." *Post-Soviet Affairs* 10:61–101.

Rogers, Everett M. 1995. *Diffusion of Innovations.* 4th ed. New York: Free Press.

Rontoyanni, Clelia. 2005. "Belarus and the East." In *Postcommunist Belarus,* edited by Stephen White, Elena Korosoteleva, and John Löwenhardt. Lanham, MD: Rowan and Littlefield.

Rose, Richard, and Christian Haerpfer. 1995. "Democracy and Enlarging the European Union Eastwards." *Journal of Common Market Studies* 33 (3): 427–50.

Rose-Ackerman, Susan. 2007. *From Elections to Democracy: Building Accountable Government in Hungary and Poland.* Cambridge: Cambridge University Press.

Ross, Michael L. 2001. "Does Oil Hinder Democracy?" *World Politics* 53 (3): 325–61.

Rudling, Per Anders. 2008. "Belarus in the Lukashenka Era: National Identity and Relations with Russia." In *Europe's Last Frontier? Belarus, Moldova, and Ukraine between Russia and the European Union,* edited by Oliver Schmidtke and Serhy Yekelchyk, 55–77. New York: Palgrave Macmillan.

Rueschemeyer, Dietrich, Evelyne Stephens Huber, and John D. Stephens. 1992. *Capitalist Development and Democracy.* Chicago: University of Chicago Press.

Rupnik, Jacques. 1999. "The Postcommunist Divide." *Journal of Democracy* 10 (1): 57–62.

Rymsza, Marek. 2007. "Polityka panstwa wobec sektora obywatelskiego w Polsce w latach 1989–2007." In *Panstwo a Trzeci Sektor: Prawo i instytucje w dzialaniu,* edited by Marek Rymsza, Grzegorz Makowski, and Magdalena Dudkiewicz. Warsaw: Instytut Spraw Publicznych.

Rzeczpospolita. 2005. "Mit mniejszego zła" [The lesser evil myth]. December 13.

Sachs, Jeffrey, and David Lipton. 1990. "Poland's Economic Reform." *Foreign Affairs* 69 (3): 47–66.

Sadowska, Krystyna. 1996. "Organizacje pozarzadowe w Polsce okresu przelomu." In *Civil Participation in the Life of Local Society: State, Barriers, Recommendation.* Krakow: Foundation of the International Center for the Development of Democracy.

Šałajeva, Alena. 2007. "Education in Belarus." In *Hopes, Illusions, Perspectives: Belarusian Society 2007.* Warsaw and Minsk: East European Democratic Center.

Sani, Giacomo, and Giovanni Sartori. 1983. "Polarization, Fragmentation, and Competition in Western Democracies." In W*estern European Party Systems: Continuity and Change,* edited by Hans Daalder and Peter Mair. Thousand Oaks, CA: SAGE Publications.

Sannikov, Andrei, and Inna Kuley. 2006. "Civil Society and the Struggle for Freedom." In *Prospects for Democracy in Belarus,* edited by Joerg Forbrig, David R. Marples, and Pavol Demeš, 57–64. 2nd ed. Washington, DC: German Marshall Fund of the United States and Heinrich Böll Stiftung.

Schifter, Michael. 2000. "Latin American Democratization: The Civil Society Puzzle." In *Funding Virtue: Civil Society and Democracy Promotion,* edited by Marina Ottaway and Thomas Carothers, 243–68. Washington, DC: Carnegie Endowment for International Peace.

Schimmelfennig, Frank. 2007. "European Regional Organizations, Political Conditionality, and Democratic Transformation in Eastern Europe." *East European Politics and Societies* 21 (1): 126–41.

———, and Ulrich Sedelmeir. 2005. *The Europeanization of Central and Eastern Europe.* Ithaca, NY: Cornell University Press.

Schmidtke, Oliver, and Serhy Yekelchyk. 2008. *Europe's Last Frontier? Belarus, Moldova, and Ukraine between Russia and the European Union.* New York: Palgrave Macmillan.

Schmitter, Philippe C. 1986. "An Introduction to Southern European Transitions from Authoritarian Rule: Italy, Greece, Portugal, Spain, and Turkey." In *Transitions from Authoritarian Rule,* edited by Guillermo O'Donnell, Philippe C. Schmitter, and Laurence Whitehead, 3–10. Baltimore: Johns Hopkins University Press.

———. 1995. "From an Iron Curtain to a Paper Curtain: Grounding Transitologists or Student of Postcommunism?" *Slavic Review* 54 (4): 965–978.

———. 1996. "The Influence of the International Context upon the Choice of National Institutions and Policies in Neo-Democracies." In *The International Dimensions of Democratization: Europe and the Americas,* edited by Laurence Whitehead, 26–54. Oxford: Oxford University Press.

———. 2005. "The Ambiguous Virtues of Accountability." In *Assessing the Quality of Democracy*, edited by Larry Diamond and Leonardo Morlino, 18–31. Baltimore: Johns Hopkins University Press.

———, and Terry Lynn Karl. 1991. "What Democracy Is . . . and Is Not." *Journal of Democracy* 2 (summer): 75–88.

Schraeder, Peter, Steven Hook, and Bruce Taylor. 1998. "Clarifying the Foreign Aid Puzzle: A Comparison of American, Japanese, French, and Swedish Aid Flows." *World Politics* 50 (2): 294–323.

Schumpeter, Joseph A. 1947. *Capitalism, Socialism, and Democracy*. New York: Harper.

Sedogo, Paténéma François. 1998. "Civil Society in Sub-Saharan Africa: How Can Western Countries Help Civil Society in Africa?" In *Civil Society and International Development*, edited by Amanda Bernard, Henny Helmich, and Percy B. Lehning, 111–20. Paris: North-South Centre of the Council of Europe and Development Centre Studies of the Organization for Economic Co-operation and Development.

SEED (Support for East European Democracy) Act of 1989. Public Law No. 101-179, 103 Stat. 1298 (1989). 101st Congress, 1st session (November 17).

Sharpe, L. John. 1988. "Local Government Reorganization: General Theory and UK Practice." In *The Dynamics of Institutional Change*, edited by B. Dente and F. Kjelleberg. London: Sage.

Shils, Edward. 1992. "On Civility and Civil Society." In *Civility and Citizenship in Liberal Democratic Societies*, edited by Edward C. Banfield, 1–16. New York: Paragon House.

Shulman, Stephen. 2005. "National Identity and Public Support for Political and Economic Reform in Ukraine." *Slavic Review* 64 (1): 59–87.

Shurkhalo, Dmytro. 2012. "Features: Ukraine's Opposition Steps Up Threats of Parliamentary Boycott." RFE/RL, November 5. http://www.rferl.org/content/ukraine-opposition-steps-up-threat-of-parliament-boycott/24761383.html.

Siegel, Daniel, and Jenny Yancey. 1992. *The Rebirth of Civil Society: The Development of the Nonprofit Sector in East Central Europe and the Role of Western Assistance*. New York: Rockefeller Brothers Fund.

Silitski, Vitali. 2003. "Explaining Post-Communist Authoritarianism in Belarus." In *Contemporary Belarus: Between Democracy and Dictatorship*, edited by Elena A. Korosteleva, Colin W. Lawson, and Rosalind J. Marsh, 36–52. London and New York: RoutledgeCurzon.

———. 2005. "Preempting Democracy: The Case of Belarus." *Journal of Democracy* 16 (2): 82–97.

———. 2006. "Signs of Hope Rather Than a Color Revolution." In *Prospects for Democracy in Belarus*, edited by Joerg Forbrig, David R. Marples, and Pavol Demeš, 20–28. 2nd ed. Washington, DC: German Marshall Fund of the United States and Heinrich Böll Stiftung.

———. 2008. "Nations in Transit 2008—Belarus." Freedom House. www.freedomhouse.org.

Sindelar, Daisy. 2012. "Ukraine: New Ukrainian Parliament Keeps Politics a Family

Affair." RFE/RL, October 30. http://www.rferl.org/content/ukraine-parliament-politics-family-nepotism/24755478.html.

Skrzypiec, Ryszard. 2008. *Civil Society and Non-Governmental Organizations in Programs and Activities of Polish Political Parties*. Warsaw: OFOP (Polish National Federation of NGOs). http://archiwum.ofop.engo.pl/files/ofop.engo.pl/public/monit_ob_wyb_OFOP/Obietnice_wyborcze_analiza_calosc_redakcja_ost.pdf.

Smith, Anthony D. 1991. *National Identity*. London: Penguin.

Smith, Jackie, Charles Chatfield, and Ron Pagnucco. 1997. *Transnational Social Movements and Global Politics: Solidarity beyond the State*. Syracuse, NY: Syracuse University Press.

Smith, Jackie, and Dawn Wiest. 2012. *Social Movements in the World-System: The Politics of Crisis and Transformation*. New York: Russell Sage Foundation.

Snow, David A., and Robert D. Benford. 1999. "Alternative Types of Cross-National Diffusion in the Social Movement Arena." In *Social Movements in a Globalizing World*, edited by Donatella della Porta, Hanspeter Kriesi, and Dieter Ruchts, 23–39. New York: St. Martin's Press.

Snyder, Timothy. 2003. *The Reconstruction of Nations: Poland, Ukraine, Lithuania, and Belarus, 1569–1999*. New Haven: Yale University Press.

Soros, George. 1994. *Building Open Societies: Soros Foundations*. New York: Soros Foundations.

Specter, Michael. 1994. "Belarus Winner Remakes His Image." *New York Times*, July 17. http://www.nytimes.com/1994/07/17/world/belarus-winner-remakes-his-image.html.

Stanowski, Krzysztof. 2005a. "Program RITA: 5 lat współpracy" [RITA Program: 5 Years of Cooperation]. http://rita.edudemo.org.pl/przydatne-pliki/doc_download/25-podsumowanie-5-lat-programu-rita.html.

———. 2005b. "The Zagranica Group's Meeting on the Role of Polish NGOs in Shaping Polish Foreign Policy toward the East." September 24. http://wiadomosci.ngo.pl/wiadomosci/128473.html.

Starr, Harvey. 1991. "Democratic Dominoes: Diffusion Approaches to the Spread of Democracy in the International System." *Journal of Conflict Resolution* 35 (2): 356–81.

———, and Christina Lindborg. 2003. "Democratic Dominoes Revisited: The Hazards of Governmental Transitions, 1974–1996." *Journal of Conflict Resolution* 47 (4): 490–519.

Stefan Batory Foundation. 2003. "Polska-Ukraina: Współpraca organizacji pozarządowych" [Poland-Ukraine: NGOs' cooperation]. http://www.zagranica.ngo.pl/files/go2east.ngo.pl/public/Polska_-_Ukraina_wpolpraca_organizacji_pozarzadowych.pdf.

———. 2005. "Stosunki polsko-ukraińskie po Pomarańczowej Rewolucji: Propozycje dla polskiej polityki zagranicznej" [Polish-Ukrainian relations after the Orange Revolution: Proposals for Polish foreign policy]. Panel discussion at the Batory Foundation. May 31. http://www.batory.org.pl/doc/dyskusja.pdf.

———. 2007. "Annual Report 2007: The East-East: Partnership beyond Borders Program." Warsaw.

Stemplowski, Ryszard. 2001. "Poland and Russia, Heading in the Same Direction." *Polish Foreign Affairs Digest* [English-language version of paper published in *Polski Przegląd Dyplomatyczny* 1 (1): 12]. http://www.stemplowski.pl/images/Opinie/ Opinie_Digest%202%20Stemplowski_1.pdf.

Stent, Angela E. 2007. "The Lands in Between: The New Eastern Europe in the Twenty-First Century." In *The New Eastern Europe: Ukraine, Belarus, and Moldova,* edited by Daniel Hamilton and Gerhard Mangott, 1–24. Washington, DC: Center for Transatlantic Relations; Vienna: Austrian Institute for International Affairs.

Stepanenko, Viktor. 2006. "Civil Society in Post-Soviet Ukraine: Civic Ethos in the Framework of Corrupted Sociality?" *East European Politics and Societies* 20 (4): 571–97.

Stewart, John. 1983. *Local Government: The Conditions of Local Choice.* London: Allen and Unwin.

Sułek, Magdalena. 2003. "Organizacje pozarzadowe na Ukraine." In *Organizacje pozarzadowe a krajach rozwijajacych sie i Europie Wschodniej,* edited by Elżbieta Puchnarewicz. Warsaw: Wydzial Geografii i Studiow Regionalnych, Uniwersytet Warszawski.

Sundstrom, Lisa McIntosh. 2006. *Funding Civil Society: Foreign Assistance and NGO Development in Russia.* Stanford: Stanford University Press.

Sushko, Oleksandr, and Olena Prystayko. 2008. "Nations in Transit: Ukraine." Freedom House.

———. 2006. "Western Influence." In *Revolution in Orange: The Origins of Ukraine's Democratic Breakthrough,* edited by Anders Åslund and Michael McFaul, 125–44. Washington, DC: Carnegie Endowment for International Peace.

Szabó, Máté. 2004. "Civic Engagement in East-Central Europe." In *Future of Civil Society: Making Central European Nonprofit-Organizations Work,* edited by Annette Zimmer and Eckhard Priller. Wiesbaden: VS Verlag für Socialwissenschaften / GWV Fachverlage GmbH.

Tansey, Oisín. 2007. "Process Tracing and Elite Interviewing: A Case for Non-Probability Sampling." *Political Science and Politics* 40 (4): 765–72.

Tapiola, Pirkka. 2006. "European Union Policy towards Belarus: An Extended Hand." In *Prospects for Democracy in Belarus,* edited by Joerg Forbrig, David R. Marples, and Pavol Demeš, 65–70. 2nd ed. Washington, DC: German Marshall Fund of the United States and Heinrich Böll Stiftung.

Taras, Vitali. 2007. "Media in Belarus: On Brink of Breakthrough." In *Hopes, Illusions, Perspectives: Belarusian Society 2007.* Warsaw and Minsk: East European Democratic Center.

Tarrow, Sidney. 1998. *Power in Movement: Social Movements and Contentious Politics.* Cambridge: Cambridge University Press.

———. 2005. *The New Transnational Activism.* Cambridge: Cambridge University Press.

Taylor, Charles. 1990. "Modes of Civil Society." *Public Culture* 3 (1): 95–118.

Thijn, Ed van, and Amanda Bernard. 1998. "Report and Executive Summary." In *Civil Society and International Development,* edited by Amanda Bernard, Henny

Helmich, and Percy B. Lehning, 17–20. Paris: North-South Centre of the Council of Europe and Development Centre Studies of the Organization for Economic Co-operation and Development.

Thompson, Mark R. 2004. *Democratic Revolutions: Asia and Eastern Europe*. London: Routledge.

Tilly, Charles. 2007. *Democracy.* Cambridge: Cambridge University Press.

Tudoroiu, Theodor. 2007. "Rose, Orange, and Tulip: The Failed Post-Soviet Revolutions." *Communist and Post-Communist Studies* 40 (3): 315–42.

Uładamirski, Aleś. 2007. "Religious Diversity in Belarus." In *Hopes, Illusions, Perspectives: Belarusian Society 2007.* Warsaw and Minsk: East European Democratic Center.

UNIAN (Ukrainian Independent Information Agency). 2008a. "Yuliya Tymoshenko Bloc Accepts All Ultimatums of OU-PSD—Tymoshenko." October 1. http://www.unian.net/eng/news/news-276014.html.

———. 2008b. "Ukraine Election Date Is Uncertain, Says President." October 22. http://www.unian.net/eng/news/news-280065.html.

United Way/Belarusian National Non-Governmental Organization. 2003. "Regulation of Activities of Nongovernmental Organizations: Change of Legislation in 2003." http://en.ngo.by/legal-regulations/legislation-change-2003/.

USAID (US Agency for International Development). 1999. "Assistance Strategy for Belarus, 1999–2002." http://pdf.usaid.gov/pdf_docs/PDABR281.pdf.

———. 2007. "Agency Financial Report: Fiscal Year 2007." http://pdf.usaid.gov/pdf_docs/PDACK333.pdf.

———. 2011. "NGO Sustainability Index for Central and Eastern Europe and Eurasia." Washington, DC.

USAID Mission to Poland, Europe, and Eurasia. N.d. "USAID and the Polish Decade 1989–1999."

Usau, Paval. 2007a. "Pro-Government Associations in Belarus." In *Hopes, Illusions, Perspectives: Belarusian Society 2007.* Warsaw and Minsk: East European Democratic Center.

———. 2007b. "Ideology of Belarusian State." In *Hopes, Illusions, Perspectives: Belarusian Society 2007.* Warsaw and Minsk: East European Democratic Center.

US Congress. 2004. Belarus Democracy Act. H.R. 854, 108th Congress, 2nd session. http://www.charter97.org/eng/news/2004/10/27/act.

———. 2006. Belarus Democracy Reauthorization Act. H.R. 5948, 109th Congress, 2nd session. http://thomas.loc.gov/cgi-bin/query/z?c109:H.R.5948.

US Department of State. Bureau of European and Eurasian Affairs. 2009a. "Background Notes on Countries of the World: Belarus." http://www.state.gov/r/pa/ei/bgn/5371.htm.

———. 2009b. "Foreign Operations Appropriated Assistance: Belarus; Fact Sheet." January 20. http://www.state.gov/p/eur/rls/fs/107776.htm.

Vachudova, Milda Anna. 2001. "The Leverage of International Institutions on Democratizing States: Eastern Europe and the European Union." Robert Schuman Centre for Advanced Studies. *EUI Working Papers* 33.

Vardys, V. Stanley. 1971. "The Case of the Crimean Tartars." *Russian Review* 30 (2): 101–10.

Vidanava, Iryna. 2007. "In the Home and on the Streets: Belarusian Women and Women's Organizations, 2001–06." In *Hopes, Illusions, Perspectives: Belarusian Society 2007.* Warsaw and Minsk: East European Democratic Center.

Volkogonov, Dmitri. 1998. *Autopsy for an Empire: The Seven Leaders Who Built the Soviet Regime.* New York: Free Press.

Wallander, Celeste A. 2004. "Economics and Security in Russia's Foreign Policy and the Implications for Ukraine, and Belarus." In *Swords and Sustenance: The Economics of Security in Belarus and Ukraine,* edited by Robert Legvold and Celeste A. Wallander, 63–100. Cambridge, MA: American Academy of Arts and Sciences and MIT Press.

Walzer, Michael. 1991. "The Idea of Civil Society: A Path to Social Reconstruction." *Dissent* 39 (spring): 293–304.

Way, Lucan. 2005a. "Kuchma's Failed Authoritarianism." *Journal of Democracy* 16 (2): 131–45.

———. 2005b. "Rapacious Individualism and Competitive Authoritarianism in Ukraine, 1992–2004." *Communist and Post-Communist Studies* 38 (2): 191–206.

———. 2012. "The Sources of Authoritarian Control after the Cold War: East Africa and the Former Soviet Union." *Post-Soviet Affairs* 28 (4): 424–48.

Wedel, Janine R. 2001. *Collision and Collusion: The Strange Case of Western Aid to Eastern Europe.* Updated ed. New York: Palgrave St. Martin's Press.

Weigel, George. 1992. *The Final Revolution: The Resistance Church and the Collapse of Communism.* Oxford: Oxford University Press.

Weinthal, Erika, and Pauline Jones Luong. 2002. "Environmental NGOs in Kazakhstan: Democratic Goals and Nondemocratic Outcomes." In *The Power and Limits of NGOs: A Critical Look at Building Democracy in Eastern Europe and Eurasia,* edited by Sarah E. Mendelson, and John K. Glenn, 152–76. New York: Columbia University Press.

White, Gordon. 1994. "Civil Society, Democratization, and Development: Clearing the Analytical Ground." *Democratization* 1 (3): 375–90.

White, Stephen, and Elena Korosteleva. 2005. "Lukashenko and the Postcommunist Presidency." In *Postcommunist Belarus,* edited by Stephen White, Elena Korosteleva, and John Löwenhardt, 59–79. Lanham, MD: Rowman and Littlefield.

Whitehead, Laurence. 1996. "Three International Dimensions of Democratization." In *The International Dimensions of Democratization,* edited by Laurence Whitehead, 3–25. Oxford: Oxford University Press.

———. 1997. "Bowling in the Bronx: The Uncivil Interstices between Civil and Political Society." *Democratization* 4 (1): 94–114.

Whitmore, Sarah. 2005. "State and Institution Building under Kuchma." *Problems of Post-Communism* 52 (5): 3–11.

Wieck, Hans-Georg. 2002. "International Organizations in Belarus." In *Independent Belarus: Domestic Determinants, Regional Dynamics, and Implications for the West,* edited by Margarita M. Balmaceda, James I. Clem, and Lisbeth L. Tarlow.

Cambridge, MA: Ukrainian Research Institute of Harvard University and the Davis Center for Russian and Eurasian Studies.

Wilde, Caryn. 2002. "The Challenge of Using NGOs as a Strategy for Engagement." In *Independent Belarus: Domestic Determinants, Regional Dynamics, and Implications for the West,* edited by Margarita M. Balmaceda, James I. Clem, and Lisbeth L. Tarlow. Cambridge, MA: Ukrainian Research Institute of Harvard University and the Davis Center for Russian and Eurasian Studies.

Wilson, Andrew. 2002. *The Ukrainians: Unexpected Nation.* New Haven: Yale University Press.

———. 2006. *Ukraine's Orange Revolution.* New Haven: Yale University Press.

———. 2009. "Ukraine." In *Semi-Presidentialism in Europe,* edited by Robert Elgie, 260–80. Oxford: Oxford University Press.

Win, Aye Aye. 1998. "The Growing Civil Society in Asia: An Overview and Proposals for Future Action." In *Civil Society and International Development,* edited by Amanda Bernard, Henny Helmich, and Percy B. Lehning, 99–110. Paris: North-South Centre of the Council of Europe and Development Centre Studies of the Organization for Economic Co-operation and Development.

Wolczuk, Kataryna. 2002. *The Moulding of Ukraine: The Constitutional Politics of State Formation.* Budapest: Central European University Press.

Wróbel, Anna. 2003. *Wspólne problemy, wspólne działania Polska-Ukraina: Współpraca organizacji pozarządowych* [Common problems, joint Polish-Ukrainian activities: Cooperation between nongovernmental organizations]. Warsaw: Stefan Batory Foundation. http://www.batory.org.pl/ftp/pub/polska_ukraina_wpolpraca_ngo.pdf.

Yekadumaw, Andrey. 2003. "The Russian Factor in the Development of Belarusian Culture." In *Belarus-Russia Integration,* edited by Valer Bulkhakaw. Minsk and Warsaw: Minsk Analytical Group.

Youngs, Richard. 2001a. "European Union Democracy Promotion Policies: Ten Years On." *European Foreign Affairs Review* 6 (3): 355–73.

———. 2001b. *The European Union and the Promotion of Democracy.* Oxford: Oxford University Press.

———. 2003. "European Approaches to Democracy Assistance: Learning the Right Lessons?" *Third World Quarterly* 24 (1): 127–38.

———. 2008. "Trends in Democracy Assistance: What Has Europe Been Doing?" *Journal of Democracy* 19 (2): 160–69.

Zagranica Group. 2003. *Activity of Polish Non-Governmental Organizations Abroad.* CD-ROM.

Zaprudnik, Jan. 2003. "Belarus: In Search of National Identity between 1986 and 2000." In *Contemporary Belarus: Between Democracy and Dictatorship,* edited by Elena A. Korosteleva, Colin W. Lawson, and Rosalind J. Marsh, 112–24. London and New York: RoutledgeCurzon.

Żejmis, Michał. 2003. "Organizacje pozarządowe na Bialorusi w swietle wypowiedzi dzialaczy" [Nongovernmental organizations in Belarus as depicted in activists' speeches]. In *Organizacje pozarzadowe w krajach rozwijajacych sie i Europie*

Wschodniej [Nongovernmental organizations in developing countries and Eastern Europe], edited by Elżbieta Puchnarewicz. Warsaw: Wydzial Geografii i Studiow Regionalnych, Uniwersytet Warszawski.

Zhuchkov, Alexander. 2004. "Problemy i perspektivy razvitiya grazhdanskogo obshchestva v Belarusi" [Problems and perspectives of civil society development in Belarus]. In *Europa Wschodnia: Dekada transformacji—Bialorus* [East Europe: Decade of transformation—Belarus], edited by Bernard J. Albin and Walenty Baluk. Wrocław: Wydawnictwo Arboretum.

Zhurzhenko, Tatiana. 2005. "Europeanizing the Ukrainian-Russian Border: From EU Enlargement to the 'Orange Revolution.'" *Debate* 12 (2): 137–54.

ZIK (Western Information Agency). 2009. "National Union of Journalists of Ukraine Names 15 Officials Who Gag the Press." October 14. http://zik.com.ua/en/news/2008/04/23/134602.

Zimmer, Annette, and Eckhard Priller, eds. 2004. *Future of Civil Society: Making Central European Nonprofit-Organizations Work.* Wiesbaden: VS Verlag für Socialwissenschaften / GWV Fachverlage GmbH.

Zimmer, Kerstin. 2006. "Formal Institutions and Informal Politics in Ukraine." In *Formal Institutions and Informal Politics in Central and Eastern Europe: Hungary, Poland, Russia and Ukraine,* edited by Gerd Meyer, 274–321. Opladen, Germany, and Farmington Hills, MI: Barbara Budrich Publishers.

Zon, van Hans. 2001. "Neo-Patrimonialism as an Impediment to Economic Development: The Case of Ukraine." *Journal of Communist Studies and Transition Politics* 17 (3): 71–95.

———. 2005a. "Political Culture and Neo-Patrimonialism under Leonid Kuchma." *Problems of Post-Communism* 52 (5): 12–22.

———. 2005b. "Why the Orange Revolution Succeeded." *Perspectives on European Politics and Society* 6 (3): 373–402.

Index

American Federation of Labor–Congress of Industrial Organizations (AFL-CIO), 68, 80, 147, 194n12, 198n43, 204n71

Balcerowicz, Leszek, 75, 212
Belarus: backsliding toward authoritarianism, 1–8; Constitution of the Republic of, 1–3, 215; cultural identity, 31, 52, 62, 99, 124; economy of, 4; Europe's last dictatorship, xxiv, 8, 228; foreign policy priorities of, 6; identity, 7, 52, 99–101, 179n19, 191n43, 222; local elections in, 3; 1996 referendum, 2; parliamentary elections, 3; political parties of, 4; presidential elections held in 2006 and 2010, 3; programs supporting culture of, 52, 57, 62, 99–101; and the Roman Catholic Church, 14, 31
Byelorussian Soviet Socialist Republic, 1, 7, 191

Catholic Church: in Belarus, 14, 31; in Poland, 65–67
Central and Eastern Europe (CEE), 21, 192n58; democratic transformation in, xii, xv, xviii, xxii, 40, 44; and EU eastern enlargement, 42; NGO Sustainability Index for Central and Eastern Europe and Eurasia, 10, 28
Charter 77, 75, 77, 88, 197n35
civil society: assistance as a major component of democracy aid, xviii–xx, 175n13; assistance strategies, xix–xx; in authoritarian states and democratizing countries, xii, xvi, 158–61; in Belarus, 8–17, 180n25; critique of assistance to, 123, 126, 130, 132, 135; and democratization, xiv–xv, 158–59, 174n7, 175n10; and durability and quality of democracy, 106; Eastern Partnership Civil Society Forum, 60; in Poland engaging in democracy assistance to, 73–84; role of in democratic transformation in Poland, 64–70; support of in Belarus and Ukraine, 84–92, 124–41, 176n21; United States' support for in Ukraine and Belarus and other postcommunist countries, 45–49; upheaval of during the Orange Revolution in Ukraine, 20–22, 183n51, 183n54, 185n79; weakness in Ukraine, 26–30
Color Revolutions, 6, 9, 12, 173n4
cross-border: collaborative work, xiv, 75, 161–62, 176n18, 199n83; different activities of, 133–35; nature of in Belarus and Ukraine, 94–121

democracy assistance: approaches (political and developmental) to, xviii–xix, 33, 42–49, 153–54; aimed at promoting free media, 52; education projects in Ukraine and Belarus, 115–19; encouraging networking internally, 132–34; external project method, xix; and geographical and cultural proximity, 141–50; impact of, 135–41; implications for literature of, 159–61; incorporating Ukrainian local authorities and NGOs, 110; literature, xvii–xxi; partnering with civil society groups, 106–8, 129–32; programs, xviii; project schemes, 125–26, 127, 128; promoting Belarusian culture, 52; responding to needs of recipient countries, 122–26; supporting grass-root initiatives, 126–29; strengthening civil society in the eastern part of Ukraine, 107–8; strengthening links between civil society groups and with the media in Ukraine, 108; strengthening local governance in Ukraine, 108–11; supporting administrative decentralization in Ukraine, 109; and young people from Ukraine and Belarus, 53, 115–19, 138
democratic consolidation, xiv, 173n5; conditions of, 56–57; and the role of civil society in Poland, 70–73, 93; Ukraine's problems with, 22–23, 102–6, 159
democratization: and civil society, xiv–xv, 158–59, 174n7, 175n10; determinants of, xii–xvii; hope for in Belarus, 14–17; and international influences, xii–xiv; literature, 173n5; in Poland, 64–73; in postcommunist countries, 198n42; third wave of, xi–xii, 160–61, 171n1
diffusion of democracy, xii–xiii, 23, 118, 121, 132, 141, 145, 151–53, 162
direct grants, xx–xxi, 20, 49, 53, 87–89, 126, 161, 175n11

Eastern Partnership policy, 40, 59–60, 187n59
European Neighborhood Policy (ENP), 43, 114, 188n24
European Partnership for Democracy (EPD), 45, 59, 189n28, 192n58